REMEMBERING RADIO:

An Oral History of Old-Time Radio

Including 14 In-Depth Interviews and the Ultimate Guide to Over 1,330 Recollections

BY DAVID S. SIEGEL

TRANSCRIBED BY MELANIE AULTMAN

FOREWORD BY J. DAVID GOLDIN

REMEMBERING RADIO: AN ORAL HISTORY OF OLD-TIME RADIO
INCLUDING 14 IN-DEPTH INTERVIEWS AND THE ULTIMATE GUIDE
TO OVER 1,330 RECOLLECTIONS
©2010 DAVID S. SIEGEL

Published in the USA by:

BEARMANOR MEDIA
P.O. BOX 71426
ALBANY, GEORGIA 31708
www.BearManorMedia.com

All photographs and illustrations are from the personal
collection of David S. Siegel.

All program titles and program descriptions are used in editorial
fashion with no intention of infringement of intellectual property rights.

ISBN-10: 1-59393-537-4 (alk. paper)
ISBN-13: 973-1-59393-537-5 (alk. paper)

Printed in the United States of America.

COPY EDITOR: DAVID W. MENEFEE

BOOK DESIGN AND LAYOUT BY VALERIE THOMPSON

Dedication

This book is dedicated to John Dunning,

Chuck Schaden, Dick Bertel, Ed Cocoran, Richard Lamparski,

Frank Bresee, and other early pioneers, whose interviews

of radio personalities provide researchers and historians

with valuable insights that shed light on the decades we

celebrate as the Golden Age of radio

TABLE OF CONTENTS

ACKNOWLEDGMENTS

Few, if any, nonfiction books are written without the need to reach out for all kinds of support: technical, inspirational, and sometimes the kind that lacks easy description. This volume exists only because of the remarkable efforts of some very special people.

Melanie Langsdale Aultman: had I not had the good fortune of learning that this terrific lady might be willing to listen to the hours and hours of interviews that I had conducted and transfer the sometimes unclear voices from audio to readable text, this book would not exist. Melanie was far more than a transcriber; she was a voice of conscience, and an inspiration.

J. David Goldin: a legend in the world of old-time radio for having the foresight to be the very first person to resuscitate the sounds of radio comedy, drama, and music by creating a market which to this day attracts thousands of newcomers to a world of entertainment they would never otherwise have known existed. It is David's remarkable website that has become the #1 source of information about specific broadcasts and used, often without attribution, by countless researchers and collectors each and every day. David was the perfect choice to provide a clear explanation of the role that oral history plays in providing historians with "how things came to be," in effect, adding meat and meaning to the bones of this book. His Foreword offers much food for thought.

Barbara Watkins: a good friend of mine for more than thirty years, and friend and constant companion to Lamont . . . err . . . I mean the very lucky Bobb Lynes. Barbara's devotion to the hobby matches that of any collector I know. Indeed, it was her encyclopedic memory, as well as her good nature, that gave me the courage to invite her to proofread the final text.

Susan Siegel: the lady who heretofore was my collaborator in every book I ever dared to write continues to collaborate with me, but in a slightly different fashion. Soon after I undertook this book project, Susan decided to run for supervisor of our town and found herself torn between participating in an election campaign and helping me to identify and organize the hundreds of oral histories that make up part of this book. Susan, I'm happy to say, won the election.

Ben Omhart: the man who founded BearManor Media and has provided us with so many books devoted to radio, film, television, and nostalgia, and at affordable prices. Had it not been for Ben, who, unlike major publishers, is willing to publish books for a limited but devoted audience, so much of radio's past would have been lost. I also offer appreciation and thanks to David W. Menefee, the gentleman who edited this book, and in doing so, saved my reputation. I would also like to thank Valerie Thompson for making my words look attractive.

Special thanks are also due to William Seeger, Stephen Pisani, Christopher Byron, and Sharon Hudson (the sons of Joan Merrill, Ann DeMarco and Ward Byron, and the daughter of Dorothea Cole) for providing photographs of their mothers and father, and to my son, Edward S. Siegel, for his technical skills for enhancing so many of these old photographs culled from a variety of sources.

My sincerest gratitude is also extended to many other wonderful people, whose generosity proved over and over again that this book has many fathers and mothers: Jeanette Berard, Fred Berney, Frank Bresee, Steve Darnall, David Easter, Jack French, Antoinette Graham, Dan Haefele, Martin Halpern, Michael Henry, Doug Hopkinson, Sandi Hughes, Walden Hughes, Stuart Lubin, Bobb Lynes, Bob Steinmetz, Derek Tague, and Jerry Williams.

FOREWORD

There's oral history, and then there's "Oral History." Back in ancient Greece, in fact, back even before then, oral history was the only kind of history. Events of the past were passed on through the generations by word-of-mouth. When Homer created his epic poem, it became a history of the last few weeks of the Trojan War. "The Iliad" was conceived and then memorized by Homer and not put into writing until after his death (the Greek alphabet had yet to be invented). The Old Testament is an oral history, much of it based on events of which there were no texts until generations later. Tribal people continue this tradition today, despite the invention of the tape recorder.

Oral history became "Oral History" with the invention of the phonograph. Recordings of North American Indians, made with acoustic cylinders, date back at least to 1895. The ability of a person to recount events from his lifetime, for the benefit of those to come, would be my definition of "Oral History." That doesn't make any interview oral history. I can imagine the first broadcast interview on that election eve in 1920, when one KDKA announcer turned to another and said, "So Charlie, who's ahead so far?" That would be "recorded history" (if such a record existed), not "Oral History."

Fast forward (in a manner of speaking) to 1936, when the Federal Writer's Project began creating oral histories in quantity for the Library of Congress. Headed by Alan Lomax, who could be considered "the father" of "Oral History," the Library began a series of recordings, many of which are catalogued at www.lomaxarchive.com. Possibly the best-known, and certainly my personal favorite, has to be the recordings Jelly Roll Morton made in 1938. Jelly modestly describes how he invented "Jazz" and illustrates his talks at the piano. It makes for fascinating listening and is prime "Oral History."

Turning the dial to WFMT in Chicago, we first come upon "The Studs Terkel Program" in 1952. For the next forty-five years, five days a week, he interviewed thousands of people from all walks of life. So why were these interviews "Oral History?" Obviously, Studs was a good interviewer and was interesting to listen to. But in addition, he kept *recordings* of his programs, and in 1956, he wrote a book called *Giants of Jazz*. This book, and the many books that followed, led him to fame, fortune, best-sellers and a Pulitzer Prize. I always felt that "talking" a best-selling book was taking an easier path than "writing" a book. But Studs' recordings were saved and publicized, and so he became a celebrity in his own right. He became a creator of "Oral History."

So now it's official. "Oral History" has come to mean a recording, either in audible form or recorded and later transcribed into writing. But a sharper definition is needed; let's take an example. On the air for "only" thirty years, from 1927 to 1957, Mary Margaret McBride was identified as "The First Lady of Radio." Her ability to rattle off a dozen consecutive non-scripted commercials for a dozen different products must be heard to be believed. During a 1957 television interview with Mike Wallace (dare I call such an interview on television "Ocular History?"), it's mentioned that she had conducted more than 30,000 broadcast interviews during her career. How did Mary Margaret differ from Studs? Why isn't she "Oral History?" She certainly interviewed interesting people, such as Carl Sandburg and Eddie Rickenbacker (who casually mentions during an August 1945 interview that he's known about the atomic bomb for some time now). She possibly interviewed more people than Studs Terkel, but few of her broadcasts have been heard. She did write two books and a syndicated column for the Associated Press, but these did not deal with the people she interviewed. So let's add an interesting interview technique and the availability of these interviews (either audibly or in print) to the qualifications needed to be an "Oral Historian."

And so we come to the present (or at least, the recent past) and this collection of David Siegel's oral history interviews and his exhaustive compilation of oral histories done by others. I've had the opportunity to hear Mr. Siegel's interviews (and seen him being interviewed on C-SPAN). While he's no Studs Terkel, he does know how to conduct a good interview. In fact, his interviews make excellent listening and reading. Asking the right question in the right way will determine how the interviewee reacts to you and the direction of the discussion. A "soft-ball" question, such as, "Tell us about your latest picture," is not oral history. A "hard-ball" question, such as those heard at presidential press conferences, is not oral history (although it may become just-plain-history if the President says something interesting). There has to be some value for those in the future for an interview to be called "Oral History."

As for the other oral history interviews listed in this volume, some were made by people who really knew what they were doing (such as Frank Bresee), and some by people who should have known what they were doing (Richard Lamparski, who could never end his program on time and frequently digressed) and some in the middle. It's time for you to join with David Siegel to find out who made history and who didn't.

J. DAVID GOLDIN
www.radiogoldindex.com

INTRODUCTION
Why a Book About Interviews?

If you're reading this introduction, it's because your enthusiasm for the programs that aired during radio's Golden Age is strong enough for you to want to learn more about the people who made it happen.

There are many books about well-known radio personalities, genres, and specific radio programs. For serious aficionados, there are multiple reference books. So, why a book about interviews? How useful or interesting can it be to read (or even hear) the recollections of folks who were involved in broadcasting: performers, writers, producers, directors, sound technicians, and the businessmen who made it all happen?

For radio enthusiasts like me, the answer is quite simple. Our interest in the Golden Age of radio extends beyond that of chuckling with anticipation as Fibber is about to open a closet door, or feeling a bit squeamish when we hear the sound of a creaking door. We gladly obey the announcer who tells us, "Uh! Uh! Uh! Don't touch that dial! Listen to BLONDIE." And we cheerfully challenge ourselves to "name that tune" before the hapless contestant comes up with an answer.

Most dedicated fans of old-time radio will admit that next to being able to listen to a favorite radio program, their greatest thrill would be that of meeting one of the people who actually participated in a favorite broadcast. Alas, with the passing of time, fewer and fewer people who were employed in radio during its golden years remain with us or are able to share their memories with today's enthusiasts. Thanks, however, to a coterie of dedicated individuals, some of whom began fifty years ago, the words and memories of many radio veterans live on—in the form of recorded interviews. By preserving the recollections of countless radio personalities, these pioneers of radio oral history have created a pool of invaluable knowledge available to both fans and researchers alike. Their interviews constitute a veritable "who's who" of radio broadcast history.

It was the memory of having listened to many such interviews that inspired me to carry on the oral history tradition, and when presented with the opportunity, conduct my own interviews, which in a modest way, add to this rich heritage.

It was while I was gathering my interviews for this book that I began to think again about the hundreds of interviews, which, to the best of my knowledge, have received scant attention from the current generation of fans and researchers. How many of these interviews existed, and who conducted them? How many collectors, researchers, and scholars actually knew about their existence? As the author of several books on radio, I was painfully aware of the limited amount of information that is often available about many programs or performers. Most important, how might people get copies or access to these interviews?

It didn't take me long to realize that there was a gaping hole in the reference material dealing with this aspect of radio scholarship; there simply was no single resource that contained a comprehensive list of extant interviews. Hence, the two-part nature of this book: Part I includes the transcribed version of the fourteen interviews that I conducted, while Part II consists of the first ever guide to more than 1,330 oral history interviews of more than 990 radio personalities.

The diverse voices that one can "hear" on these pages offer a unique insight into the human side of radio.

DAVID SIEGEL
JUNE, 2009

PART I
INTERVIEWS

Chapter 1
PARKER FENNELLY
(1893–2004)

INTERVIEW: AUGUST 27, 1977

Was it really thirty-two years ago? Shortly after moving from upstate New York to Westchester County, and filled with enthusiasm for everything related to old-time radio, it did not take long before I learned that a well-known radio personality lived nearby. Overcoming my natural shyness, and following several phone calls to the Fennelly household, I introduced myself and literally begged for an opportunity to meet with Titus Moody, the legendary resident of Allen's Alley.

Either out of pity or to put an end to my incessant phone calls, I was finally invited for a visit. And there I was, portable cassette recorder in hand, sitting on the back porch on a warm summer afternoon with Parker, eighty-six years old at the time, and his wife Catherine. In a most gracious manner, Parker began to share with me a lifetime of memories, from his earliest days of the stage to his radio appearances in a wonderful series called *Snow Village Sketches* (circa 1937) in which he and Arthur Allen appeared as a couple of cantankerous small-town New England characters. I learned a great deal that afternoon, both from Parker and his wife, who never hesitated to chime in with a memory of her own.

New Yorkers, who pay attention to television ads, will no doubt recall Parker as the Pepperidge Farm spokesperson. And movie buffs might remember Parker playing opposite Doris Day and Jack Lemmon in *It Happened To Jane*, or replacing Percy Kilbride in the final *Ma and Pa Kettle* film. As for me, I will always remember his voice greeting Fred Allen with the phrase, "Howdy Bub."

DAVID: Now you said you were on a radio program in 1929. It was my impression that commercial radio didn't really begin until 1927 or 1928, so you must have really been there at the birth.

PARKER: Now we came out here in either 1929 or 1930, I'm not quite sure. I had been doing some radio before then. I think I started in New York in about 1929.

DAVID: Your wife told me, I don't know whether she was

giving any secrets away, that you're eighty-six-years-old, or eighty-six years young.

PARKER: She's a little off. Eighty-five.

CATHERINE: I didn't say that!

DAVID: Okay, don't start a fight here.

CATHERINE: That wouldn't be the first one.

DAVID: The reason I raise the point—did you start in the theater? Were you on stage before you went to radio?

CATHERINE: He was a Shakespearean actor for many years.

PARKER: I started as a Shakespearean actor. Is this on?

DAVID: It's on. If you want me to turn it off, I will, or if you're concerned about what you say . . . .

PARKER: I'd rather you shut it off and ask me questions and then I will answer them. It doesn't make any difference if you can stand it.

DAVID: You've got to realize—I still think that people think of the radio stars, and I consider you a star . . . .

PARKER: Well, some how or other.

CATHERINE: I can't image any young people interested.

DAVID: I think you'd be surprised at the number of people who . . . .

CATHERINE: I think I would be.

DAVID: That's why I offered to take you, if you would like to travel, to Connecticut on October first. There's going to be—I offered this last year also. As a matter of fact, I think it was around October.

PARKER: I know you did. I know you did. And Jay—what's his name over there . . . .

DAVID: Hickerson. Jay Hickerson.

PARKER: . . . invited me to come over. No, I thank you.

CATHERINE: He never goes anywhere. What do they do?

DAVID: Mostly nostalgia. People talk about the old radio programs and quizzes . . . .

CATHERINE: What's the use of Parker going if you're doing that right now?

DAVID: Well, the use of your going—what I'm saying is I'm not a selfish person. I want to share your husband, because there are so many people who I think would be so happy to see him.

PARKER: It only makes you feel older. Makes me, I mean— not you.

CATHERINE: *One.* It makes *one* [laughs] . . . .

DAVID: You were telling me that you were a Shakespearean actor before you got into radio.

PARKER: Yes.

CATHERINE: Now listen—I want to tell you this. Parker was so down on radio that we didn't even *own* one. He didn't want to have one of those silly boxes in the house. My mother lived in Chicago. I went out there and she had a radio. I came home and I said, "It's great. It's wonderful." "No, no, that's no way for an *actor* to do. That isn't for an *actor*." Real actors looked down on it terribly in the beginning.

DAVID: There's no way to blackmail you, you know that.

CATHERINE: . . . until they began making money and then they thought better of it.

DAVID: What was your first radio show? It wasn't the *Snow Village* show?

PARKER: It was a series, [inaudible] *of Men*. I think the first sketch in that series I ever worked in was based on Service's poem, "The Cremation of Sam Magee."

DAVID: That's Canadian or Alaskan?

PARKER: Alaskan, I think. That pertained to fire, you see. It was sponsored by something like a furnace company or something like that. Maybe a coal company, I'm not sure—furnace I think. The same authors who were writing that series wrote *Soconyland Sketches*, which eventually turned into *Snow Village Sketches*. Because I worked in the one series, I went into the other series. And we—when I say we—Arthur Allen, and I, and several others did *Snow Village or Soconyland Sketches* off and on. Not always fifty-two weeks, but off and on for nineteen seasons. I think it was nineteen; over nineteen years. At the same time, Arthur and I did a series which was on five days a week, and we did two or three broadcasts a day of it because, at that time, you would do a delayed service for the coast and the Middle West.

CATHERINE: That was fifteen, and *Snow Village* was sixteen, and then he did two or three others. He did about twenty broadcasts a week.

DAVID: Was this all for the same network?

PARKER: No, different. CBS, NBC and WOR.

CATHERINE: He lived in New York. I lived out here.

PARKER: And we were sponsored on the series *The Stebbins Boys (of Buckport Point)* by Swift in Chicago, the meatpackers. And then things commenced to go wrong and they offered us a chance to renew it at a reduced price. I wouldn't do it and it went off the air. Very few people knew about *The Stebbins Boys*, but *many* people through the years, in the letters that I've had from people talking about the old days—five out of six would speak of *Soconyland* or *Snow Village Sketches*, although I did literally *thousands* of radio sketches. And they speak of Fred Allen.

DAVID: Are you originally from New England?

PARKER: Maine.

DAVID: Sometimes you think of actors on TV or in films being typecast—the typical villain or the pretty boy. It seems almost that you played the role of the country . . . .

PARKER: Yes.

DAVID: Was that constant, or did you ever break that typecast?

I also thought I heard your voice on a mystery series, *The Thin Man*, or *Mr. and Mrs. North*.

PARKER: I was on *The Thin Man* a number of times. Not regularly, but off and on. Incidentally, the man who produces *The Mystery Theater* . . . .

DAVID: Himan Brown.

PARKER: . . . also did *The Thin Man*. I mean produced it. Claudia Morgan was the girl. Two different ones played the man, I think. I can't remember his name now. I've worked with so many.

CATHERINE: Parker did Broadway shows, and even wrote several. He had several plays produced on Broadway.

DAVID: I also thought I saw you on a movie a couple of years ago—a Doris Day movie. Were you in a Doris Day movie?

PARKER: Yes, *It Happened to Jane*.

DAVID: Yes, I remember I was in Washington at the time. I was a radio buff at that point. I heard the voice. We were in a hotel room . . . .

CATHERINE: But the one that people remember now because it's so recent, *The Russians are Coming, The Russians are Coming*.

PARKER: Did you see that? I was in it briefly.

DAVID: Yes, yes. I don't remember seeing you in that, but . . . .

PARKER: I was an old man with a hearing aide, whose daughter is hung up on the wall by the Russians.

It's very brief.

CATHERINE: But very funny, very funny. And then, well, another one that is fairly recent is the one that Pam's children looked at the other night—*Angel in My Pocket*. That's really quite funny.

PARKER: That was with Andy Griffith.

CATHERINE: Well, that's only how many years ago?

PARKER: Six, I guess, maybe.

DAVID: Did you travel out west to do that, to California?

PARKER: Oh, yes. I've been out there many times. I made about twelve movies.

CATHERINE: One Hitchcock. I don't remember which it was.

PARKER: Yeah, I was with Hitchcock. *The Trouble with Harry.*

CATHERINE: Oh, yes.

DAVID: When you do a film, do you think they're choosing you? I don't mean to say anything that may prove offensive, but do you think they're choosing you for your voice or for the character that you . . . .

PARKER: I would think for the character—I would think so. Many years ago I was with Kate Smith for a long time.

CATHERINE: Wrote it.

PARKER: I wrote some material and there used to be people out in the alley at the stage door, principally to see

Kate Smith, of course. As I came out, I heard some girl or woman say, "He always plays the farmers (laughter)." Oh, and you asked about before radio. I was with Walter Huston, the first time Walter ever played on Broadway. He had been in Vaudeville at The Palace, but he had never been in a legitimate play before. I knew him very well. You know he was John Huston's father. Well, ask me something (laughter).

DAVID: I just don't want to interrupt. I'd rather hear you speak than me.

PARKER: Well, I have nothing . . . .

DAVID: I guess this is a question most people would ask: how did you get started with "Allen's Alley" and Fred Allen?

PARKER: Well, I worked on some special hour program and Fred was the emcee. I think that was the first time I ever met him. From that, he had me on his program. "Allen's Alley" was on the air before I ever joined. I was with him three and one-half seasons, one-half season of television, which Fred was never happy in. It wasn't a good program. I think he liked the last one that we ever did on the air in television. I think he was happy in that, but previously he liked radio, I know. And he liked Vaudeville. He had been in Vaudeville for years. He never was happy in television, and so it didn't last.

CATHERINE: He wasn't successful. You're never happy if you aren't successful.

DAVID: I was just talking to my wife this morning about Fred Allen and Jack Benny as two contemporaries and their famous feuds with one another. But Jack Benny seemed to just meld right into TV.

PARKER: Yes, he did.

DAVID: Fred Allen, for some reason, I remember his last few years on the radio he was always critical of TV on the radio. He was critical of the quiz programs particularly. He had one announcement where he got on the air and said, "If you're listening to my program and they call you for one of the quiz programs and you miss a prize, my insurance policy will pay you."

PARKER: It's true. He did. He carried his own insurance.

DAVID: They say that his wife, Portland Hoffa, or I don't know what her name is, but it was Portland Hoffa on stage I guess—that she has been very unhappy or bitter about radio, or about the collectors of the tapes, for example. I know Jack Benny, when he was alive, there were a lot of people out in California who wrote to me and said that he was always active, always successful. But as successful as he was, he would let people—people like myself—strangers—just come into his house, go down into his basement, and tape—make copies of his programs because he wanted to share them with people. And Portland Hoffa, the widow of Fred Allen, has just the opposite point of view.

CATHERINE: Oh, well Fred was very generous to Parker. He just gave him everything because everybody wanted to use that name (Titus Moody), and he kept asking Fred if it was okay. And finally, he wrote him a letter and said, 'It's yours. It's *you*. Nobody else can do it."

PARKER: Portland married a man named Joe Rines, and they live in California most of the time. I knew Joe very briefly because he was an orchestra conductor in Allen's own program. But he eventually married Portland. We generally have a Christmas card from them in California. I have heard that maybe the husband is very careful about things now rather than Portland would be. I don't know about that. Fred was very generous with *everybody*. Incidentally, only a couple of weeks ago, one of the people who used to be on "Allen's Alley" before I was, died.

DAVID: Alan Reed?

PARKER: Yes. His real . . . .

DAVID: Falstaff Openshaw.

PARKER: He was on, I think, one or two programs I worked on with Fred. He had left as a city character the year before.

DAVID: His name was Bergman was it?

PARKER: Teddy Bergman was his real name. Alan Reed was his stage name. He did very well in California. He did *The Flintstones*.

DAVID: Fred Flintstone—the voice.

PARKER: I saw him once when I was out there and he got to be very heavy. He was inclined to be heavy. I read his obituary. Minerva Pious, Mrs. Nussbaum, you know, lives in New York now. I went to Cape Cod for some anniversary thing, and Minnie was there and Pete Donald. Pete Donald did Ajax Cassidy, the Irishman, and Senator Claghorn was Kenny Delmar. And he was also at Cape Cod.

CATHERINE: They all went up and did a show up there.

PARKER: That's the last time I saw him.

CATHERINE: And who was it that did Fred Allen?

PARKER: On the air, you mean?

CATHERINE: No, no, up there at Cape Cod.

PARKER: Well, don't know anything about him. I'd never seen him before.

CATHERINE: Was he anything like Fred?

PARKER: Yes, yes, he was very good.

CATHERINE: And did he do Jack Benny too, that night?

PARKER: Yes. Jack Benny was an artist. He had good material. He knew how to handle it. He was one of the greatest.

DAVID: You talk about material and you said you did some writing for Kate Smith. In terms of the success of the radio program, what weight would you place on the comedy writers or the material in terms of that versus the delivery?

PARKER: About 75 percent, I think! It used to be, I don't know that it is now, but some of the people who would write—I knew about rural things more than I did about city things—and some of these authors who would write rural things. I was thinking the other day. This is not in radio or television; this is theater. I worked in *Carousel* in New York. Did you ever see *Carousel*?

DAVID: Yes.

PARKER: I did the Startender, (Starkeeper) you know—the old man up on the ladder? You know *Carousel* was adapted from the Hungarian . . . .

DAVID: Molnár?

PARKER: . . . and was converted to New England. But I could have written—with no ego—I could have written better dialog. Not the music and the songs, naturally—the lyrics. But the dialog, I thought, could have been improved a good deal. It was a great show. I think *Carousel* is a great musical.

DAVID: Wonder if the public really paid much attention to the dialog, or if they were just enthralled by the music?

PARKER: That was great I thought. I saw the original *Lilliom*, and Eva Le Gallienne did it. I think they could have used better dialogue, but that's neither here nor there. They did all right with it.

CATHERINE: Well, that's interesting about Eva. I mean Parker liked her so much. He likes everybody that he works with. He never has any trouble. And naturally they like him.

PARKER: John Cecil Holm, H–O–L–M, wrote in conjunction, in collaboration I guess, with George Abbott, *Three Men on a Horse*. You know the old comedy? And others. There was a book called *The Southwest Corner* laid In Vermont or New Hampshire. John Cecil Holm dramatized it. We did it at Saratoga in the summer theater, and then we did it in Philadelphia and in New York with Eva Le Gallienne, and she was very nice to work with. That was the first time I ever met her, knew her.

She was very nice to work with. She has been praised wonderfully in *The Royal Family*. They revived that with Eva as the old actress. Are we running out?

DAVID: It'll run another minute or two, I'm sure, and then we'll flip it over. I could listen to you for as long as you're patient enough to speak.

PARKER: I've been looking for you all my life (laughter).

CATHERINE: Is it over now?

DAVID: Have you ever considered writing an autobiography?

PARKER: No. Sometimes, somebody has said that. I said, "Nobody would read it but the grandchildren and I doubted if . . . ."

CATHERINE: They were always at him to even talk. He won't talk like this for any of us. We're supposed to know it all. But, you know you *forget* after so many years. You really and truly forget it all. We have twin girls. They are always, whenever they come—now next week, Jane will come down from Connecticut for a week. She's always at him to let her take notes or do something. He just brushes her aside and says, "Why don't you go out to a movie or why don't you go out to lunch?"

DAVID: To your own daughter, huh? That's cruel. I would think that there would be interest in your—you've known so many famous people.

CATHERINE: You have to have a little bit of egotism to write a book about yourself, and Parker—although he has a very good opinion of his *ability*—he knows just what it is, but he doesn't have that kind of egotism.

DAVID:	No, but there are probably a lot of stories that he could tell about people like Ms. Le Gallienne.
CATHERINE:	Now that's true, if he ever sat down to do it, but he'd rather fool around writing a play. He'd much rather write a play than write about himself.
DAVID:	Have you written . . . .
PARKER:	Yes, I wrote one, which I sold to George Cohan. Do you know George Cohan?
DAVID:	George M. Cohan. *Seven Keys to Baldpate.*
PARKER:	Yes. And he played the leading character and I gave him the proviso to change it any way he wanted to suit himself, because nobody else would evidently buy it and he did and he did it in Boston and New Haven and in New York. But it was a flop. But the other one, in New York, was a mystery play called *Cuckoos on the Hearth.* And that ran, I think, 129 performances.
DAVID:	What year was that? Do you remember?
PARKER:	Oh, gosh, it was in the 1940s, and then it was published by Dramatists Play Service. It has been done—well, I can't say in every state—but it has been done all over this country and in South America, and in Hawaii, and in Japan.
CATHERINE:	Where did Leo see it when he was in the service?
PARKER:	Japan.
CATHERINE:	(laughs) It seems so ridiculous!
DAVID:	You wrote that in the 1940s, and they're still

putting it on—still doing it?

PARKER: Very seldom now, because it's dated. It was about the war. I mean, that entered into it. The man was an inventor, and he invented something used in the war, so it's passé now.

CATHERINE: I'll tell you what it *did* do, among other things: it kept us in salt, I would say. Not much more, for fifty years, but it made Percy Kilbride.

DAVID: Pa Kettle!

CATHERINE: Parker wanted to play the part himself, but it *made* Percy Kilbride.

PARKER: I wrote the part for myself, but I was tied up with radio in the evenings, regularly under contract. Percy did the part and he got notices that long in the papers. I took him to Hollywood, and he did about eight of those *Ma and Pa Kettles*, and then he retired. I went out to do the final one. It *was* the final one. The audiences naturally were looking for—Percy was a small man. He was funny, but . . . .

CATHERINE: But not legitimate at all.

PARKER: I never did another one. I never once saw it. I never wanted to see it. I knew it wasn't good, but I got paid for it.

DAVID: Marjorie Main was still in it.

PARKER: Catherine had known Marjorie up in Fargo, North Dakota in a stock company before I ever saw Catherine or Marjorie. And then Marjorie was out here at our house and eventually I worked with her in *Ma and Pa Kettle.* So I knew her very well. She died not long ago.

CATHERINE: Parker was saying last night that if they ever did the life of Bella Abzug, Marjorie, if she was alive, would be a natural for it because she looked very much like—well, of course she'd be very old now because she's as old as *I* am.

DAVID: Were you on the stage also?

CATHERINE: A very, very short time. I mean, there's only room for one, unless you're a Lunt and Fontaine.

PARKER: There was the great team of all time, Lunt and Fontaine.

CATHERINE: I couldn't run a home . . . .

DAVID: He's very ill.

CATHERINE: . . . and take care of twins . . . .

PARKER: He died.

DAVID: It must have been this last week, then. Within the past week or so, I remember hearing about him being very, very ill.

PARKER: I saw him when he was a juvenile, thin, young, in Boston. He used to work at a stock company in Kestrel Square. He said in an interview that he worked for $10 a week I think, or $15. That was before Equity and any scale.

CATHERINE: You worked for almost that little.

DAVID: Speaking of Equity and scale and that sort of

thing, I thought I heard you say that you found, after a while, that radio paid better than Shakespeare, better than the theater.

CATHERINE: He gave up Shakespeare because he had a family to send to college.

PARKER: It was steady, and the theater might last two weeks. In fact, I did a play in New York called *Live Life Again.*

DAVID: Many of the interviews that I've heard from some of the people who were in early radio claim that the only way to make money in radio was to play many different roles. They'd get something like $15 or $20 for each performance and sometimes they'd be on and off . . . .

CATHERINE: Don't you believe it! I'll tell you a story and this is true. I was very resentful when Parker was young and handsome and had this beautiful speaking voice.

DAVID: Now he's old and handsome.

CATHERINE: . . . that he was playing, and he's always played— that same character. Always. I happened to go into the Peekskill Post Office and somebody—some mail clerk, hollered something at me about one of his characters, and I resented it. So I said to Parker, "It's about time you stopped playing *that* character. You can play anything. You can play Hamlet. You can play anything." So he said, "You go down to the advertising agency and tell them what you think about," and he *never* in his life had let me interfere in any shape. But I knew this girl very well, so I went down and poured out my soul to her. And when I got all through, she said,

"When all those pretty boys are in the actor's home, Parker will be working." And that's just what happened.

DAVID: I don't want to compare you to someone like Boris Karloff, but I heard again on tape, an interview that was done by a British radio fellow of Boris Karloff just a year or two before he passed away. One of the questions that was asked of Karloff was, "Did you ever resent being cast in the monster roles?" And Karloff's response was, "No, because prior to that I was a character actor, but I never really made any good and it was the monster roles that kept me and my family going all of our lives."

CATHERINE: If you're in it to make money, or you are in it for fame, and want to go hungry, all right, but I mean if you want to make money at it . . . .

DAVID: But you see there are people who not only collect radio programs, but there are also quite a few interviews of the stars that are available. These are fascinating. Has a fellow named Richard Lamparski ever tried to get in touch with you?

PARKER: No, I never remembered the name.

DAVID: He has written three or four books called, *Whatever Became Of?*

PARKER: Oh, I have one of his books.

DAVID: Invariably, he will go around and interview people, who have been very famous and who dropped out of the public life to find out what they are doing. Some of them are still in the field.

CATHERINE: Some of them are in the actor's home.

PARKER: I'll tell you something. When I was young, there
           was an actor around New England named Alexis
           Luce, L–U–C–E. "Lexie Luce," they called him. He
           was a very good leading man in stock company and
           so forth. As I told you, we did this series, *The
           Stebbins Boys*. Not for very long, but we did it two
           to three times a day. Years afterward, when it had
           been abandoned by the advertising agencies, I got a
           letter from a man in Bangor, Maine or somewhere
           in Maine, asking about the rights. Who owned the
           rights to the series *The Stebbins Boys*? He said he
           was interested in getting a friend to use it on a
           Maine radio station. This is before television. Lexie
           Luce said he now drove the rural delivery mail
           route. He was looking for something to do in
           radio. I don't know how it turned out. I just turned
           it over to the author. And by the way, I told you
           the author of the historical sketches on the
           Soconyland Sketches lives on—what is it, Henry's
           street?

CATHERINE: Harmon.

DAVID: I better write that down. Is he still there?

PARKER: No, he died.

CATHERINE: I told you, there's nobody still alive except this
           one girl. Rosie Russell is one girl that Parker
           took out of high school and put her in his
           company in Washington, D. C. Somebody sent
           me the thing out of *The Post*. It was a big
           interview with her and asked her how she ever
           got into radio. She said, "Parker Fennelly helped
           me get into radio." She's actually the one still alive,
           isn't she, Parker? Directors, authors, Assistant
           Directors (laughs) . . . .

PARKER: I think so. And the original Director—he died a few years ago.

CATHERINE: Jerry? He lived in Harmon.

PARKER: He lived in West Croton isn't it? His wife, his widow still lives over there, or did.

CATHERINE: You see, when people came out from New York, Harmon was absolutely the limit. You couldn't commute any farther than that. Besides, you got wonderful service, you know. They changed the engine there and you got terrific service. When we were looking for a house, I looked in Pleasantville and all around and Parker said, "This is the limit." I mean the thought of riding on the train that long when you just came out of New York—that's why they all came out here.

DAVID: I see the bread company has got somebody else now trying to imitate your voice.

PARKER: Pepperidge. I was with them a long, long time— twenty-something years. I used to go all over the country to their sales meetings, but I haven't been with them for about three years. I tell you, Campbell's Soup owns Pepperidge Farm. It's a different set-up now. You probably know the story. Mr. and Mrs. Rudkin lived near Norwalk. He was a Wall Street man and she was a housewife, I suppose—a mother. She had three boys. The story that I had always heard was that one of the boys was ill, and for some reason she commenced making homemade bread. Things weren't any too good at that time. He used to take some into town either to give—anyway, I think I'm right about that. I know that she'd put it in local stores and that led to it enlarging. So when I first was with him, Mr.

Rudkin was alive and Mrs. Rudkin and two boys. One lives in Paris. At the time he did, anyway. The other two boys were with the firm. So I knew the whole family very well. And then I was in Chicago. We were there for a sales meeting. The word came that Mr. Rudkin had died. One of the sons was with us. He came back. It wasn't too long before Mrs. Rudkin died. Meanwhile, she had sold the business but retained some to Campbell's Soup. Campbell's Soup is a very thrifty organization. They're all right, but I never had many dealings with them. Anyway, we came to a parting of the ways. I didn't mind. I enjoyed going around to the sales meetings because they were nice people. Money was no object. I'm talking about the time the Rudkin family had it. They would give these huge dinners and cocktail parties for the local food brokers, the bread people. That was long enough. I was with them a long time.

DAVID: What was the last work that you've done in terms of the profession? Have you been pretty well retired for the last couple of years?

PARKER: Yes. I haven't done anything lately.

DAVID: Would you take something on if you had the opportunity?

PARKER: I doubt it. I don't know. They wouldn't send for me now—not me being as old as I am.

DAVID: The reason I asked—I assume that you have an agent.

PARKER: No, not anymore. I did on the coast. I had two and one moved to retirement and the other one handled—do you know when you see him Andy Griffith? He's a very, very nice person, very nice.

DAVID: Oh, yes, sure. He's selling Ritz Crackers now.

PARKER: He should be a very wealthy man because of all of those old television programs that he did with Don Knotts. Do you know Don Knotts? I made a picture with him, I think. It wasn't such a bad picture, but it wasn't terribly good. I don't know who devised the name, but Don Knotts played a character named Figg F–I–G–G. I can't remember the first name. Anyway, Figg. The name of the picture, of all things, was *How to Frame a Figg*. Now anybody could have thought of—but anyway, it was quite funny in spots. Don told me—I hadn't seen him for many years. He said, "You know when I saw you last or you saw me last? It was at WOR and I was one of the children, or one of the "boys" in *Bobby Benson*. That used to be a radio . . . .

DAVID: I remember Bobby Benson.

PARKER: . . . well, he was one of the younger characters. Why didn't you bring your wife along?

DAVID: Do you know who wanted to come along? I have a nine-year-old boy, and I didn't take him with me to the convention last year. When I told my wife yesterday that I was coming here to see you, his question was, "Is he a famous man?" I said, "Yes, he is. He's a very famous man. Not everybody knows him, but he's a . . . ." I spoke to my mother last night. She wanted to know if I was coming to see her. She lives in the Bronx. And I said, "No. I'm going to be busy. I'm going to be visiting Parker Fennelly." She said, "Oh, I remember Parker Fennelly. He was on many radio programs. So my son wanted to come get your autograph.

CATHERINE:	Well, I tell you, the girl who has these tapes and lives right next door is the one with the nine-year-old son. Now Parker, will you explain to—*how* did Nancy have those tapes? Who was it who gave you—was it the man up at Cape Cod?
PARKER:	A man I met in Cape Cod.
CATHERINE:	That he didn't know.
PARKER:	He was a collector like you.
CATHERINE:	You probably know him.
PARKER:	He sent me some tapes. I didn't have a player. We took them up to the neighbor's to play—of *The Snow Village*.
CATHERINE:	Right next door.
DAVID:	Did he give you many? Did he give you one or two or several?
PARKER:	I think there are four altogether.
DAVID:	It's possible that I may have them.
CATHERINE:	I never heard them. I never went up. Jane, our daughter, lives in Connecticut. Parker went up and listened to a couple and he said, "I think the Ross' were getting bored with that, so I called a halt." And they kept them. It must have been a year ago isn't it?
DAVID:	Do you drive? Do either one of you drive?
CATHERINE:	Do I drive? Parker drives. I lost my license after sixty years because of my eyes.

DAVID: Are you far from Route 202 here or from Route 6? I would be delighted to have you as guests in my house for dinner one night if you'd like to come out. I'd consider it an honor. I would be happy to play any of the tapes that you might be on and I won't be bored. I assure you of that.

PARKER: I heard them for the first time in many years. One was about Hiram Neville and the boy going fishing. Do you have that?

DAVID: Yes. That's the one where he plays hooky from school.

PARKER: Truant, right. I thought that's the one you meant when you said—the other one I can't remember.

DAVID: I think it's one where they have to pay for a window in the church. One of them is too cheap. One of them is supposed to be a skinflint. You were the skinflint?

PARKER: Can you turn it (the tape) off and start again? Because I'm going to say some things . . . .

DAVID: If you want me to. (Resuming tape).

PARKER: The phone rang. I went to the phone and he said, "This is Hans Conried. I've listened to you for many years. I've just come back from Europe and am staying overnight in New York. I said that when I was in New York again I'd call you up and tell you." And he did. I never saw him in my life and he never saw me, but I mean he's an eminent actor. For him to take the trouble to call up someone he's never known or seen, I think that was very nice of him. I never saw him when he was in New York.

CATHERINE: I wanted Parker to go and see the show or send a telegram or something.

PARKER: It didn't last long.

CATHERINE: If it had lasted, it would be all right to send the telegram.

DAVID: I think recently I read that Molly Picon moved to Croton.

PARKER: Oh, really?

DAVID: She is living with her sister, and she was in our newspaper. I don't know if you get the same newspaper that we do. There was a festival about two weeks ago. They had a feature story about her. They say she's eighty years old. Do you know her?

PARKER: No, but I've watched her on interviews and read about her.

CATHERINE: Well, long before you came out here, Jackie Gleason had a house just over the mountain there—a great, big, spectacular place. Columbia bought it from him.

PARKER: CBS. I tell you, he was remarkable, when he had that series. I worked with him twice, maybe. He had the most amazing memory. He could go through a thing once or twice . . . .

CATHERINE: Parker said he never saw such a memory in his life.

PARKER: One other—Ralph Bellamy. He had that same kind of camera memory. It was amazing.

DAVID: I would think that going from radio to anything else, where in radio you can read your script.

CATHERINE: That's why they loved it, that's why they loved it.

DAVID: It would be such a pain in the neck to have to start remembering.

CATHERINE: They could run from one studio to the other and *read* it.

PARKER: I'll tell you who used to live over on Mount Airy. Do you know Mount Airy? Everett Sloane. He must be in some of the tapes you have because he worked in so many. And especially he worked for Himan Brown.

CATHERINE: You know, Mount Airy, many, many years ago when we first came out here was a real, real artist's colony. I mean all kinds: dancers, singers, and real artists that do this.

DAVID: People tell me in Croton that there were a lot of Communists who lived up in that area also.

CATHERINE: I wasn't going to add that, but that was true (laughs).

PARKER: Fay Bainter owned land up on Mount Airy. Do you remember Fay Bainter?

DAVID: Yes, yes.

CATHERINE: There were an awful lot of theatrical people here then, because, as I say, they thought they were *really* getting as far out of New York as they could reasonably live.

DAVID: It's a good hour by train.

CATHERINE: Forty-five minutes—about forty wasn't it—at best?

PARKER: Forty-nine on the Express.

CATHERINE: When Parker was working so much in New York, he kept a room in a hotel and just came out here weekends. Well he couldn't—I mean, the last broadcast for the coast was . . . .

PARKER: One o'clock.

CATHERINE: Yes. So how could you get a train? He once had trouble with the income tax people because they said, "Who on earth would be listening to radio at one o'clock in the morning?"

DAVID: Well, I can recall as a kid, turning on a radio in the daytime and listening to a soap opera. Then, later at night, you know, sometimes when you drive at night in New York, you'll get stations as far west as Chicago.

CATHERINE: Sure.

DAVID: You said you did *Snow Village* for nineteen seasons?

PARKER: Off and on.

DAVID: And *Fred Allen* for I don't know how many seasons.

PARKER: Three and one-half. Three in radio and a half-season of television.

DAVID: What would you say, although those three years—I think probably, for people who remember radio, I would guess those three years have left a greater impression than almost anything else that you've done. Do you find that true?

PARKER: Well, they've all died off. The ones who used to listen to the original broadcasts are dropping off like flies.

CATHERINE: There are only a few people like you.

DAVID: What programs were you on, other than *Fred Allen* and *Snow Village*, on any steady basis?

CATHERINE: Julia Sanderson and Frank Crumit used to go to Boston. After he did his *Snow Village*, he would get on an all-night train to go to Boston and broadcast up there with Blackstone Cigars.

PARKER: Well, one I was on a lot was *Grand Central Station.*

CATHERINE: That was daytime, wasn't it?

DAVID: Saturday afternoon I think.

CATHERINE: You remembered!

PARKER: And there was one I did for Kroger grocery company in the Middle West. It was called, *Mary Foster, the Editor's Daughter.*

CATHERINE: How many years, Parker? How many years?

PARKER: Thirteen years, I think.

DAVID: Did you play her father? I have several of those.

CATHERINE: For thirteen years. We used to kid about it, because Parker has a cousin Mary. You passed by her house on Hunterbrook Road. Mary Rothsford (now), but she *was* Mary Foster. We used to always kid about this, *Mary Foster the Editor's Daughter* and laugh uproariously.

DAVID: Did she play the part?

CATHERINE: No, no. She's not an actor. That was the character's name. I was out in Chicago. My mother lived at the Edgewater Beach in Chicago. I turned on the radio, and I hear Parker. And I thought, *What on earth is that? I never heard that program. Why that's Mary Foster, the Editor's Daughter.*"

PARKER: It wasn't heard in New York. Kroger's brand . . . .

DAVID: I have a few of those programs. If you haven't heard that for a while—when I tempt you into stopping by the house—I want to play that one for you.

PARKER: For a brief time it was on WOR here, but that was long after.

CATHERINE: Thirteen years he did it, and I had never heard it until I went to Chicago. I wasn't sitting around *wishing* I could hear it or anything (laughs).

PARKER: I'll tell you, a number of months ago, our dog was stolen, and they used to take paid ads on the local radio station in Peekskill. I called up to find out if I could put an ad on. They had discontinued it, sort of. Anyway, he didn't seem much interested but he said, "Maybe this is a news story." And he put it on the news just because he heard my name. From that, a man who has a program on WLNA in Peekskill called me up and asked me if I would be interviewed. I wasn't very anxious to.

CATHERINE: We found our dog, so we had to.

PARKER: So I told him the story, and I'll tell it to you. There used to be a member of a garden club that Catherine belonged to. The woman was very deaf and probably never heard or listened to the radio. She maybe never wanted to, but she wanted to be polite. When she saw Catherine occasionally, she would say, "I always forget. Is your husband Lum, or Abner (laughs)?"

CATHERINE: Parker, tell him the story about when you were making personal appearances and you were walking along with Arthur up in Albany. It's quite a long story. It was like that.

PARKER: Did you ever hear the program *Sunday Night at Seth Parker's?* Phillips H. Lord?

DAVID: I think I have one program in that series. Wasn't that a religious . . . .

PARKER: Yes, Sunday evening.

DAVID: I have one excerpt, one program. Were you on that one?

PARKER: No, no. I guess I won't tell that one. I don't think I should. It's about a man who's dead.

DAVID: Don't speak ill of the—we're not supposed to do that. Some people who have talked about Phillips H. Lord have not spoken too kindly of him.

PARKER: I can understand that.

DAVID: Mr. Gang Busters.

PARKER:	That's right. He was very successful; a great businessman.
DAVID:	Didn't he also do *David Harding, Counterspy*?
PARKER:	I think so, I'm not sure.
DAVID:	Were you on *Counterspy* at all? There must be people out there trying to imitate your voice.
PARKER:	Well, there used to be an actor. He had a restaurant.
CATHERINE:	He was the only one. When Parker couldn't do a radio show, he would always recommend—he was a young boy, wasn't he Parker—a fairly young guy. And another one who does the *best* imitation of Parker, but he wouldn't do it—is, you know, the boy with Jack Benny.
DAVID:	Oh, Dennis Day.
PARKER:	I couldn't tell if it wasn't myself.
CATHERINE:	He is absolutely marvelous—absolutely the best. There's nobody like him.
DAVID:	I've seen pictures of him recently. As old as he is, he looks very young for his . . . .
CATHERINE:	He does the commercial. He was quite young when he went with Jack Benny, wasn't he?
PARKER:	He has about one hundred children, doesn't he?
CATHERINE:	More or less.
PARKER:	His real name is McNulty, I think, and he had a great many children.

CATHERINE: It was a wonderful tie-in because he would come on *The Jack Benny Program* following the *Fred Allen* program and do Parker, this imitation, and it was absolutely marvelous.

PARKER: One program followed the other. Jack's followed ours.

CATHERINE: None of us could tell the difference. He's the only person that doesn't make one little slip. Any of these people who do these imitations, there's always just something they do.

PARKER: I remember on *The Benny Program* Jack comes into the room and sees Dennis in my character reading a book, and Jack says to him, "What book are you reading (whatever his name was)?" *Titus Moody.*

PARKER: I don't know that they used the name. Dennis said, "Oh, a sad book." And Jack said, "What is the name of it?" Dennis said, *Forever Amber.* Jack said, "That isn't a sad book." Dennis said, "At *my* age it is!"

CATHERINE: He was wonderful. Absolutely perfect.

PARKER: He's a very nice person, too. I heard there's a program on WOR radio at noon. Jack—*Critic's Circle*—Jack O'Brian. He generally interviews people connected with the theater or television or concert field or something. He had an agent on yesterday, a man who had handled a great many celebrities, and Jack asked him, "Who was the highest priced artist making appearances?" And he said, "Hope. Or at least one of the very to—Bob Hope." He was on Fred's program more than once, I think. I remember one time in particular. He couldn't be there for the afternoon rehearsal on

Sunday because he'd gone up to West Point or somewhere to do a program. He loves to work, evidently. It can't be the money. He has so much money.

DAVID: He must be in his seventies now, Bob Hope. Well, there are some people, I guess, who if they didn't work—we all know people who retire who suddenly—it's the worst thing they can do.

CATHERINE: He would never do anything unless he read the script and it was something he wanted to do. He's turned down more things than he's done.

PARKER: That was not in the beginning.

CATHERINE: He isn't money mad. That's why he's living (laughs).

PARKER: You remember Jim Farley if you're a New Yorker.

DAVID: *Postmaster General.*

PARKER: Yes. He was supposed to have one of those camera memories—who never forgets a face or a name. And Fred used to have guests on the program. Not theatrical people necessarily, but he had Jim Farley. Farley wasn't there for the Friday rehearsal, but he was there for Sunday dress rehearsal. He sat in a row of chairs no farther away than that chair from me. It was in the wintertime. He had seen us get up and do our little stunt, so he couldn't fail to see and hear us. I was walking along the corridor of the RCA Building. They took Jim Farley down in the musician's elevator so as to avoid the autograph people, you know. He was getting out of the elevator, putting on his overcoat, just as I came up to him in the corridor. I had been with him a good many hours, so I said, "Good night, Mr. Farley." And he said, "Oh, hello. How are you today?" Like he'd never seen me in his life.

DAVID: He's a politician, though. You should remember that.

PARKER: Yes. He only remembered politicians, evidently. He certainly didn't remember me.

DAVID: People who could scratch his back . . . .

PARKER: That's right, that's right.

CATHERINE: You ought to tell some of the jokes on *yourself* apropos of *that*. Because Parker can't remember / (laughs). He was walking through Grand Central one night, rushing for a train. Some guy walked up to him and he shook hands, or put his hand out to shake hands with him, and said he hadn't seen him for a long time. All the guy wanted was a dollar. He'd never seen him before!

PARKER: He misled me because he said, "Hello Partner." I thought he said, Parker, you know. And I said, "How have you been?"

CATHERINE: (Laughs). He has a *million* of them where he hasn't remembered people.

DAVID: Do any of the radio performers or TV people—I'm sure their union has been successful in getting them coverage for programs that have been done again and again and again, but I wonder if any of the people in their fields are getting residuals. Is that part of the radio business?

PARKER: Yes. It came into being with the AFRA. It was originally The American Federation of Radio Artists, A-F-R-A. Then, television came in and it changed to AFTRA—A-F-T television and radio. They established rates and rules as the years went on. Back to a certain time, you get residuals, not before a certain date.

CATHERINE: I'm always glad when somebody says, "Oh, I saw one of those old movies." Good. Well, we'll eat *this* week.

DAVID: That's what I mean. When I saw that movie in Washington, does that mean that some people ended up getting money as a result of that because it's playing?

PARKER: Which one was it? Oh, the Doris Day. After a certain time, it burns out. You meant about television programs when you spoke of it, didn't you?

DAVID: Right, because they don't repeat radio programs, so you wouldn't get anything for radio programs.

PARKER: No. And the repeats on television. You see, I've done so few that have been repeated, I couldn't say. I think for instance, *The Hollywood Squares*. Did you ever see that?

DAVID: Yes.

PARKER: All through the summer, they're repeats. Now I think those people get a certain amount. I've done so few television programs. I've done pictures that have been repeated on television, and it's a descending scale of residuals. At first you get a certain amount through the years. After a time it runs out.

DAVID: They say that some of the people who are doing commercials are doing better in commercials than if they had their own program.

PARKER: Yeah.

DAVID: The commercials are just repeated over and over again.

CATHERINE: Well, you see now Parker has severed his relationship with Pepperidge, but he still gets the residuals from when they *use* his old commercials.

PARKER: Which is very seldom.

CATHERINE: We can't speak to him during income tax time because he insists upon doing his own. So I said to him this year, "Oh, it's wonderful. You don't have to pay anything now; you're not working." And he said, which he shouldn't have done, and he thought better of it afterward, and was sorry he said it. "I made more money this year than I did last." Because they used his programs so all over the country.

PARKER: But now they don't.

CATHERINE: These residuals are very nice things.

PARKER: We look at the news at 6:00 p.m. and that girl that does the lip quencher ad—in an hour and a half, she's on twice, at least. Sometimes three times, I think. Now just imagine . . . .

CATHERINE: But way back, Parker, when you were doing so many, many radio shows, there was no such thing as residuals then.

PARKER: No.

CATHERINE: See, that's where the union comes in good.

DAVID: I don't imagine there are too many radio programs that were rebroadcast. TV programs during the summer they'll rebroadcast them again.

PARKER: There are some stations, as you know, that use old-time radio programs, but there will be no residuals.

DAVID: Don't they have to pay—you can't just put a tape on radio and broadcast—don't they have to pay the original producer or someone's got the copyright on that?

PARKER: I would think in some cases NBC owns the rights. In other cases . . . .

DAVID: The sponsor, in other cases, would own the rights.

PARKER: Right. Standard Oil might own the rights to *Snow Village*. I don't know that. I know I don't get anything, naturally.

CATHERINE: When we first started in show business, there was no Actor's Equity. So you could be stranded out in the middle of no man's land, and if you didn't have a check from home, there you would be. Parker fought tooth and nail. He wasn't gonna be like a ditch digger and a carpenter and join a union, but it's been a wonderful godsend to actors, that union. He didn't want it. Oh, he fought it. He said, "No." He wasn't joining any union. Well, this is an altruistic way of looking at it, but when it comes down to hard . . . .

PARKER: I was only a small fish, but there was a big fight in New York. George Cohan refused to go in for Equity. He founded a union—an organization called The Actor's Fidelity League, and they were rivals with Equity. But eventually Equity won out, and there was no more other union. All these off-Broadway theaters and off-off Broadway theaters, they have a deal with Equity, I think, that some Equity actors can work with non-union. But only off-Broadway, not on Broadway. Catherine spoke about—I'm not sure she did—we have a grandson who has been acting in an off-off-Broadway show. That show has closed, but the same theater, the same outfit, is doing right now, or were last week—you know the theater has not only changed in the quality of the plays, but in the titles of the plays. I never heard such titles. The one they're doing this month, or have been doing, is called *Consider the Roaches*. Would you want to see a play called *Consider the Roaches*?

David: If I were a bit perverted, maybe.

Catherine: Parker wouldn't go to see Michael, but I went with his mother and we drove in and went to a Sunday matinee. There were two Equity girls in that show.

David: Do you miss very much the excitement of radio or did you find radio as exciting as TV?

Parker: Oh, I suppose I miss it, but I'm used to not missing it now. I did enough, I think.

David: Some of the people who have been interviewed talk about their dreams of a Renaissance of radio coming back.

Parker: I doubt that.

David: The only two programs that I know are being done now are *The Radio Mystery Theater*. I don't know if you've heard any of those—and there's a program on Saturday and Sunday called *The General Mills Adventure Theater for Children.*

PARKER: For children. I didn't hear it. I heard it announced on the radio.

DAVID: I haven't heard any of the programs. A friend of mine who has been tape recording them says it's for children, but adults who like adventure would enjoy it as well. Whenever I try to get my daughter to listen to a tape, she always complains because she can't see it. She likes to be able to see the characters.

CATHERINE: Well, you see that generation is conditioned to that. They probably don't like black and white at all. And yet I have two neighbors, both with swimming pools, so you know they can buy anything they want, and they don't have anything but black and white. But they are older people. Parker always thought, and still thinks, that you can imagine things better than you can look on television.

DAVID: Arch Oboler talks about that quite a bit when he's interviewed, particularly when you are doing something of a frightening nature. With sound you can create an image that is more frightening than you can with . . . .

CATHERINE: You can, you can. Parker, tell him the story about when you used to have an audience up in The Fishbowl, and the little old lady who wrote to you and Arthur for years finally came down from Upstate New York.

PARKER: She was a *Snow Village* listener. I think she probably had been a school teacher. She used to write little notes when we went off the air to find out when we were coming back—these beautifully-written letters. Once, she wrote that she was visiting her daughter or niece or something in Jersey. She lived in Connecticut, and was visiting across the river, and could she come over and see a broadcast. There's nothing more boring than watching a broadcast, but we called her or wrote her or something, asking her to come over. It so happens that at that particular time, which was one summer, we were doing fifteen-minutes versions of *Snow Village*—parts of programs cut down so it was done in a small studio with not many people in the cast. We took her into the control room and she saw the final rehearsal and the broadcast on the air. She came out through the studio and we took her to the elevator. Now here was a woman who had been listening for years and imagining the church, and school and grange in the small village. Her only remark was, "I should think you'd be bored to death doing this." All illusions gone! And that's true of radio (laughter). That's all I have to say.

DAVID: Okay, I probably should be leaving now.

PARKER: No you shouldn't. I didn't mean that. I didn't mean that.

DAVID: I was quite serious in saying that if you do get out—I really don't know what your schedule is—but if you do get out and you can find your way, at least as far as that mall, where the theaters and where that restaurant is, we're just about five minutes from that spot. I'd be so happy to have you as a guest.

PARKER: I still have a license, but I don't usually drive much because Mary—our girl who lives in Brooklyn—we hear from her every day or every other day. She goes to the supermarket and she takes Catherine and brings her home. So I don't generally drive, but I have a driver's license. I don't like to drive at night and I never was a *good* driver. Long ago I put many thousands of miles . . . .

DAVID: Well, if you want to take advantage of the offer, I'll pick you up and take you.

PARKER: Well, thank you. That's good of you. I appreciate that. My first experience in the theater, I think was in Boston. (Johnston) Forbes-Robertson, who was long before your time of course, was the greatest Hamlet I ever saw. He did repertory. He did *Hamlet* and Shaw's *Caesar and Cleopatra* and *The Passing of the Third Floor Back* and another one. I, along with some others, went down and got one dollar—fifty cents maybe—and I'd go walking along in the crowd scenes. In those days, radio needed crowd noises.

DAVID: We call them spear carriers.

PARKER: That's right. I remember being in the mob in *Caesar and Cleopatra*. After the scene in which we had carried spears or something on stage and yelled at the proper cue, the curtain went down. This great man—he was an elderly man then, but he was a model. He had the courtesy to come over to these rag-tag bums off the street and students earning fifty cents and say, "Very good boys."

CATHERINE: (to their cat) "You want to come out, Othello?"

PARKER: You see we have a Shakespearean cat, Othello (laughter).

CATHERINE: Well, he's in there yowling at me while I'm talking.

DAVID: Does he have a Desdemona to keep him company?

CATHERINE: That was Mary. I was telling her about those
              tapes and she said, "Why don't you get those tapes
              back and *they* have something to play them on."
              (inaudible) see even any show in Boston, let
              alone a Broadway show, and yet he knew he
              wanted to be an actor.

DAVID: How did you get started?

CATHERINE: He always wanted to be.

PARKER: I went to school in Boston, but before that I
              always wanted to (inaudible).

CATHERINE: Very well could have been. He used to go down to
              the post office in this town in Maine where he was
              born. Once, he was getting playbooks and the
              Postmaster said, "Some more of those damn
              dialogs?" They probably thought he was as freakish
              as we think some of these Pop stars are.

DAVID: Have you ever been back to your hometown?

CATHERINE: He owns a house up there.

PARKER: My brother died a few years earlier. Before that I
              hadn't been back for forty years.

CATHERINE: No, he won't go back. We own a house up there,
              and I want to go back in the summer.

DAVID: Do you correspond with anyone from your
              hometown?

CATHERINE: Oh yes, more or less. I send Christmas presents to
              them.

PARKER: At Christmas. They're all dead except on the hill.

CATHERINE: Oh, they write and *beg* him to come. He has relatives . . . .

DAVID: It must be people. Every town has a famous . . . .

CATHERINE: They don't look at him *that* way. They like him. They love him.

PARKER: I wouldn't know about that.

CATHERINE: But he would take shows up to Lakewood.

PARKER: Lakewood is the second oldest summer theater in the country. I wrote three plays that were done out there.

CATHERINE: He'd go there because it was work. Well, it's a joke, but it's the truth. People would say, "You've been to Europe and you've been here and there. Why won't Parker go?" Parker won't go anywhere unless he gets paid and *this is the truth.*

PARKER: (Laughs).

DAVID: Well, it's only for you. Who does he spend the money on except for you?

CATHERINE: No, no, no. That's got nothing to do with it. If he got a call, an SOS right now from Hollywood, he would be on the next plane. But if I said, "Let's go up to Maine and look things over . . . ." "Oh, I don't want to travel all that way (laughs)." No, he won't go anywhere unless he gets paid. He was down in New Orleans for thirteen weeks. And he'll say, "I can't close the house. What about the animals and people breaking in?" For thirteen weeks, nobody broke in. The animals didn't die or anything. Because it was acting and he wanted to do it. They're all a little strange. You talk about you and your wife getting along in spite of your temperament. They're all a little strange, but you learn to live with it. You take the bitter with the better.

PARKER: I was telling somebody the other day. Fred Allen, as you know, used to have guests on his program, and Fred, being a very courteous person, went to see Bela Lugosi, you know, who played Dracula, at his apartment with a man from the William Morris Agency, I suppose. It was fairly early in the forenoon. And Lugosi had just been getting cleaned up and he came to the door and he had cut himself shaving and the blood was (laughter).

DAVID: Oh, that is a rich one. That's good.

CATHERINE: You know, Fred Allen, for all his success and all of his money, never owned a house, and never owned an automobile, but he walked down the street every night from his apartment towards Times Square, and he'd have $5 in this pocket and $10 in this pocket and $1 in this pocket, and just handed it out.

PARKER: He had a regular retinue of followers who depended on him.

CATHERINE: The most generous person in the world. Imagine he never owned a *car*. Never went to Europe.

DAVID: He didn't need one.

PARKER: No.

CATHERINE: He didn't *want* anything like that.

PARKER: He used to go to Old Orchard, Maine in the summer and many years ago somewhere in Jersey.

DAVID: Wasn't he from New England also? He had kind of a twang.

CATHERINE: Boston.

PARKER: His name was Sullivan, but he took the name Allen because he was going to be on an amateur program and they did it alphabetically. At least that's what he said.

CATHERINE: He was a juggler, wasn't he? Did you ever read one of his books?

DAVID: No.

PARKER: He was a juggler, but . . . .

CATHERINE: In Vaudeville.

PARKER: The funny part—as long as I was with him, I don't think I ever heard him say a dirty word or swear word. But in doing recorded programs, there was a sound effects man, who used to be a pianist in the pit in a Vaudeville house. He told me he never appreciated Fred Allen because he used such filthy language under his breath, whispering for the orchestra. I never heard it when Fred was on stage.

DAVID: You probably knew him at a different time in his life. You know sometimes as you mature, you change. I have a tape recording, not only of some of his programs, but also of an interview done of Fred Allen where he talks about almost regretting being in show business, wanting another life. He wanted to be a writer or . . . .

PARKER: And he could write very funny material.

DAVID: Didn't he write a lot of his own material?

PARKER: Yes. They had writers, but I think he always circumvented it.

CATHERINE: He asked Parker to sit in on his—but he didn't want to get involved in that at all. In one of his books, he speaks about "Allen's Alley" and how he said he could always write for Parker better than for any of the other people.

PARKER: He was from New England.

CATHERINE: He knew what he could do and Parker always changed anything he didn't like in *any* show that he was on. He *always* rewrote it the way he wanted it (laughs), but he didn't want to get into that part of it. Well, he did it for Kate Smith. He did it for a year and he didn't like it.

DAVID: Kate Smith, I understand, has a summer home in Lake Placid.

PARKER: Yes, she used to live there. I guess she still does.

DAVID: Abbott and Costello started with Kate Smith. *The Aldrich Family* started with Kate Smith. Were you one of the characters on her program, or did you just write her . . . .

PARKER: Both. And Abbott and Costello were on when I was on.

DAVID: Was that in the early 1940s?

PARKER: I would say so, yes. I'd have to look up the dates.

DAVID: Do you keep a scrapbook of . . . .

CATHERINE: No! He doesn't even have a program or anything (laughs). He doesn't want any pictures of Dorian Gray around. He didn't want to look back, he wanted to look ahead. He threw everything away. We haven't a script as far as I know. If we have, it's well hidden.

PARKER: I will tell David what I told somebody the other day. I have written a mystery play called *Cuckoos on the Hearth*. It was tried out near Gloucester, Massachusetts, and in New York. At that time, we had a boy who didn't live too far. Anyway, he was in his twenties. I suppose he was in New York so much he had to take care of the place. His mother was English, and I think his father was a local around here. They probably never went to the theater in New York, but he was a great driver. He was a great mechanic. So I had tickets for my play in New York.

CATHERINE: We were very fond of him. We wanted to do—we thought it would be a great thing for him to go and take his family to a Broadway show, especially one that Parker had written.

PARKER: I gave him tickets for himself and his family— enough for all of them. He used to come about three to four times a week, and the next morning, I saw him. I didn't expect him to rave over the play or anything about it. There were a couple of damns or a damn and a hell. Nowadays, a teacher in Sunday School, you know—I didn't open the subject, but all he ever said about the play was, "How'd you ever know those swear words (laughter)?"

CATHERINE: That was the comment. Of course, they didn't like it. They weren't attuned to Broadway shows. We were *stupid* to even *think* that he'd like it.

PARKER: I never knew . . . .

CATHERINE: Parker directed at Beechwood for a couple of years.

PARKER: In Scarborough.

CATHERINE: Yeah, The Beechwood Players. We've always maintained—you give away free tickets and people don't like the show. They think, "Well, I paid all this money and I've taken a lot of trouble to think it out." If you just give them tickets they don't like it. It's human nature, I guess.

DAVID: If you give them something, it's probably not worth anything. If they have to pay for it, it has to be worth something.

CATHERINE: That's just exactly it, but it's hard when you have the tickets and can give them to feel that way, but you really should.

DAVID: You have to know who you're giving them to also. There are some people who would give their eye teeth for the opportunity.

PARKER: Turn that off.

Chapter 2
JOAN MERRILL
(1918–1992)

INTERVIEW: MARCH 15, 1981

Once in a while, I hear from a relative of someone who appeared on a radio program asking if I have a program on which their relative appeared. Such was the case early in 1981, when I received a phone call from a gentleman, who identified himself as Israel Seeger, an attorney. He was engaged in a sentimental hunt, and had heard of my collection. Israel, or "Tex" as he liked to be called, was the husband of Joan Merrill, who just happened to be a vocalist on the Edgar Bergen radio program. He went on to explain that when he served as a naval officer in the Second World War, he would listen to AFRS transcriptions of his wife, when his ship was not involved in combat. Over time, most of those transcriptions were either lost or damaged, and thirty-seven years later, he was anxious to replace them.

As luck would have it, I was able to provide "Tex" copies of several of the Bergen programs from 1944 and 1945 that featured Joan Merrill. Rather than ask for any financial compensation, I instead requested an opportunity to interview his wife about her experiences as a radio performer. Postscript: the photo of Joan that accompanies the interview was provided by her son, William Seeger.

DAVID: I am very lucky. I have two charming guests in my house today—Israel "Tex" Seeger and his wife, Joan Merrill. Joan is a very lovely, charming lady, who used to be a vocalist with *The Edgar Bergen and Charlie McCarthy Show*, and I would like to ask Joan some questions about her experiences as a radio performer.

JOAN: Just one correction . . . .

DAVID: Yes, ma'am.

JOAN: (slight giggle) I was the singing *star* of the *Edgar Bergen* show.

DAVID: Spoken like a star. Let me ask you this—I asked some of the questions earlier—how did you first get into show business, Joan?

JOAN: Well, I've been singing since I was a little girl. I don't ever remember *not* singing, and just continued on until suddenly, one day, something very important happened in my life. I did a recording called "How Did He Look?" for RCA Victor, or a subsidiary, Bluebird Recordings, and that's how it happened.

DAVID: Somebody heard that recording.

JOAN: Oh, yes.

DAVID: Two million people heard that recording—at least two million people.

JOAN: Over two million people bought the record, yes. Unfortunately, at that time, we didn't have—we weren't presented with "gold records." So that was the only drawback I can think of right now.

DAVID: But somebody in the accounting office was adding up the pennies, nickels and quarters . . . .

JOAN: Oh, yes.

DAVID: Also, somebody from the Bergen show had to have contacted you or your agent. Could you tell us how that got started and how you first met Edgar Bergen?

JOAN: Well, they had heard my record. They had seen me perform on Broadway and in the various clubs, and they asked to interview me, and of course, I was very interested in going on their show. We had about one home broadcast in New York, and then flew out to California, where we traveled from one Army base to a Naval base. This continued for the full year I was with the show.

DAVID: Could you tell us something about some of the famous performers—almost as famous as you—who performed as guests on the Bergen–McCarthy program—any anecdotes . . . .

JOAN: They were *all* so wonderful. One in particular I'll always remember. Linda Darnell was a beautiful, beautiful, beautiful girl. We shared this large dressing room just before the show. My sister, who is a very beautiful woman—at that time a girl—and I were making up in front of the same mirror. Unfortunately, because I got finished making up *my* face, thinking that *I* looked rather well, and I looked at my sister, and I thought she looked *beautiful*, and we both looked at Linda Darnell, and then we looked at ourselves again. Then, we added more rouge, and then I added more mascara, and couldn't beat *that* beauty. She was really something outstanding; a lovely, lovely girl. Most of the guest stars were very charming, very warm people.

DAVID: I find it interesting hearing you talk about the makeup before the programs. Some of the popular movies in the 1940s, which featured excerpts from radio programs, seemed to always show the radio performers going on with tuxedos and formal gowns, and yet one thinks that the audience in many cases being limited to a studio audience, the performers might not have been that interested in their appearance. It was their voice rather than their physical appearance.

JOAN: Oh, no. Oh, no. Particularly when you're broad-casting for the boys in the Army or the Navy, one must look their best for them—always, always. We were always very particular how we looked.

DAVID: Can you talk a little bit about the rehearsals for the programs that require a great deal of time in terms of rehearsal?

JOAN: We started to rehearse on Thursday for my vocal numbers, and Ray Noble and I would sit down and work out our arrangement, or rather *my* arrangement, together. On Sunday, we would meet early in the day, and we would go over the dialogue, sitting in an office doing that, of course. It entailed not too much, because you had a bunch of pros there. It was my first experience with speaking lines on radio, but they were real pros, so it wasn't too difficult, and it wasn't too time-consuming.

DAVID: What was Edgar Bergen like to work with? He is, of course, a legend in show business. Can you tell us anything about the Bergen personality?

JOAN: He was a very wonderful, wonderful man, very sweet man, very gentle man. He was very quiet until he put the dummy on his lap—Charlie McCarthy—and then he became alive. I think that what happened was that his personality came out of the mouth of Charlie. It was fascinating to watch and to listen to.

DAVID: Did he write any of his own material?

JOAN: I'm certain he did. They had a staff of writers, yes, but I'm certain he had a great deal to do. And then, as we went along, we would correct anything we felt could be done in a better way.

DAVID: I was going to ask you about Ray Noble earlier, but I don't want to cause you to say anything that might be embarrassing in terms of the kind of individual he was to work with.

JOAN: Well, he was a fine musician. He was a fine arranger, and he was a good actor; he was great. Everyone was rather very nice to work with, very nice to work with, particularly the guest stars.

DAVID: Can you tell me at all about any of the other radio programs you might have performed on?

JOAN: I had been on *The Fred Allen Show* as a guest singing star, and I had been on one that Steve Allen had on—*Songs for Sale*, and I had been on a show—I was a guest star on Rudy Vallee's radio show.

DAVID: All of this in the mid 1940s—1944 . . . .

JOAN: Right, uh-huh. I had toured on the road with Rudy Vallee for about six months.

DAVID: When you say toured . . . .

JOAN: . . . doing theaters throughout the country . . . .

DAVID: . . . as his vocalist.

JOAN: No, as my own act. I had my own act, and he had a whole package; he had a whole show. He had a dance team, and a dancer, and a comedian.

DAVID: Did he emcee the program?

JOAN: Yes, he sang, as well.

DAVID: I guess sometimes one doesn't know the right questions to ask in order to elicit as much information as would be of interest to radio hobbyists, but I think anybody who listens to the Edgar Bergen programs, or the Rudy Vallee programs, or Fred Allen, basically wants to know as much as they can about what it was like to work with these people—what it was like basically in terms of the routine of being a radio performer.

JOAN: Very interesting, very difficult, and of course, to one who had been in show business, it was an everyday occurrence, so it's rather difficult for me to pick out any one thing that might interest the people listening. It's a marvelous business. It's a fantastic business. People are so interesting. Don Ameche, for one, is just about one of the nicest men I've ever met in my life. He, too, is a gentle man with a *marvelous* sense of humor—just great to work with. Basically, what it boils down to is sitting down and rehearsing, and stopping and correcting certain lines, feeling that you have a better idea, and it's very difficult, actually, to try to define precisely what might interest people listening because, as I say, it was an everyday occurrence to us—just being together—getting ideas from one another.

DAVID: Do you find—I may be projecting something that doesn't exist—the role of the vocal star, or the vocalist on a particular program, differs in who was on almost throughout the program? You have a spot . . . .

JOAN: Right.

DAVID: . . . and then there's some comic relief, and then there's a commercial, and then you have a spot . . . .

JOAN: Exactly. I had two spots in the show: one at the beginning of the show and one towards the end of the show, at which time, I would have dialog with Charlie, and then go into my song.

DAVID: When you had that dialog with Charlie, did you think you were talking to Charlie or Edgar?

JOAN: No, I thought I was talking to Charlie. One never looked at Edgar when Charlie was talking to you. He was a character.

DAVID: How old was Charlie at the time? A teenaged boy?

JOAN: Well, I guess he was a teenaged boy.

DAVID: Charlie used to work with Marilyn Monroe.

JOAN: Charlie flirted with everybody and he was one of the cutest characters.

DAVID: It didn't feel like Edgar Bergen flirting with you?

JOAN: No, it was Charlie, and it may very well have been Bergen, because as I told you earlier, he was a very quiet, quiet man. But as soon as Charlie opened his mouth, he was anything but quiet.

DAVID: Charlie, of course, has a much different personality than Mortimer or Effie Klinker.

JOAN: Yes.

DAVID: Did Bergen change when he had Mortimer or Effie, or was he the same Bergen?

JOAN: He was the same Bergen. Naturally, the voices were different. The characters were entirely different.

They were fantastic to look at, as well as to listen to.

DAVID: Did he have more than one dummy that he would bring just in case something happened to Charlie? Did he have a backup?

JOAN: I'm certain he must have had a couple.

DAVID: You never saw Charlie getting any makeup or Charlie getting any paint jobs?

JOAN: No, no. Charlie was always spic 'n span and ready to go.

DAVID: Always wearing his full dress outfit. At the time, as I recall, they used to sell McCarthy dolls. They were very popular. Did you ever own a Charlie McCarthy doll?

JOAN: No, I had him every Sunday, and that was enough for me. He was cute.

DAVID: Have you had any regrets, in terms of leaving the Bergen program, or not being on radio beyond . . . .

JOAN: No, because I had made moving pictures, and later I appeared on television shows. I love to perform in theaters and night clubs. I like the rapport that I have with the audience, and no, I didn't miss radio quite honestly.

DAVID: Do you miss it today, when you turn on the tube and hear nothing but either the news or . . . .

JOAN: I don't believe so, because there's television now, and there is no need for shows on radio. I have listened to some shows on radio that I find are quite interesting, but for the most part, as you say, they are news programs and record programs, which I listen to quite frequently, but I think television is certainly here to stay.

DAVID: Shall we embarrass Tex and ask him if he would like to comment on listening to his wife in the South Pacific?

TEX: It was really great. I had taken with me to the South Pacific in 1945 quite a number of the air check records Joan had taken off the air of songs. I had occasion to play them for the crew on the battleship *Iowa* when we were at sea. I used to play them over the public address system to entertain the crew. It got great responses, and we would also have the opportunity there to hear the shortwave rebroadcasts of *The Edgar Bergen Show.*

DAVID: Were they popular on the ship?

TEX: Oh, yes. We got those, and we got shortwave direct from the States, at times, and then we had the Armed Forces records that they sent out to the ship on 16-inch records that we had to play on a special record player that we would listen to. I used to make it a practice, whenever I got time off, to play it on the radio—not the radio—the loudspeaker system on the ship, so they would broadcast throughout the whole ship to entertain the crew with my wife's singing. It was quite a thrill. I'm getting a kick now out of collecting old Edgar Bergen shows—looking for some I no longer have the reproductions of because a lot of them got worn out and broken while I was overseas. Some that Joan had here got broken, as well. We're trying to track down people who have the old Edgar Bergen shows of November 1944 to May 1945.

DAVID: If anyone ever listens to this tape (laughter) and has a Bergen and McCarthy program with Joan Merrill—now you have the ones that have Linda Darnell, Orson Welles—but if there are any others that surface and we can get them to you, we will do our best.

TEX: There was one in particular that I'd like to get—the one with Rudy Vallee as the guest. I remember very distinctly he had two great songs on it: "Accentuate the Positive" and "Saturday Night is the Loneliest Night in the Week."

DAVID: I remember that one quite well.

TEX: That was the last broadcast I heard on New Year's Day of 1945 before I went overseas. There were others that Joan did where she did great songs— "Night and Day" for one—that I haven't been able to locate. I'd love to get my hands on them.

DAVID: We will hunt for you. Joan Merrill, thank you very, very much for being patient, cordial, and sweet and everything else.

JOAN: Thank you, David. Right back at you.

DAVID: My pleasure.

Chapter 3
WARD BYRON
(1910–1996)

INTERVIEW: JUNE 9, 1984

I first met Ward Byron at the Friends of Old-Time Radio Convention in October of 1979. The convention program for that year lists the names of some thirty-four guests, including folks like George Ansbro, Ralph Bell, Hyman Brown, Raymond Edward Johnson, Mandel Kramer, Peg Lynch, Grace Matthews, Alice Reinheart, Rosa Rio, and Arnold Stang, to name just a few. Not surprisingly, guests with the highest name recognition were surrounded by fans whenever the opportunity presented itself. Others were either ignored or given only perfunctory attention by attendees.

I freely admit that the name "Ward Byron" meant nothing to me, at the time. Reading the program, which identified him with such programs as *The Chesterfield Supper Club with Perry Como, The Fitch Bandwagon,* and *The Phil Harris and Alice Faye Show,* motivated me to seek him out, a decision which proved most fortuitous.

Whatever it was that opened a veritable floodgate of memories, had me listening with rapt attention. Ward and I met again at another FOTR convention in October 1983 where he told me about his involvement in other programs such as *The Chamber Music Society of Basin Street* and his connection with some of the nations most famous big bands such as Jimmy and Tommy Dorsey, Duke Ellington, Benny Goodman, Woody Herman and Harry James.

By this time, having managed to conduct a couple of prior audio interviews, I suggested that Ward's memories should not be lost to future generations, who would want to know more about radio's past, and invited him to visit me at home, where I might capture those memories. Several months later, Ward acted on my invitation, and what follows are the recollections he shared with me.

DAVID: Hello. This is Dave Siegel, and I have the distinct privilege of having as my guest on this Saturday, June 9, 1984, Mr. Ward Byron. Ward has been associated with The Golden Age of radio, and has a particularly rewarding relationship with some of the world's greatest jazz musicians as they shared their talents with radio audiences. Ward, can you tell us how you got started in show business in general and in radio broadcasting in particular?

WARD: Okay, Dave. It's a pleasure to be here with you and to be in this library of yours, or I should say storehouse of tapes such as I've *never* seen before. I've never seen such a collection. I'm *overpowered* by it. The fact that you've dug up things that I've been looking for years is just icing on the cake on this visit, and seeing you. But now, you ask about getting into radio and all that. I don't know how interesting that would be, except that as a kid, I had a kid band—a college band, allegedly—went to Europe with them in 1929 and 1930. We played on the Cunard Line, and so I always had a love of music. It was a case of should I go to college or should I go in for music? And the music won out. Not from the standpoint of a performer, but from the standpoint of being *behind* the microphone. I went with WEAF, and 195 Broadway, at that time, that was owned by AT&T, so I was with NBC six months before NBC was born. So, from that I learned the fact that I had loved music and had even studied voice for quite some time. I was going to be the next John Charles (Thomas) Byron, and found out that I'd much rather be behind the microphone. So, in fact, my voice wasn't up to it, let's face it. So that was the start, and then it went up when NBC was formed to 711 5th Avenue and became the Red and Blue Network. As you remember, Red being WEAF combined with the Westinghouse Station of WJZ, which was the Blue Network. So, from there on, I got mixed up with Raymond Knight, who was probably the fount of all comedy in television, radio, or whatever. The electronic medium, let's say. He was the real source of it all, because Ray did a show called *The Cuckoo Hour*. Now this predated any of the Jack

Bennys, Eddie Cantors, or anyone of that type, and it was a nonsense, wild, crazy show that I loved. I went in for that and got to know Ray well. Finally, we became partners, and I left NBC and went with Ray, and did the program with him, and we did a daytime serial, too, for kids. So, that's back in the early 1930s.

DAVID: Do you remember the name of the daytime serial that you did?

WARD: Yes. The daytime serial was *Wheatenaville* or *Billy Bachelor and the Twins*. If any recording of that could be found, I think it should be destroyed immediately, if it hasn't already self-destructed. As a matter of fact, though, it was not a soaper the way other soapers were. It was a comedy soaper with kids. He was a bachelor with two children, and he played it for laughs and humor rather than any of the weepies that came with most of the soaps. So I'm getting way off the track. The thing that brought me up to see Dave was the fact that he had *Chamber Music Society of Lower Basin Street*. Now there is quite a history to this that involves a lot more than my participation in it. That is the fact that it's almost a person going full cycle and involving people full cycle in this thing that could become rather interesting to anyone studying radio, because some of the things, I think, were the first time they ever happened in radio. I had left Raymond Knight in 1935 to go to NBC in San Francisco—KPO and KGO. That's the Red KPO and the Blue KGO. Now on arrival out there, I ran into a chap, Jack Meakin, who was Associate Director and Arranger for Meredith Willson, and Jack and I became the very closest of buddies. He was doing a program called *Bug House Rhythm* that had been created by Jack and Boyd Joe Thompson.

Now Joe Thompson has a show of his own on the public radio station in San Francisco. I don't know the call letters. Do you know, Dave? Anyway, it's in San Francisco and it's called *Joe Thompson's Music Room*. He and Jack had dreamed up this idea of treating the gut-bucket, low-down jazz of the day with the dignity of an appearance by Toscanini, but announcing things in a very straight way. Well, I had just come from New York where Ray Knight and I had done three years, once a year, a program at the Metropolitan Opera which was called *Operatunities*, and we had the full cast of the Metropolitan Opera—the entire cast and orchestra and everyone to work with, and it was one of the greatest fun times of my life. In fact, no one remembers it, because it was not broadcast. It was just for the Metropolitan Opera Fund, and quite expensive the tickets. We packed it wall-to-wall each year with this burlesque parody of the opera. Well, the surprising thing was that people never realized that opera stars are human beings, and they like to laugh, and they don't have to be bowed to and said "Madame so-and-so." Lily Pons was "Lily," and a great gal, a wonderful gal. She loved 52nd Street, where we'd take her in the old days to hear jazz, because no one would *think* of her doing things like that, but they loved to participate in this show. Well, it turns out that that was practically the same idea as Joe Thompson and Jack Meakin were doing with *Bug House Rhythm*. So now, Joe left for some reason. I don't recall whether he left the company or went away. Anyway, I took the program over. So, I had it from 1936 to the end of the series, when I left KPO and went with Music Corporation of America. We did the program with Jack Meakin as the orchestra leader, who became Dr. John Brunker Meakin. Archie Presby, the announcer, became G. Archibald Presby, and we were very purist in the presentation of this whole idea—the fact that we never allowed any laughs. We had commentary on all the numbers and the names were given. Never Duke Ellington, but Edgar Kennedy Ellington, and we never allowed laughs or clowning in the program. So, weeks would go by, and we'd get letters from people saying we didn't know you were kidding. And all of a sudden, it would dawn on them what was going on, and they would roar and laugh at the thing. Well, it was perfect for my type of enjoyment, because I had just come from the Metropolitan Opera with all the seriousness that things were treated in those days by announcers speaking with awe about the performers. We had Wagner and Milton Cross, who was a wonderful guy. I loved Milton. We were ribbing Milton. We were doing it with kindness, but ribbing the whole pretense of classical music was the general idea. Now, the thing that makes, I think, an interesting story is the fact that I left NBC to go to the Music Corporation, and Jack Meakin left, I guess, KPO, about six months or a year later. He came to New York and tried to form a band, but just didn't have too much success with that. In fact, you need an awful lot of backing for that. He had a wonderful band, actually. But he finally was looking for work, and I introduced him to the Program Director at NBC. So, the next thing you know, he's an NBC producer in New York. So, I was on the road with *The Fitch Bandwagon* you may remember, which played all over the country and played every name band in America. I was called one day by the Program Director, who said, "We'd like to bring back that *Chamber Music of Lower Basin Street.*" And I said, "Great. I'd love to do it." And they said, "Well, it's a sustaining program. You know what it pays." As a matter of fact, I think it was about $25 for a script, but I said I'd do it for *nothing*, we had such fun. So, I wrote the script for it and to the first program for the idea of *Bug House Rhythm*, rather, and a week later, the Program Director called me, practically in tears he was so embarrassed. He said, "Ward, I don't know how to even tell you this, but what happened at the program meeting was that one Lewis Titterton, who was head of Continuity Acceptance at NBC, stood up at the meeting, and said "Yes, I think it's a great idea to bring back *Bug House Rhythm*, but does Ward Byron own that thing?" He said, "Now Ward is an old friend of mine, but I'm working for NBC. He's not. Now, doesn't NBC own this program? Why do we have to have Ward Byron do it?" So, he said Lewis won the point, and his writers were to take the program over, and he said, "I just can't face you, having gotten you into this." I said, "Well actually, so there's no embarrassment, and so you won't feel bad, here's a present. Here's the first script." So I gave him the first script.

DAVID: Do you remember what year this was, Ward?

WARD: Yes, that would have been—it started in 1940 or 1941. I don't remember which, but it's one of those years. So anyway, he said, "Well, we'll take it." And I said, "Now, on one condition. I'll give you this and then you don't have to be embarrassed. Whenever I'm in town, I want to go on the program for nothing. I don't care if it's pay or not, I want to be the intermission commentator/musicologist just for kicks and for fun." And so he says, "You got it." So, every time I was in New York, I would go on in the intermission spot with *Chamber Music Society of Lower Basin Street* and I was introduced, I believe, as Dr. Ward Byron, musicologist, who will read from his five-foot book of shelves on how to tell a downbeat from a boiled owl.

DAVID: You're really saying that they stole the program from you.

WARD: They didn't steal it because it was their show. I did it as an employee of NBC. They owned it.

DAVID: When it was *Bug House Rhythm*.

WARD: When it was *Bug House Rhythm*. So, they brought it back. They did change the title, though. So anyway, I would go on with my commentary and do a ridiculous spot of intermission the way the opera would have their intermission with Milton Cross, and then they'd go on to an opera quiz and all that, so we kept that intact. However, it had turned into not the purest show that *Bug House Rhythm* was, because they allowed an audience to laugh, so no one was led astray by hearing this nonsense and wondering what it was all about. They even had Zero Mostel and noted comics on. Everybody became Doctor instead of just Dr. John Brunker Meakin, the leader, which we were doing of course. Dr. Damrosch—Walter Damrosch in his day—we were referring to that sort of presentation. Now getting back to it, I keep wondering, but coming back to the thing that I say goes full cycle. The remarkable thing is, as I think back, when I'd come on and do my intermission spot. Here I am, in New York on the microphone out front, and Dr. John Brunker Meakin is the producer sitting in the booth, who had been the original Dr. Meakin of *Bug House Rhythm*. So, he's looking at me through the glass window and I'm out there, which is such a strange switch in radio, and as far as I know maybe it's the first time it ever happened. Maybe it should be the last.

DAVID: A little role reversal.

WARD: Yeah, complete role reversal.

DAVID: How did you get involved with the Fitch radio show?

WARD: *The Fitch Bandwagon*, I think, is memorable at least to me, heaven knows. For six years, it provided a very good income and a way of life traveling all over the country and even Canada, doing a different name band every week. Of course, in six years, we repeated many of them. The Dorseys would visit again, and Benny Goodman, and all of the biggest name bands would be on once or twice a year at times. But the story of how it originated might be interesting to those who follow the devious methods of radio broadcasting booking. MCA had gone to the Fitch Company in the Chicago office of MCA with an idea. They said for X number of dollars per week, we will produce—deliver one of the top named bands of the country—1938 it was—to 1939. Name bands were pretty big. Records were booming. The Dorseys and Goodmans and all were kings of the mountain. So, they said, "Great, we'll do it." The remarkable thing to people in these days is the fact that the contract was signed with the starting date of September, I believe, of 1938. It was all set, but they had no program. They came to me because I had been working for MCA. I had done the Elizabeth Arden show with Eddy Duchin, Buddy Rogers, and a few of those, so they said, "You've got a program." I said, "What is it?" We're going to call it *The Fitch Bandwagon*. I took it over from there and I did the script. Then, they said we better have an audition. So, we auditioned the first original script of *The Fitch Bandwagon*, which was to be Guy Lombardo. Well, Guy was a little too big to audition. Why should he go through all this script and doing lines and so forth and the history of his life and band? So, The Fitch Company wanted to hear approximately what it would be like, so Frankie Masters in Chicago did the very first show and he played Guy Lombardo. The members of his band played Carmen, and Lebert and so forth, and we did the script as though it was Lombardo. The Fitch people were down in the clients' room of The Merchandise Mart in Chicago. They heard the thing, and said "great," so we went on the air, and it went on for six years. The thing that I think would shock all of those engaging in this pursuit these days is the fact that there were no lawyers, no long contracts, no six auditions with the client changing things here and there. It is just remarkable to think how casually the show went on. Was that the story you wanted?

DAVID: Well, that's the story I got (laughter).

WARD: In other words, you *don't* want it.

DAVID: It's a good one. I'm interested. I think anyone who loves old radio as I do, in learning about as many of the broadcasts that you were associated with, any little human interest stories that you can give us about them. For example, you've indicated that you've been on Bug House Rhythm, and you practically created the program whether you say so or not. I got the feeling that NBC swiped Chamber Music from you. You were active with the very, very first Fitch shows, you did that daytime kids' serial *Wheatinaville*. What other programs have you been associated with, Ward, and in what manner? You've written some, directed some. Have you done any production? What are some of the other shows you've been involved with?

WARD: Actually, Dave, I wrote and directed all my shows. The only time I didn't write programs was when I got into television. I did the Ameche-Langford show—*The Frances Langford-Don Ameche Show*—out of the Little Theater next door to Sardi's.

DAVID: Was it *The Bickersons*?

WARD: No. *The Bickersons* was their radio career. They used it in guest appearances once in a while, I think, in television. We didn't do *The Bickersons*. There was some contractual problem with the thing, but we had Tony Romano. He had traveled with Bob Hope and Frances in Europe. We were on five days a week, but now *that* I had writers for. But the distinction of *that* show is that I think it was the first real television exposure—although he had done single, dramatic shows here and there—it was the first real exposure of Jack Lemmon. Jack did a sketch on the thing five days a week with his first wife, Cynthia, and it was called "The Couple Next Door." It was a *joy*. Jack was one of the most talented people in the world, so that's the distinction that show had.

DAVID: When radio people think of *The Couple Next Door*, they think of Peg Lynch and Alan Bunce.

WARD: That's right, but we stole the title. I think it was "The Couple Next Door." Maybe I'm misquoting. Anyway, it was a segment of the Ameche-Langford show out of the Little Theater on 44th street.

DAVID: That was television . . . .

WARD: Yeah, that was television. That I didn't write—I had writers. I was just Producer. I did write *The Paul Whiteman's Goodyear Revue* in 1950-52. That was in television, out of the biggest studio then in New York for television—ABC Studio at 66th Street. NBC didn't come in with the Brooklyn facilities until a year or so later, so we had the largest studio facility for television in the country at that time.

DAVID: Speaking of Paul Whiteman, as you know, you're credited with writing some of the early Whiteman radio programs, *Forever Pops* programs, and *Stairway to the Stars*. Can you tell us a little bit about the programs and about Paul Whiteman? What was he like to work with?

WARD: *You're* the one who told me I did those, and thank you for doing it. I'd forgotten all about them. I'm delighted to have the shows. I remembered that I did them. I have a faint recollection of them, but there's nothing faint about the recollection of Paul Whiteman. He was a giant in the industry, and someday will really be given the recognition he deserves. Maybe a complete hour special on television should be done for him. There's a very excellent book out now by Tom DeLong called *Pops: The Biography of Paul Whiteman*. People don't realize what an influence this man was in the industry, in the business. They think of him as King of Jazz. Then, they say, "He wasn't jazz." All jazz musicians resent that title. Jazz was an all-encompassing title in those days. Jazz meant ragtime, popular, anything in the world. That's how he got tagged. Paul didn't like the King of Jazz title himself very much, but I'll tell you one story people never brought out and that is that to this day, probably, every popular musician alive doesn't realize how much they owe to Paul Whiteman for their position in life. Now, back in the 1920s, when Ragtime and Jazz boys came up the river from New Orleans, St.

Louis, and Chicago, they were *not* the Ozzie Nelsons. They were *not* the Rudy Vallees. They were not college bred. They were not Ivy League. They were the poison ivy league. They were a different breed of cat than we got into in the 1930s. So that when—if you recall the old movies—when a band played at Rector's, or any of the famous places in New York, they'd be on a balcony or in the back of potted palms. They kind of hid them as third-class citizens. You just never considered them as part of a party. Now, I know, because in the 1920s, I mentioned before a little band we called College Band, because one boy was from Brown, another from Princeton. Brown—we liked the name, so we called it The Little Brown Jugglers. I'm sure we were hired by many of the nice social parties in Long Island and Jersey, not on the strength of our music, but on the fact that the hostess figured she probably didn't have to count the silverware when we left. You know, that was the criteria for choosing a band. Now, along comes the much-publicized concert—justifiably publicized of the Aeolian Hall recital, where Pops did the first concert of popular music in which Gershwin presented "Rhapsody in Blue." Well now, in that audience, you had Walter Damrosch, who was known as the Dean of Popular Music, opera, concert, and so forth. You had these people of that sort—Deems Taylor—rubbing shoulders with jazz musicians and the audience. Everybody came; it was a mixture. But after the concert, a strange thing happened. The jazz musician came out from behind the potted palms. He became no longer a third-class citizen, and a better class of people went in for music because it was no longer considered low-brow. To this day, of course, it might have happened without Pops in some other way, but by gosh, he was the first one to really start the movement going, where people

accepted musicians as their fellow human beings.
They no longer hid them. So, that is one of the
things people should remember about Paul
Whiteman. As for himself, he was a Rabelaisian
character. There's no doubt about that. When
someone spoke of Jackie Gleason or Dean Martin
on consuming alcohol, Pops would say, "Hell, I've
spilled more than they drank!" He was a lusty guy.
There's no hiding anything about it. It fit him. He
was a big man, and lived a big life, and was a big
picture in everything he did. I can think of one
story about him. After one terrible episode, he'd
become like a little boy, who'd been caught with his
hand in the cookie bowl. He was so contrite and
felt so *badly* after having misbehaved and had a
little too much to drink. For days, he would just
condemn himself and say what a terrible person
he was and how *awful* he was. So, one day, we're
having lunch after such a session, and he was
continuing to run himself down and how life has
been good to him and why is he such a no-good
bum, and I'd say, "Oh, come on." Suddenly, he
brightened. "You know, Spook—he called me
Spook—because everything Pops said had a reason.
I wrote for him, therefore, I'm a ghost writer,
therefore I'm a Spook. So, my nickname was
Spook. So he said, "You know, Spook, with Detroit
and assembly lines and interchangeable parts, good
Lord, wouldn't you think that by this time, we
could unhook a person at the throat and bottom
and put in a whole new set of plumbing?" And I
said, "That sounds very logical, Pops." I wanted
to get back to a script we were working on. He
sat there and kind of thought it over, and then a
beautiful smile came over his face. He said, "You
know, when they do, I'm going to go out and ruin
it all over again (laughs)." So, how can you hate a
man like that?

DAVID: That's amusing, particularly since some of the stories that are told about Paul Whiteman are told in relationship to his early contacts with Bing Crosby and how he was more the master and Bing Crosby was the cut-up. The stories that I've heard deal with Whiteman getting on Crosby's tail for some of the things that Crosby and his crew would do. Now you're telling me that Whiteman was just as capable of cutting up as the people who worked for him.

WARD: Sure he was, but then after all, he's the boss, and he did have to get after Bing on many things, many episodes. Also, I think Bing owed a great deal to him that people don't realize. Now, I'm sure Bing might have developed it by himself—his wonderful use of words, his throwing around little catch phrases. That was developed by a lot of writers for him, too, who saw his love of language. But Pops was that way, and I think Bing would have caught a bit of it from him. Everything with Pops was a swing-a-ring-a-rooer. He had a wonderful way of speech, of things you'd never think of describing scenes or something. He'd have colorful speech. I think Bing picked up a great deal of that from him. Granted, I think he developed it further and perfected it further than Pops did. But Pops was a wonderful slinger of words in that kind of style. Now, Carroll Carroll, the writer in Hollywood of many, many radio shows, is one of the great writers of all time out there for my money. I used to think Carroll must have slept under Bing's bed—hid in the closets 'cause he got to use in the scripts the language that fit Bing so perfectly, and I think he picked up a lot right from Bing's own expressions and didn't have to tailor them for him. All of that was very much a part of Pops Whiteman's speech, too. The same kind of thing, but not as highly developed.

DAVID: You also indicated you worked with Perry Como on the Chesterfield show. How did you get to develop that relationship with Como, and what was it like working with him?

WARD: Well, Perry—I had worked with him, of course, before I did the Chesterfield because when he was singing with the Ted Weems Band, I'd done one, two, maybe three programs during the six years of Fitch. So I knew Perry from that, and knew him quite well. But I think what happened was saving money. Perry was to go out and do *If I'm Lucky*, a motion picture with Vivian Blaine. He was to do a movie there and go to the coast. That meant that *The Chesterfield Supper Club* had to be put on from the coast. So, to save sending a writer, a director, and a producer out, they said, "This guy claims to do them all," which I had been doing, so I went out as probably a money-saving device, where I wrote, produced, and directed the shows. I went along with Perry on that trip and continued on when we come back to New York, and stayed with him right until I left to go back into television in 1949.

DAVID: You talked about money earlier, when you commented on $25 a show that you got for some of the earlier programs. For those of us who are interested in the economics of radio, we know that there were stars that made quite a bit of money— the Eddie Cantors and the Al Jolsons. What were the economics of radio for those people who were in the background? Was there a great deal of money? How did it develop? Was it—did AFTRA have anything to do with changing any of that? Could you maybe talk about the role of AFTRA?

WARD: No, not so much. AFTRA didn't have that, although later in the Writer's Guild, they have jurisdiction over such things these days. I'd say writers and producers did well on the big shows. The $25 I mentioned, Dave, was for a sustaining bit—a little filler program, which was all *The Chamber Music of Lower Basin Street* was at that time. It was, I believe, on the Blue Network. Maybe it was on Red. I think it played both at times. Certainly, the man that wrote it that I told the story about taking over the script—his name was Welbourn Kelley, a very, very good guy. Good writer. He took it over, but he was employed by NBC. He was in the script department, so I don't know what his salary was, but I'm quite sure he didn't make any money doing the program. But because I was an outsider and contributed my spot, they had to pay me something, and it was about $25 because it was a sustaining program.

DAVID: What you're saying, then, is that if someone were just on the NBC staff, whether as an announcer or a writer, they would take whatever assignments came to them and would not necessarily receive extra remuneration for that show.

WARD: Oh, no. That's not so. The sustaining shows—they were not paid for. They just received their salary. But nearly all were auditioned for the bigger shows. *Cities Service*, or any show that came along, would have auditions for announcers, and they got an extra fee from that client for doing the show, so all the bigger commercial programs had their own announcer. My announcer in New York for *Fitch* was Jack Costello, if you remember, and on the coast, I had Larry Keating and Dresser Dahlstead. We paid them a fee, although they were on staff there. But because they had been offered by NBC to the auditions and they won the part, they got paid for it.

DAVID: Were you involved in active production during the Petrillo period and during the strike of the musicians?

WARD: Oh, yes. Very much so, because those were the days when everybody remembers we were all playing "Jeanie with the Light Brown Hair" and "There's a Tavern in the Town." Arrangements had to be made of all the old standards, folk songs—everything else that was not controlled by ASCAP. We were getting pretty tired of the material, so I went through that period. But in fact, that was the period that created BMI, who the networks sponsored or furthered their cause. For the first time, ASCAP had competition.

DAVID: What was BMI?

WARD: Broadcast Music Incorporated. They are now very, very big. They have a tremendous library, and many of the artists signed with them, who were not getting any work with ASCAP out on strike. That became quite a problem for programming, because things were beginning to sound pretty much alike.

DAVID: Ward, rather than asking about specific programs, can you tell me who were some of the musicians that you really felt a pride and a pleasure working with, and who were some that you perhaps preferred not to work with, but had to nonetheless, and perhaps why. I'm putting you on the spot because, as we said earlier, people like to hear some of the gossip of the days of yesterday.

WARD: Well, I'd say that all in all, most of them were great. There were ones that if your musical taste was not the same, you'd try to duck them. The greats were really great. I'd say one of the greatest, and of course you can't say he doesn't get the credit because he does, is Artie Shaw. Artie was absolutely head and shoulders over the usual crowd of musicians in that he had so many other avenues to his talents. Controversial or not, sometimes he'd drive you crazy with his persistence in following some damn thing that nobody else was interested in, but he was extremely well-informed and was an all-around talented guy. I hate to use the old expression "a Renaissance man," because it's used lightly everywhere, but for people that want to use it lightly, Artie would be qualified for that, because he was a very amazing guy, and anyone who's heard him talk knows that. He'll talk for any subject endlessly and interestingly too, I might say. For the musicians, I think Tommy Dorsey and Jimm—Tommy, Jimmy, and certainly Benny Goodman are among the tops. Harry James. Oh, I loved Harry James' trumpet, although I can tell one story that maybe musicians don't know about him. Once a year on the old *Fitch Bandwagon* we did the Ringling Brothers, Barnum and Bailey Circus and that was an interesting thing. It had nothing to do with name bands, and it was one of the most popular shows each year. The leader was Merle Evans, who had done it for I can't think how many years. It must have been thirty, forty years.

DAVID: Wasn't he the ringmaster?

WARD: No, he was the band leader. Ringmasters they changed occasionally, but Merle Evans had the Ringling Brothers Barnum and Bailey Band, and the stories that he told about musicians—how they're out in the rain and the cold—they're parading. They're doing everything in the world and still batting out these powerful marches and gallops that they play for circuses. It took the stamina of an Olympic athlete to be a circus band musician.

The reason I bring this up is that I just thought of it when I spoke of Harry James. One day, I was talking with Merle about how his musicians were playing a waltz—"La da da da de, de de de"—then a whistle blows, and they go "Da da da da da da" without a cue of anything musical in front of them. They'd blow that loud whistle and they'd shift into another type of music to fit the act that was going on. It was, as I say, a superior performance by athletes to keep up with these guys. So we were talking about the various ones, and I said, "Well, could any of the dance musicians today, Merle, would they be able to live this life that you guys put up with?" He said, "No. Well, yes, yes—one—Harry James. That's because he was born under a tent. He was the son of circus performers in one way or the other, but his early days were in the circus, which I thought was an unusual story about stamina among musicians.

DAVID: You had mentioned a little while ago—not on tape, that Paul Lavalle is still rather active. I was a little surprised, but happily surprised. I remember him, as I'm sure most do, with The Cities Service Band of America.

WARD: That's right.

DAVID: Did you ever work with Paul?

WARD: Oh yes, yes. I knew Paul. He had been a regular staff musician with NBC at 711 5th Avenue until he began to get programs of his own. Whether or not he stayed on staff then, I doubt it. I think he probably went independent, but he did *Cities Service* for a long time and became almost a member. Maybe he was on the Board or heaven knows what. I think he was employed by Cities

Service long after the program went off the air. I know he was employed to go around and form bands in universities and towns all over America sponsored by Cities Service. It was one of their promotion things. Now, in recent years, maybe that developed from *Cities Service*—that type of presentation, but each Thanksgiving Day Parade was The McDonald's Band of America, where there were two kids, I think, two from each state in the union, and they had to audition to win that honor. It was a *tremendous* band. They did a *wonderful* job. I think for the last year or two, Paul has no longer been the bandmaster for The Bank of America and for McDonald's.

DAVID: I was not aware of that at all. We had a youngster from our high school, as a matter of fact, who was selected for this organization.

WARD: What high school is that?

DAVID: Croton-Harmon High School.

WARD: Croton-Harmon—good.

DAVID: A little local commercial—we had a youngster who was selected for that band, and it never occurred to me when I learned about it that Paul Lavalle was associated with it.

WARD: When was that?

DAVID: Two years ago, I think.

WARD: Well, he might have done it two years ago. I don't know whether he's been out of it more than a year or two. But that was Paul's, and he's living very comfortably. I think for the whole time after the

Cities Service he was still on their payroll—four years after it went off the air. Part of that probably was as consultant and as a touring Goodwill Ambassador in music, forming bands, and aiding or conducting bands in various cities under the aegis of Cities Service.

DAVID: If you would, Ward, tell me about some of the vocalists that you've worked with. Not only who they were, but what they were like to work with.

WARD: Gee, I think I worked with all of them—certainly not in favor now with the MTV movie thing, TV videos, or any of that. But the Helen O'Connells, the Margaret Whitings—just mention them. I'm going blank. But any one of them—Doris Day I had for thirteen weeks and had done our shows with *The Fitch Bandwagon* when she was with Les Brown. But there was one of the summer series for thirteen weeks. Les Brown was the attraction on the show along with guest artists. Doris was with him at that time, so for thirteen weeks, she was a *beautiful* child—just a *wonderful* girl. And to show you what a beautiful, wonderful concept I have of talent and how I can pick 'em, I'm so *proud* of this fact. Doris was pretty young then, and she came in one day crying, and often she'd just not be in a mood to rehearse. She didn't like it at all. She'd had a slightly unhappy marriage. This was before the publicized bad marriage. She was crying, and she was so beautiful, and such a nice kid. I said to her, "Doris, do you realize the rest of your life you're going to be hanging your clothes on steam pipes and miserable dressing rooms all over the country? You're not meant for this life. You shouldn't pursue it at all. If I were you, I'd look for something else. Get out of it, because you sing beautifully, but this is not for you (laughs)." See how I pick 'em? About ten years after that, Capitol, I think, had a big reception for her at Danny's Hideaway, and I was invited to that. She was there with her then husband, Marty Melcher. She was greeting all the people in a group, and I came up in back of her and just whispered in her ear, "Doris, you ought to get out of this business." She turned around and said, "You! Ward!" So you see I really pick 'em.

DAVID: She remembered your advice.

WARD: Yeah (laughs). Oh, dear. So, as I say, it's good I'm not a talent scout.

DAVID: When you had actors or comedians who were guests on some of the programs that you worked with, did you continue to write the scripts or were there kinds of partnerships in terms of script writing? Did you work with any other writers?

WARD: No. Most of the shows I did were my own, where I did the writing, direction, and production. But when I got with the B. O. Company (Batten, Barton, Durstine & Osborn Advertising Agency), and did Lever Brothers and what else? I can't think—Phillip Morris and that. Then we had writers and I just kind of rode herd on them. Speaking of comedians, you spoke of Zero Mostel a while ago. I'll never forget Zero on some program in the 1930s, and I don't know what it was. I wasn't there and I know nothing, but he had gotten a bad blackball by going on and on and stretching his part. He really loused up a show in timing and everything else by not sticking to the script. He was funny. He was bringing down the house, but it got so bad that people couldn't depend on him. They weren't going to take him, and so his agent, whoever it was, I forget whether he was MCA or

William Morris or what, had trouble booking him for quite a long time. Then we came up on a Lever Brothers show when I was at B O. They booked Zero on for me with the *promise* that he was going to stick to this—well, wise-guy. Byron said, "Yeah, he'll stick to it, I know." So, I prepared a big "stretch part" we call it, a big blank, maybe a minute or two, where I knew he was going to fill that. You just couldn't depend on him not doing it. So, we went on, and Zero played it right to the letter, and I was stuck with a minute or two at the end of the show with nothing going on. Ray Bloch was the orchestra leader. I know he played the theme over and over again. The announcer announced and ad libbed all the people who were on and it seemed like an hour dragged by, getting that show off the air. I never had had that experience before of being out more than five or ten seconds on a show, but this one was a nightmare. And all because Zero did exactly what he said he was going to do.

DAVID: A few years later, Zero Mostel was one of those people who had been blacklisted for association with left wing organizations. Did you know him at that time?

WARD: No, not really. That was about the only show I ever did that Zero was on. I think it was for Lever Brothers.

DAVID: What was Ray Bloch like to work with?

WARD: Oh, Ray Bloch was an absolute little dynamo. He was one of the most capable production directors that I'd ever worked with. One of the fastest and best. It would be like Al Goodman used to be in the very early days of the Rudy Vallee type show. Al was very good, but Ray was a craftsman.

Everything was prepared and done, and if an emergency happened, he'd handle it. His very speed and ability to get a show on and off with no trouble at all, probably gave him the reputation of not being a very artistic musical director with great feeling and depth for his music. You didn't have time for that. This wasn't Carnegie Hall. It was radio, and he was one of the best.

DAVID: Speaking of Ray Bloch, he worked for Edgar Bergen and Charlie McCarthy for a while. Did you ever work with Bergen and McCarthy?

WARD: No, I didn't know Ray did.

DAVID: Oh, I thought he did. I may be giving some misinformation now.

WARD: No, Bobby Armbruster was the conductor that I recall—might have been someone before him. Was it Ray Noble?

DAVID: Ray Noble.

WARD: Yeah, Ray Noble was earlier when they used the name bands.

DAVID: There were constant jokes about his baldheadedness.

WARD: That's right, but then he was followed in the latter part for a long time by Bobby Armbruster.

DAVID: Can you tell me about any of the comedians other than Zero Mostel that you might have worked with? Did you ever work with Fanny Brice?

WARD: No, never with Fanny, no. But you see, in San Francisco, I had such a run of them I can't remember

them all. The only one I can think of is Morey
Amsterdam. That I had with Meredith Willson.
When I went out to the coast, what I was brought
out there for actually in 1935 was their top show
called *The Carefree Carnival*. It had been on for a
couple of years before I was there—on and off. It
was never steady, but it was their big show. Their
big variety show was *The Carefree Carnival*. Well, I
think because I was with Raymond Knight who
was noted for comedy in New York, when I wanted
to go to the coast, and had applied and been
accepted, I think they said, "This is the guy we'll
put on with *The Carefree Carnival*." So that's when
I started with Meredith Willson and *The Carefree
Carnival*. That was an hour show that I had to
write, direct, and produce. An hour, which no one
would ever *think* of doing today, with the gang of
writers you have, but I finally got help, and I'm
glad you reminded me of this one, because I wanted
to pay tribute to him. About 1936, 1937, they said
I was going to get help—have a writer coming in
and he'd be up one day to see me. I didn't know
when it was, so I was up in some little piano studio
with a piano recital guy, and I was falling asleep
there, and the announcer was falling asleep in the
corner, as the piano recital went on, a typical filler-
sustaining show, and the doors opened to the studio
and a guy walked in with the brim of his hat
turned up like an old farmer and his belt pulled
way below his stomach, so it hung out. He looked
like a real farmer. I think he even had the straw in
his mouth and walked right into the studio, walked
up to the mike, and said, "Calm is the night. Calm
is the day. Come Rover, come Rover," and walked
out (laughs). I fell off my chair. The announcer
didn't know what to do and said, "We've had a
slight interruption," or something like that. That
was Ransom Sherman.

DAVID: Oh yes, yes.

WARD: He became my co-writer, and of course, performed on the show, too. I never had a better and funnier program to work on than working with Ransom. He was a benevolent Don Rickles. I've never heard that used before, and maybe no one knows what I mean. He wasn't as hard-hitting as Don Rickles, but he was a put-on artist. Everybody he'd talk to—he knew a great deal more of their subject than they knew, and he was very definite about it. He'd come in with just enough knowledge to confuse everybody, and he'd stand in front of a window, where some girl was demonstrating a product, and that was a sight to see. He'd have a straw in his mouth and his belt pulled way down. He'd put his nose to the window, and he'd watch everything they'd do, and you could see that they were saying to someone else, "Hey, get a load of this guy out here," and pretty soon, there were a lot of people there watching this character out there, and he's got the person by this time so confused that's doing the demonstration, but Ransom was just wonderful. I think he's retired now. In fact, I just got his address a couple of weeks ago. I'm going to write him a letter.

DAVID: He has been a guest on many, many programs as a comedian, and I think he had his own show for a while.

WARD: Sure. He had started out maybe before this, but the first I was aware of, there was a show out of Chicago called *The Three Doctors*. That was Ransom Sherman and I can't think who else. Then, of course, after my *Carefree Carnival* days, he came back to Chicago and did the *Club Matinee* with Garry Moore when Garry was in Chicago.

DAVID: Where do you think he's living now?

WARD: I have his address at home, but I can't think where it is.

DAVID: Do you know what state it is?

WARD: Gee, I can't remember.

DAVID: West coast or New York?

WARD: Yeah, west coast, or it's in the mountain area somewhere—the mountain zone.

DAVID: I have a feeling there are a lot of people who would love to be able to speak to him and get some of his memories.

WARD: I'm going to write him a letter, or give him a call in the next week or so.

DAVID: You mentioned *Carefree Carnival*, and I raced over to my files and see that you're right—Meredith Willson was on that. I have a program where Vera Vague was one of the comedians.

WARD: Vera Vague was my gal out there because she was strong. Her name was Barbara Jo Allen, and a lovely, wonderful gal. She pretty much wrote her own script for it. I edited and went over it with her, but she was so creative, and so good, and of course, out of *Carefree Carnival* got *The Bob Hope Show*. Another one there that is not recognized by anyone much because she was short-term was Helen Troy. She was *Suzy of the Switchboard*. She did an act like the girl of today in television—what's her name? The comedienne who does that . . . .

DAVID: Oh, yes, I know who you mean.

WARD: . . . that funny voice—"ringy-dingy." Well, everyone knows when I say that, Helen was that type, but she was long before her, and was *Suzy of the Switchboard*. She was a *darling* girl. She was just great. Now, she came from *The Carefree Carnival* to become *Suzy of the Switchboard* as a regular on the Eddie Cantor Show for six months—a year maybe. One contract, I don't know.

DAVID: Several people had switchboard operators. Jack Benny had the two switchboard operators.

WARD: The old ladies, yeah.

DAVID: When I think about Vera Vague, I also think about Brenda and Cobina. Do you remember those two girls?

WARD: Yeah, I remember them. Never worked with them; didn't know them at all.

DAVID: Blue Jay footpads. Was that the company that sponsored the show when you were with it?

WARD: Yes, yes, yes. Blue Jay, yes. They were for one season or one contract. I can remember Ransom doing a phony commercial for Blue Jay on the thing.

DAVID: Were you on live on most of these programs?

WARD: Oh, these were all live.

DAVID: Or were any of these programs prerecorded?

WARD: Now you've brought up a subject that I think I'm not unique in, but I'm among those who suffered this problem. I missed all the switches, as though fate had me destined to work hard. I left Perry Como in 1949. If you check your records, you'll find out that in some part of 1949, early or late, was when Bing Crosby won his fight with ABC. He had his Ampex because he was interested in that, and forced them to accept his shows on tape. So, I went from doing two shows a day—as you know, they used to have the second repeat show for the west coast. I'd do 7:00-7:15 five days a week, and then three days to a week later, Monday, Wednesday, and Friday with Como. We'd finish at 7:15 and have to wait around until 11:00 or 11:15 at night. We'd have to go to Toots Shor's and sit round and just wait and come back and do the show. Well, a couple of months after I left, they went to tape. Everything went to tape. Now, in the meantime, I'd gone into television, and I did *The Paul Whiteman Goodman Revue*, and oh, a couple of others—the Langford-Ameche show, five days a week. Beating our brains out on live television was fun and exciting, but pretty darn difficult. So, I left them to go with the Lennon and Newell Agency. At that time, I left in 1952 because ABC was awaiting word from Washington on their merger with Paramount, you may remember, and they had to get approval for the deal, and so for a couple of months, we went black, as they say in television, went dark in our various outside theater studios because nothing could be done. We were spending no money, just treading water until the approval came. I said, "Gee, I don't want to sit around waiting for this. They're going to suddenly look at me and say, "What are we paying *this* guy for?" I had wanted to go into agency work and to try that, so I went to the Lennon and Newell Agency. Now, I'm at Lennon and Newell probably six months, and in came tape and film for the commercials. When we started, commercials were done live. Pretty soon, everything went to tape, and I said, "I missed it again." So, I'm sorry you brought that up. It makes me think how hard I had to work.

WARD: A true pioneer. I was fascinated to hear earlier about the organization you belong to in New York—The Dutch Treat Club, because you had mentioned that as a member of that organization you have developed friendships with some people who are legends in radio and in other fields, particularly Alexander Woollcott, Lowell Thomas, Robert Benchley, and others. Could you kind of talk a little bit about some of these individuals in terms of your own impressions of someone like Woollcott or Benchley?

WARD: No, I never knew Woollcott. I told you the story of how I was pulling the thing that I thought I was getting away with—telling a story personalized to my own tailoring, when he did it on the air and finally brought me up short. I said, "I can't use that anymore." So, I never knew him. I saw him because he was doing *The Town Crier* at that time. I was with NBC at 711 5th Ave. Benchley, too, I only bumped into him a couple of times at the Garden of Allah in Hollywood, but I never knew him well. I know his son, Nat Benchley. Nat and I became very good friends, but the others were radio people at this club where Lowell Thomas was our President. It was a bitter blow when we lost him a couple of years ago as President of the club. There was John Charles Thomas, Bobby Armbruster, Gene Lockhart, any of the top stars of the day. Many of them were members of the club. We worked with some of them, but knew most of them.

DAVID: When you were on live, other than the time you
             were a couple of minutes short because you expected
             Zero to clown around and he didn't, can you recall
             any flubs that might have caused anyone any
             embarrassment?

WARD: Oh, yes, yes, but they can't be told on the air. Most
             of the flubs . . . .

DAVID: We're not on the air now.

WARD: I think—oh, there's one, and it's not radio, but it's
             so aligned with it I'd have to tell you. I would
             gladly pay I don't know how much, but right now
             I'd pay $100 to anyone that has a kinescope of it,
             but I don't think it exists. I don't think we made
             kinescopes. In 1950 or 1951, I took the job of
             doing the commercials. I was Executive Producer of
             Television at ABC, but Robert Kintner, who many
             people will remember his name, was President of
             the company, and I was given permission to write
             the commercials for the famous old radio show,
             Can You Top This? This was a strange thing. They
             said, "You can do it and accept a fee, because they
             don't know how to convert their radio commercials
             to television."

DAVID: Who was the sponsor? Do you recall?

WARD: The sponsor was Mogan David Wine. That's what
             it's coming to. Oh, boy. They had an agency, Weiss
             and Geller, in Chicago, and they said, "Great, we'll
             pay you." I forgot what it was, but it was pretty
             good loot to readapt the commercials. Well, with
             these nice old gentlemen, Senator Ford, Joe Laurie,
             Jr, Harry Hershfield, and Peter Donald as emcee.
             All of them have had a touch of the grape every
             now and then to the point where they were pretty

good at it. They would practically get sick at my commercials because they advertise what I was given to advertise—Mogan David Longfellows, a highball out of this sweet wine, Mogan David, on the rocks, Mogan David all sorts of ways. And they'd clown around in the background terribly. Not their type of drink. So, I got pretty tired of writing these commercials and was looking for a new way to do it, a new way to put them on. Suddenly, I thought, *Wait a minute. I'm going to do a Lucius Beebe type of thing—a man of distinction, with his elbow on a mantelpiece—everything but the patch over the eye.* I said, "I'll do an *elegant* commercial." So, there's a thing called a mirror box. You have mirrors made into a corner where they meet like corners of a wall. You put something in that corner of the mirror and you shoot at a certain angle with a camera, and you see thousands of them stretch out. It's a camera illusion. So, I said I'd put the glass of Mogan David there. Well, that worked for a while and everything was fine. And they said could I do more inventive commercials. Suddenly, I thought, *Now I'll do this Lucius Beebe act.* So, I wrote a commercial in sheer elegance, starting out to the effect that when you think of eavesdropping, that's by the ear. That's an aural pursuit. I wondered with this new medium of television—which it was then—*could we eavesdrop by television? Well, let us see.* With that, the camera cut down from the apron down to the floor of the theater we were in. You wouldn't see the audience when we shot down at that angle, because they're twenty feet back from the apron. I needed an actor. I thought, *Why should I pay an actor? I'll do it myself.* So, I had a club chair arranged with an end table with all the ingredients on it and a reading lamp. I'm in a dressing gown with my back to the camera, and I've got a book there, and I stretch my arms out and hold the book out and put it across my knees and reach over to the ingredients on the table.

DAVID: Live?

WARD: Live. All the time, the announcer is droning away. "Now this gentleman is at home. Aaah. He seems to be spending a pleasant evening, and he seems to be a gentleman of good taste because we see on the table to his left the sparkling decanter of Mogan David Wine, and we see the tall glass, the ice cubes, but does this gentleman know the proper way to mix a Mogan David Longfellow? Let us see." So, the camera now tightens up to the end table with the ingredients there, and he says, "Yes, he does know. He's poured half a glass of sparkling Mogan David." Now three, four cubes of ice from the ice bucket, which I placed with the tongs in. Now a touch of seltzer, of soda. The soda was like those professional bottles that are sealed at the top. You don't see them around very much, but they were very heavy glass. You know what they are. So anyway, it seems that Sam, the stage hand, kept that bottle on the steam pipes down the stairs. So it came in, and I said, "Now a touch of soda." And I hit the soda. It went down one side of the glass, up the other, and ice cubes, Mogan David wine, and all went at least seven feet in the air (laughs) all over me—dripping down my arm. All the camera could see was my shoulders shaking. I was breaking up. The audience broke up. The three old boys on the show hung on to each other and got into hysterics. While all this *chaos* is going on, the announcer is saying, "And so this gentleman is spending a relaxing evening at home, enjoying the better things of life (laughter). And the "TD" we called him—the Technical Director—a high-hat name for the engineer, had fallen under the desk practically. He couldn't reach the things. The Director of the show was broken up. He was roaring with laughter. It took us, I would say, a good minute to get back on the air. Now, imagine if I had a tape of that for home consumption.

DAVID: That was appropriate for *Can You Top This*. If you were doing a more serious program, they might have thought that was a plant.

WARD: The pay off—all those in this business will appreciate the P.S. to this. I said, "Well, I've blown that. I'm not going to get that check anymore, putting on these commercials for Weiss and Geller and Mogan David." *Never* heard a word. I think that they thought something went on that they didn't understand, and didn't want to admit that they didn't get it, so I got away with it.

DAVID: I've listened to a lot of the *Can You Top This* shows. I'm sure you have, also. I've sometimes wondered whether or not those shows were actually rehearsed, whether the jokes that Senator Ford and Harry Hershfield and Joe Laurie, Jr. told, presumably to match up the joke that the contestants sent in, were off-the-cuff, or whether they were jokes that they had ready.

WARD: Sometimes, they were off-the-cuff, but most of the time they'd say, "taxi joke." They'd say, "One thing is going to deal with a small boy in school. One deals with a woman hanging out laundry." A "laundry" joke. You'd get a topic, but they wouldn't rehearse what they were going to say, actually.

DAVID: But they knew the topic in advance.

WARD: I'd say most of the time they knew the topic, but sometimes they'd spring one on them just to see what would happen.

DAVID: They had a supply of jokes at home?

WARD: They just knew them in their heads. They were "rememberers." Harry Hershfield was one of the most delightful storytellers, great as an emcee at dinners and parties. He was just perfect.

DAVID: They did a lot of dialect stuff on the air. Did they do their dialect stuff on TV, as well?

WARD: Yeah, yeah. Every now and then, they'd go in for the dialect stuff.

DAVID: Speaking of dialect, and this may be a sensitive question, but I'm going to raise it because we talked about this earlier as well. Nowadays, if anyone dared to play *Amos 'n Andy* on the radio, they'd probably be banned from the air. There was a great deal of dialect type of humor on the radio in the 1930s and 1940s. Jack Benny with Rochester and *Amos 'n Andy* and several others. You told me off tape before, a little story about a situation involving a Black musician.

WARD: Count Basie.

DAVID: Could you repeat that?

WARD: Well, there's not much to repeat, except the fact that they wanted my script to have Count Basie refer to the emcee as "Mr." Reddy. His name was Tom Reddy. Everyone else called him Tom, and I wouldn't have it. We won that fight. It was just fear of NBC, and the client, that the southern stations would resent it. They didn't want to lose the audience or anything, which is so different today. That's been beat. I'm 100 percent for what has happened there, that we don't have that problem anymore. But I'm also very, very regretful of the fact that you can't have the Webber and Fields and the Amos 'n Andy's and so forth. The super-sensitivity of races, of minorities, they seem to be *looking* for things to be hurt over. The great, great comics of all times could tell racial stories, but not on the air, not on television. They do it in public. They've lost a great literature of comedy. They've lost a complete field that should be done, but I think, if anything, it makes you appreciate the minority and the races more than, "Oh no, this will insult them." I think it's sheer nonsense and I feel very badly about that. Oh, I was on the road with Jessel for a year. I didn't tell you that. We did a co-op show.

DAVID: Was that when he was married to Norma Talmadge?

WARD: Norma, yes. Norma went along with us and so forth. Well, Jessel would tell the greatest stories on a Hungarian. Of course, his Jewish stories were great. Now, why aren't they allowed? If Georgie can tell them, then they seem to be accepted, although not often. They don't want to go in for that. They're careful about it. I just think there's much too much of that sensitivity.

DAVID: As a writer, what kind of censorship existed in the radio? How many days prior to broadcast did you have to submit your script and were there many changes made in scripts and if there were, what were some of the reasons?

WARD: The reasons were clients, advertising agencies, or the stars themselves. That is the story where I probably was the—I just disturbed all my fellow writers, producers, and directors. They probably *hated* me for it just—I don't mean hate in the true sense. They'd say, "Oh *you*, boy!" I tell you the truth. I had the Fitch thing for six years, and I would go out to the coast to Lord and Thomas. That was what the agency was before it became Foote, Cone, and Belding. Many of my very good friends worked there and at other agencies. I'd walk into a meeting where they had teletypes practically from the ceiling to the floor that they'd written change this, and get this paragraph out of here, and so forth. The greatest example would be George Washington Hill, who rode herd on his programs as no one has ever ridden herd before. These guys were tearing their hairs out having to rewrite at midnight, and get it ready for tomorrow, and get it approved back to New York, and all this. I'd look at them and say, "Well, I have to go home and write the *Fitch* script for the day after tomorrow, or something, and I'll be in Chicago." I would write the script. I would mail a copy to the agency, which was a Davenport, Iowa agency, and then I'd go two days later to the hotel that they'd know I'd be in and I'd look. "Any mail?" Yes. There'd be two commercials written out with not one word in them. I'd insert them anywhere in the program that I wanted, and I'd go this way week after week. Sometimes, I'd pick up the phone after a show and call the Fitch Company or the agency and say, "Hey, are you fellows listening?" They'd say, "Oh, no, everything's fine. We're happy." So, these friends of mine would say, "*How* do you get away with that?" I said, "I don't know. That's the way it started." And for six years, I don't think—I can't recall any time when they sent anything other than a suggestion about, in this commercial could you get so and so, or in this commercial, would you put it to follow this? Once in a while, they'd do that, but otherwise I don't remember anything ever being dictated. When I saw what all my fellow workers were going through to get a program on the air, I had—for eight years—I lived a charmed life.

DAVID: Do you think that was the result of the Fitch people being so liberal, or was that . . . .

WARD: I can't tell. They were a strange; they were a wonderful gang; they were Midwestern. The radio to them—they were selling enough Fitch Shampoo to float the Queen Mary. Oh, I got a great rib from Meredith Willson on that. He said, "We had a wonderful time spot." It was the greatest. I followed Jack Benny and I was followed by Edgar Bergen. What a time spot in there. So, Meredith, in some interview somewhere said, "Well, Byron and that *Fitch Bandwagon*—you could read the Brooklyn Telephone Directory in that spot and get a rating." So, I wrote back to him and said, "When you find the person that reads the Brooklyn Telephone Directory for this number of points and Hooper Rating"—we had Hooper then—I said, "I'll hire them." It's true. I'll admit it was a wonderful time spot, *but* they had that same time spot before the name bands came in there, and they didn't do anything. It was not that big.

DAVID: When the name bands went off, was that when Phil Harris went on?

WARD: Yep. Phil was one of our pets anyway. I did several shows with him. They wanted to emanate from Hollywood and I didn't want to go and live in Hollywood. That was number one. Number two, I think they were ready to change me, too, by that time, because I was getting interested in other things. So, there were no hard feelings. In fact, I had the last member of the Fitch family, whose name is Lucius Fitch, who lives in Sun City. Is that Arizona?

DAVID: Yes.

WARD: He writes to me. He's compiled a very fine book. I think I told you about it on the phone, Dave. It's a vanity press thing of the Fitch family, about all the records of the company and what they did in radio and so forth.

DAVID: I'd love to have a copy of that.

WARD: I'll get you a copy of that. So anyway, we've kept a very good association since, but I don't think they ever came up. Phil Harris and Alice. Phil and Alice it was finally called. It wasn't the *Bandwagon* anymore. I don't know whether or not they topped our ratings or how much they topped it. It was a very popular show, but they swung in the same hammock I swung in.

DAVID: Elliott Lewis, I think, was on their show.

WARD: Yes, Elliott. A very dear friend of mine at the time I was in Hollywood. He was married to Cathy Lewis.

DAVID: She has passed away.

WARD: She did.

DAVID: The little boy who played in *The Great Gildersleeve* was on that show also, Walter Tetley, who I think also is gone.

WARD: Oh yes, I knew Walter Tetley. He was one of the characters on my Ray Knight kids' show about five days a week that I told you about.

DAVID: Was he on that? I think of Walter Tetley as being just a teenager when he was on with Gildersleeve.

WARD: Walter Tetley was small in stature and he never changed much. That voice. He was one of the most *talented* radio performers that ever lived. He could be this little kid forever and ever. I'll never forget my best description of Walter Tetley. He was thirteen, fourteen, fifteen, when he played with me on *Wheatenaville*. Some years later, he went out to Hollywood, and he was out there doing everything. Heaven knows what. Gildersleeve, and as you say, *Phil Harris*. Did everything. He was the sort of guy you wanted to murder, because as a kid, would read a line, and you didn't like the reading, and you'd start to push the button to say, "Walter, would you do . . . ." And he'd wave and say "Don't call." And he'd do it over exactly what you wanted. He knew it before you'd tell him.

DAVID: He had such a distinctive voice, though you could never . . . .

WARD: Oh, yes. He was so good. On his age: people never could figure out how old Walter was because they had him placed as twelve-thirteen, when he was probably in his thirties (laughter). My best memory of the conflict over his age was provided by Ben Grauer. We were sitting around one night, and someone said, "Wonder how old Walter Tetley is? He's got to be about twenty now, doesn't he?" And Grauer said, "Twenty? Walter was a busboy at the last supper (laughter)!" Oh, dear!

DAVID:	He was on Wheatenaville.
WARD:	Yeah. Not as a steady character, but he played on it many times—played many characters. Our regular performers on that were Ray Knight and a girl named Alice Davenport. Maybe I've got her name wrong. It was Alice something and I think Davenport. But there is another Alice Davenport, a famous old radio performer, but I don't think our Alice did much more than *Wheatenaville*. She married after that. Then, the boy was Bobby Jordan, who showed up on *The Dead End Kids* later.
DAVID:	Billy Halop.
WARD:	He was on the show at times. He was a part of it. And the little girl was Emily Vass V-A-S-S. The Vass family.
DAVID:	That's funny. There's a relative or member of the Vass family who lives in Croton.
WARD:	Oh, really?
DAVID:	I had never heard of the Vass family, and some time ago, a local minister, who was a friend of mine, loaned me some records that the Vass family had made.
WARD:	They were great.
DAVID:	I played them, and most of the people who know radio don't seem to have ever heard of the Vass family.
WARD:	I know. It's too long ago. But they were lovely people, the mother, girls, and a couple of boys. I forget how many, but I knew all the girls. Emily

Vass was the youngest. The thing that always intrigued me was that you referred to them as the Vass family. If only half of them showed up, how would you refer to them?

DAVID: (Laughs) I'm not going to repeat that, even on tape (laughter). That's good.

WARD: Anyway, in fact, one of the sisters married a neighbor of mine in Douglaston, Long Island. Her name was Water or Waters. A very lovely gal. They were a swell family.

DAVID: If you're interested, I may be able to put you in touch with one of the members of the Vass family today.

WARD: I have a picture of all of them at home. First ask if they remember me.

DAVID: Ward, what was the theme of *Wheatenaville*?

WARD: Just like a soap opera, except without the suds. There were no tears.

DAVID: Teenagers basically? Adventure story?

WARD: No, a bachelor bringing up two kids and finally marries. We had a marriage on it as all things did. He married Alice Davenport, and it was just fun.

DAVID: Was that sustained, or did you have a sponsor?

WARD: No, that was commercial. That was Wheatena. *Wheatenaville. Billy Bachelor and the Twins.*

DAVID: Silly question for me to ask with a title like that. How many years was it on?

WARD:	Two I think. Two. We used to have to go down to somewhere around Camden and read a week's scripts to the client and just have them approve. They'd fall asleep at the tables, as we were droning on, taking all parts in the thing and reading the scripts. Never much trouble with that; never many changes or anything.
DAVID:	Did you do any other radio work that was not related directly to music? Any other drama or was that . . . .
WARD:	Yeah, pretty much. I'm trying to think. I supervised a lot of them at B. O. Agency, for instance. I was Eastern Radio Director, when *FBI in Peace and War* [both sing] Bom, bom, bom, bom bom bom bom bom. You want to know how that happened? I'll tell you that story, see. You get me into these things.
DAVID:	That's my intention.
WARD:	They had that theme, which was "Love of Three Oranges," and so forth. I forget where they rated, but the show was way up in the ratings. I forgot where, doing more than good, but they weren't selling the product. And if you remember, the product was LAVA Soap. So, Milton Beal, then the President, said to me, "You've got to get what we call sponsor identification. We need sponsor identification to this thing. So, at that time, they were just coming in—experimenting with a thing called Sonitone. That doesn't sound right. But anyway, they were the little microphones that you put at your throat, and you'd talk over a musical note. You'd give a word and it would come out in music, or with a musical tone, rather. What the devil was the name of the thing? It never got over.

It wasn't too successful. So, I thought, *Well, we'll try that*, but it didn't work out. So, I got a base. I think I can almost remember his name: Harry Stanton, I think, was a bass/baritone singer, and I put him in a big echo chamber with kettle drums outside. BONG – BONG. Had them tuned to the thing, and got it the same tone as the theme itself and had the bass and echo chamber say L–A–V–A, L–A–V–A BOM BOM BA BOM BOM in the . . . . I think within a month we came from one of the lowest sponsor identifications to one of the highest with just that little L–A–V–A.

DAVID: The one gimmick. Lava Soap Company must have loved you.

WARD: You bring up these things that I haven't thought of in years.

DAVID: If I can tickle your memory in any other way, I'd be delighted to do so.

WARD: Well, I think you're going to have to tickle me off this chair and into my car. I'm going to have to take off, Dave.

DAVID: Ward, I have rarely enjoyed an afternoon as well as I have this afternoon. I want to thank you so much for visiting, and for sharing memories with me. I don't know how many other people will get to hear this tape, but I know that those who do will have enjoyed it as much as I because they are all people who love old radio.

WARD: Good. I've enjoyed it in this room with all your tapes. I'm so impressed I can't see straight. I never *knew* there was a collection like this. Well, it's a goldmine for me with things for the future that I'm trying to prepare for, and I have absolutely no memory of things unless someone spurs me into it like you mentioned the L–A–V–A BOOM BOOM DA BOOM. I never would have thought of the story if you hadn't. I'd forgotten.

DAVID: Ward Byron, thank you so much.

WARD: Thank you, Dave.

Chapter 4
FRANK NELSON
(1911–1986)
AND VEOLA VONN
(1918–1995)

INTERVIEW: OCTOBER 20, 1984

In 1982, while attending the Friends of Old-Time Radio convention held each year in Newark, New Jersey, I had the pleasure spotting one of the most effervescent professional couples in the radio business, Veola Vonn, and her husband, Frank Nelson. As luck would have it, a staff member of my local cable television station was also attending the convention as my guest, and she had had the foresight to bring along her video camera and microphones. Thus prepared, I approached Veola and Frank and asked if they would be kind enough to let me interview them. They graciously consented, and what follows is the only interview I was able to conduct at an old-time radio convention, and the only interview that was also captured on camera.

DAVID: Frank and Veola, we're not going to be very formal, but I would like to ask both of you how you got involved in acting, and very, very specifically, radio acting, and even more specifically, radio comedy.

FRANK: Well, you want to go first, Veola? Go ahead.

VEOLA: Well, okay. It's very difficult to be short with this, because it's sort of a long thing. I got involved in the business when I was five years old, and went into Vaudeville and radio. Specifically, my first radio job was at KHJ and it was on a children's hour. I did cartwheels over the air.

FRANK: Don't ask her why she did cartwheels over the air, because I don't want to know. I've never found out, as a matter of fact, and I don't think I would now.

VEOLA: From there, I went into Vaudeville as a little kid, had my own act—went up and down the country—went into dancing, and dancing led into radio station KMTR-KWB, and from that into real, real radio. I think my first job was on

Big Town—Edward G. Robinson, and then *The Joe E. Brown Show*, and from there on, it was just absolute gravy.

DAVID: Frank?

FRANK: Well, actually I started when I was very young. I was living in Denver, Colorado, and I was doing amateur theatricals and occasional things with a stock company at the time. I was still in high school. Somebody told me that KOA was doing an audition for some kind of a series and why didn't I try out? So, I went out to KOA and walked in, and the Program Director looked at me and said, "What are you here for?" I said, "Well, they told me you were having an audition." He said, "No, no, no. This is about a thirty-five-year-old man married to about a thirty-year-old girl." It's a story about this couple, and it ran for about twenty-six weeks. I said, "Oh, well, thank you," and I started to leave. He said, "Well, wait a minute. Have you ever read on a microphone?" And I said, "No, no I haven't. He said, "Well, you've made a long trip out here to the edge of town. Maybe you'd like to stay and read." I said, "Well, sure, sure." So I stayed, and there were about thirty of us, and we read. The next day, they called back twelve. The next day, they called back four. The next day, they called me up and told me I *had* it. I played the thirty-five-year-old man with the most beautiful thirty-year-old redhead you ever saw in your life, and if I'd had any brains, knowing what I know today, I might have enjoyed myself more. But I did the best I could with it. That was really my start. After that, I came out to Hollywood. I went from dramatic into announcing and back into the dramatic again.

DAVID: You were on *Entertainment Tonight* a few nights
                ago. Your trademark, probably the most famous
                line that certainly is associated with Jack Benny
                and Frank Nelson, was you slowly turning around.
                Could you do it for your fans?

FRANK: Y-e-e-e-e-s? W-e-e-e-e-l-l how are y-o-o-o-o-u? Yes,
                I'll tell you how I got into comedy, because you did
                ask that up front, and I kind of missed with my
                answer. I was basically a leading man, and I was
                working opposite stars getting $25 and they were
                getting $3,500. I was good enough to work opposite
                them, but not good enough to get any money and
                not even good enough to get credit, because they
                wouldn't give us any credit in those early days.
                Nobody knew who did anything. Then, it dawned
                on me that I could make a lot more money if I
                could do comedy, do it well, and deliver on it. You
                could make about four or five times as much as
                you could as a leading man. That's really what led
                me into it—greed, sheer greed (laughs). So, I started
                doing comedy. That was a great joy. In radio, every
                day was a brand new day, because there were no
                reruns for the twenty-seventh time that you see
                today in television. Everything was fresh every day,
                and you could do whatever you were capable of
                doing vocally. It didn't make any difference whether
                you were short, tall, fat, thin, old, or young. That
                made a great joy out of it, and I continued to do
                dramatic parts, even after I started comedy, until
                we got into television. Then, of course, I was
                trapped by the *Jack Benny* character, and really,
                everything I've done in television has been some
                kind of an offshoot. It may be a gentler approach
                to it, but it's always, once in a while, just for fun,
                I'll go in and start reading quite strange you know.
                They'll say, "Well, what we had in mind was . . . ."
                And I say, "Yeah, I know exactly what you had in

mind." And we end up doing the *Benny* character anyway.

DAVID: You were on the radio for years before you were on the Benny program. Could you tell me how you were selected for Benny's show, and what it was like working with the cast of *The Jack Benny Program*? Also, how did the shift from radio to TV affect the cast, Benny and the entire production?

FRANK: Well, the way I got on the Benny show is that I had worked for John Swallow at KFAC-KFAD in Los Angeles. John became the head of NBC. Now, NBC didn't even have a building in Hollywood at that time because all of the major shows emanated from Chicago and New York, and they had not yet decided that there was enough in Hollywood to reverse the lines. It was very expensive to run shows from west to east. Jack came out to California to do a picture. Of course, he was doing his show in New York, and they wanted to keep him alive on that show, so we did a five-minute insert, and John called me to do it. What it was—we were on a train coming out to the west coast. Jack, of course, is bragging about the fact that he's going to Hollywood, and he's going to be a big star in pictures, and so on. My character is non-committal, but very polite to him and so on, and the sketch finally ends up with Jack saying, "Well, you seem like a very personable young man. Quite possibly I can do something for you out there. My name is Jack Benny. What is your name?" And my answer was "Clark Gable." That was the joke. So, the following week, we did another five-minute insert, and then Jack went back east. Then after a period of time, I don't remember how many months, he brought his show to the west coast, and I started doing just casual things with him, you know, just parts.

DAVID: Aren't you the voice of the famous train conductor?

FRANK: No. Mel did the "Anaheim, Azusa and Cuc—amonga."

DAVID: Was that Mel Blanc? I'm sorry.

FRANK: No. What happened—the way this character developed—as I say, I was just doing casual characters for him. Then one day, the writers said, "Hey, we're going to try that again." I said, "Try what again?" They said, "Remember last week? You stretched the "S" and it got a big laugh?" I had to think back, and I said, "Oh. Oh yeah. I don't know why I did it. I just happened to do it." So, they started writing it in. Then, we went from there to the "Oh, oh," and so on. The first time we did the "Oh, oh" was funny. Jack had a line, "You really hate me, don't you?" In rehearsal, I said, "Oh, *do* I!" and just left it like that. When we got to the show and Jack said, "You really hate me, don't you?" and I said, "OO-oo-oo-ooh DO I!" It just absolutely broke him up. We knew I was going to do it, the writers knew I was going to do it. Jack didn't know it until we got to it, and then I did the "Weeeeells" like he did the "Well!" So, we just kept it going. You asked what it was like working with the people. In radio, everybody knew the characters. It was a family to them. As soon as Jack said, "Oh, mister!" they knew I was coming on. They'd hear "pickle in the middle," and say, "Oh, there's Mr. Kitzel." We just had an easy, easy cast. They worked well together. Jack knew exactly what he was going to get from everybody, so there was really no direction on the show. Theoretically, you would figure there was, but there wasn't. We'd sit around the table on Thursday and read the show. Then, they'd do any rewrites they wanted to do, and you'd come in on Sunday, read it once, go on mike, do a dress rehearsal, and do the show.

DAVID: Were members of the cast of a program like that socially friendly? Some of them are not with us any longer. Rochester is gone, and of course Jack and Mary, but Phil Harris is here, and there are probably several others—Dennis Day. Do the folks who worked together—have they, after the show, stayed as friends?

FRANK: Well, we're friends, but socially—Los Angeles is real spread out, and I go to see my daughter. That's a sixty-mile round trip, and she's in the Los Angeles area. I go to see my son. That's an eighty-mile round trip. Actually, I never socialized, I believe, with any of the people on the show, unless Jack had some kind of a big affair, or something like that. Now, Jack and Mel Blanc socialized. They were very close friends. Outside of that, I don't know, but all the rest of them we just met because you're running from show to show. In the radio days, we were doing six to seven shows a day. We simply didn't have the time to do that, nor were you close enough together. Some of the people were fifty miles apart, and yet they worked the show together.

DAVID: No residuals on radio. How about television? Many of the programs are still being broadcast on CBN and other networks. Are you enjoying some of those residuals?

FRANK: That's another story. I intend to get into that and try to find out who's getting the money for that, because we are not getting it. I'm sure that somebody is being paid. I don't think those shows are on the air for nothing. They're supposed to be paid, but simply not. It's like old-time radio. You see, there were no rebroadcast rights with old-time radio. When you did a radio script, if they repeated that script for any reason, and the only reason that they would repeat a radio script ever was if someone in the cast was ill, and they had a recording of it, they'd repeat one from several weeks before because they simply couldn't do a live one that week. Outside of that, you never heard of a repeat in radio. They had no rights to do that. They had to negotiate, or pay the full, original fee in radio. Yet, you see and hear countless radio shows today. Of course, on some of them, the copyrights have run out, and therefore, there's no claim by anybody, but the real thing is that you can never find out where they were released—or who did it. How did they get there? Usually, it's because somebody recorded it maybe for themselves, gave it to a friend, a friend of a disc jockey somewhere gave it to him, and he said, "Hey, that's great. I'll put it on the show." Next thing you know, it's all over.

DAVID: Many of Jack Benny's programs came from his personal collection. I'm told that he was one of the most generous people in terms of being willing to share his own programs. While he was still alive, he would permit people to visit him and to record some of his programs. They are available back to the 1930s. I have some Jack Benny programs in my collection that were done back in his first or second year on the air, back in 1933-1934 all the way through 1938-1939. The sound quality on some of them is terrific. I'm going to be criticized by our director if I don't give Viola an opportunity . . . .

VEOLA: *Veola.* Eddie Cantor always used to call me Viola.

Nobody called me Veola. I've changed the spelling three times and it was *still* Viola, so I've given up. (Frank laughs).

DAVID: Were you as steady as Frank was on any particular program, or were you a guest star only?

VEOLA: No. I tell you, I had an enviable place in that golden time, because I looked lovely, my body was lovely, you had an audience. I slithered and wiggled across the stage and got to the mike just in time to say the line, and everybody fell apart because we dressed for women, dressed for the audience. There were about 250-300 people in the audience, and as soon as they saw me approaching, they started to go "woooo." It began to build, and I'd go up and say, "Hello, Blue Eyes." And Jack said—what did he say, dear?

FRANK: "I always dream about her." (Laughs).

VEOLA: On the Benny show, I did Spanish, French, I did Southern—and when Mary was not feeling well, I would stand by. They'd redo the script, and I would do it, and on all of the other shows, as I started to say, I was a femme fatal foil. I sang with Dick Powell on the *Bergen and McCarthy* show. I sang with Crosby. I did a lot of singing and acting, too. It was just a very thrilling part of my life.

DAVID: What about Eddie Cantor?

VEOLA: Eddie Cantor! *The Eddie Cantor Show.* Yes. Eddie was wonderful. I won an audition, got on the show, and heard Deanna Durbin, Pinky Tomlin, Jacques Renard and his Orchestra, and of course, the Mad Russian, Bert Gordon. We took the show to New York. We even performed in two convention halls at that time—Cleveland and the Philadelphia Hall. Each was 12,000 people, and they were *stacked* with tiers all over. It was very thrilling.

FRANK: Excuse me. The kid—I don't know—she doesn't know even enough to tell you that what she did was Mademoiselle Fifi. Oh, good lord!

VEOLA: Oh, well. I just assumed. Yes, yes, yes. Mademoiselle Fifi.

DAVID: Tell us about Mademoiselle Fifi.

FRANK: I just told you about Mademoiselle Fifi. That's what he hired her for, though—put her under contract.

VEOLA: Yes, it was the French. French was always my love, but I did the Spanish ones. I sang with Gildersleeve. I was Gildersleeve's Spanish girlfriend. (Singing) "Bésame, bésame mucho . . . ."

DAVID: Were you on with Willard Waterman or with Harold Perry?

VEOLA: I was on with both.

FRANK: You know the story about those two?

DAVID: Enlighten me.

FRANK: Hal Peary and Willard Waterman were both Chicago radio actors long before *Great Gildersleeve*. They were just actors like we all were. You went in and did X number of shows, and we did different characters. They both did that character as one of the things that they did on the local Chicago shows. If whoever got there first happened to think that character would play, they would be the character. So, when Hal Peary quit the show, Willard Waterman walked right in and nobody knew that Hal had left. That's one of those things where Willard didn't come in and do an *imitation* of Hal Peary. It isn't very nice, but he just did the character that they had both done when they were just actors in Chicago.

DAVID: Not only do I get to hear old radio programs from my collection, but as a result of organizations like SPERDVAC, FOTR, and people like yourselves, and Hal Peary and Willard Waterman, I get to listen to the stories of your lives. I think it was Hal Peary who wanted to buy the program or a piece of the program from Kraft. They weren't willing to sell it to him. He thought that by leaving, he would perhaps make a better deal. Obviously, it didn't work out. He also appeared in some of the Arch Oboler *Lights Out* programs. There's a very fine one where he plays a dentist who's getting even with a man who has made love to his wife. Imagine being in a dental chair under those circumstances (laughter).

FRANK: I'll tell you an Arch Oboler story. I got a call from Arch one week to do the lead opposite Helen Mack. So, I went down, and Helen had a speech about this long, and then I said, "Oh?" And then she had one about this long, and I said, "Aaah." Then she had one about this long, and I said "Mmmm." And this is the way it went through the script. So, the following week, I'm doing a *Lux Radio*, and there's an actor on the west coast, Lou Merrill, who did a lot of work. Lou was on the show. They used to call us "The Gold Dust Twins" because both of us were running from show to show all the time. So, Lou said, "Hey, I'm on

Oboler this week." I said, "Oh, when you see him, tell him that the fellow who adlibbed opposite Helen Mack last week said hello." He gave him the message, and I didn't work for Arch for two years. He got so mad about it. I reminded him of it when we were doing something to honor Lurene Tuttle out there at an affair, and I said, "You remember, Archie?" He got mad. He didn't think that was funny at all.

DAVID: Mr. Oboler is probably the only person in the field of old radio who does challenge people today that are replaying his broadcasts. He is well-known for that. Most other radio personalities, I think, are honored and enjoy the fact that collectors and some of the non-profit stations are playing those shows, but Oboler, I understand, goes after them with a passion.

FRANK: And he does. There's one reason: he keeps copyright on everything, and he challenges anybody who uses it. But he doesn't know, and he's not going to see this program, so I'm going to tell you—about 1976, wasn't it honey? We were asked to go to Washington, DC, to appear for the Smithsonian on the Mall. *Working Americans* was the title, I think, of the whole thing. We were to do something about radio. When we got there, I said, "Well, what is it you want us to do?" They said, "Oh, what do you want to do?" I said, "Oh, good Lord. I thought you had material for us. You had things you wanted." And they said, "Oh, no. Whatever you'd like to do." I said, "Well, what do you have on the radio today?" And they said, 'Well, we have a news man, a sound man, we have a sportscaster, an engineer . . . ." So, we talked, and I said, "I have an idea if we can find some material. Let's show them what was taken away from them—something that they no longer have—comedy and drama in radio, because it just doesn't exist anymore. Now, if we can just get some material . . . ." So, we start running around Washington. "Where are you going to find scripts? Who are you going to go to?"

DAVID: Library of Congress.

FRANK: No, we went—what was the name of it? It was a library of old-time radio, and we started thumbing through things, going through this material. We found an old thing from the 1930s of an old Midwest couple sitting on the porch rocking. We picked that. Then, we picked another thing, which was Arch's. It was a cute little sketch. It's a young man on his way to his wedding, and you think, of course, that the girl is his fiancée. Uh-uh. The girl is a baby abandoned in the back seat, and you hear a baby crying. He stops on the way to make a phone call. An old man lets him in and then the young man says, "Do you like children?" "Yes." "Oh, that's wonderful, because we've already got a baby!" And you hear the baby cry from the back seat. So, anyway, we did that, and then we reminisced and told stories. We told about things that happened that you couldn't get back, you know—where something went out over the air and there was no way to get it back again. Yeah. Real bloopers. I made some of those on radio.

DAVID: Will you share a few bloopers with us, Frank?

FRANK: Well, let's see . . . .

VEOLA: You used to set fire to somebody's . . . .

FRANK: Oh, well, we did that, setting fire to the script. Everybody did that. The newsman's working and you come in and light the thing, and he's trying to get it out and he can't. Yeah, we did a lot of those bad things, but talking about actual bloopers on the air—we had a very dramatic show out there called *The Witch's Tale*.

DAVID: *Old Nancy* . . . .

FRANK: Yes, *Old Nancy*. Oh, you know it. Alonzo Deen Cole. So, anyway, I was the leading man on *The Witch's Tale*, and I came to the end of this first act, a highly dramatic scene. My line was, "You've killed my boy." And I started to say "son," and I tried to change back, and what came out was, "You've killed my *soy!*" And I'm dying, and Lindsey McHarrie was the director, and he sent a note out to me, and just as we were going to start the second act, I flipped this thing open and looked at it and he said, "My little *soy*, how have you *bean?*" (Laughter). And I thought, I'm not going on at all, I tell you. Those things kill you. Somebody breaks up and you catch their eye. You're dead. I've seen things where the whole show is dissolved. (Laughter). Mel Blanc had a problem one day with—I've forgotten who the announcer was—oh, Ken Niles. And Ken had a very high-pitched laugh. He was reading something about Pepsodent, and all of a sudden, he goes (laughs) "Pepsodent is (laughs) and he says, "Mel, take it." Mel had never looked at it, but he picked it up and just read it because Ken couldn't do it. He was through. He was finished. And oh, Dr. Christian . . . .

VEOLA: Oh.

FRANK: His name? Jean Hersholt. When you did that, there were people who really thought he was Dr. Christian. They almost revered the man. When you did his show, it was kind of like being in church. Art Gilmore was the announcer, a very lovely man, and a very restrained, gentlemanly type. He would talk to the audience, and they all just sat there enthralled by Jean, and so on. Jean worked in a spotlight and Rosemary DeCamp worked in a spotlight. There were two spotlights on the stage, and that's all the light. Now, this week, Rod O'Connor, who we called the "Dirty Old Man of Radio," was the announcer. He weighed about 300 pounds, and could tell you more dirty stories in thirty minutes than you could possibly assimilate. So, Rod is replacing Art, because Art is on vacation. He goes out and makes the speech and does a nice job of that. Now, Jean gets to a line, and his line is, "There was Judy, peeking through the keyhole." And then, he continues the line, because Rosemary can't talk until he ends the line. The balance of the line is what she responds to. So, Jean says, "And there was Judy, peeing through the keephole." (Laughter). Now, there's a pause, which you wouldn't believe. Rosemary is sitting there, frozen in her spotlight. Jean is looking at his script and going— you could see it all going through his mind—I couldn't *possibly* have done that!

VEOLA: And the audience . . . .

FRANK: The audience doesn't make a sound. Now, had there been any other audience except for Jean Hersholt, they would have yelled, but for Dr. Christian? No. So there's dead silence. Now, the funniest part of the whole thing is—over at the side of the stage, behind the curtain, is Rod O'Connor. He is jumping from one foot to the other and cramming grapes into his mouth to keep from bursting out laughing. Finally, after about a ten-second pause, Jean went on with the line and

Rosemary was able to pick up the script. I'll never forget that as long as I live. "There was Judy, peeing through the keephole." I don't know whether or not you can use that, but there it is (laughs).

DAVID: We have a very liberal community. I like to start out asking you both questions and then give you a chance to share your personality with the rest of the folks attending this convention. If you can tell us, perhaps, some of the favorite people you worked with—other than Jack Benny and perhaps Eddie Cantor—people folks would remember. What are you folks doing today, commercials, voiceovers? How are you enjoying life in the 1980s?

FRANK: I'm still doing commercials. I just did some the other day for Detroit, which was strictly the Benny character. Of course, I did a campaign about a year back for McDonald's, where I was the spokesman for them. I've been doing a cartoon series for Hanna-Barbera. I did a series a couple years ago called *Dinky Dog*. Last year I did one called *Monchichis*, in which I was the Wizard, or the "Wizzer," as they called him. On *Dinky Dog*, I was the uncle of the two girls, and of course, the foil for the dog. Dinky Dog was a huge dog. We have just gone on the air with a show called *The Snorks*. The reason we're called "Snorks" is because we have little snorkels because we live under the sea. I am the Governor of Snorkland. So, I do those kinds of things if they find me. They have to hunt for me, because I'm not really looking for anything. And of course, Mamma's home working over a hot stove. You know we don't let her get out very much.

VEOLA: (Laughs).

FRANK: Keep her home. Keep her locked up in the closet.

What about your favorite people, Veola?

VEOLA: Well, favorite people—very difficult, but I would say, naturally Benny, of course, as you said. Bing Crosby, Bob Hope. I loved Abbott and Costello. I worked in the movies with them. Oh, golly, there were so many . . . .

DAVID: Do you remember Fanny Brice?

FRANK: Oh sure, sure.

DAVID: She was the Baby Snooks character so many of us remember and love. Can you tell us anything at all about what Fanny was really like to work with?

VEOLA: Well, I don't know whether you knew that Hanley Stafford, my first husband, was Daddy.

DAVID: No, I did not know that.

VEOLA: Yes, so I was very, very close to them. I worked the show, too, and *Blondie*. Of course, Hanley was Mr. Dithers, and this one here, my now husband, was Herb Woodley.

DAVID: That's terrific. I am learning a great deal today.

VEOLA: We worked with all the people during the war, even went on bond drives. It was a very exciting period.

DAVID: There was talk about Fanny Brice having trouble getting away from the Baby Snooks character. Is that just legend?

VEOLA: Getting away?

DAVID:	That sometimes, when she was off the air, she would still play or still pretend . . . .
VEOLA:	Oh, no. Fanny was a realist. She was a mixture of elegance and gutter, she really was. She came from the Lower East Side, and when she would go to the dressing room, she would lie down and belch a lot. I mean she really did. She was just herself. When we bought our home, Fanny decorated it. She got up into the area where we were—we had a beautiful view of the city—and she says, "Oh God! Kid, look! I've got goose bumps from looking at the view." And she'd pull her skirt up. She was just basic. She'd come to the house, and she'd cook potato pancakes when we had only a stove in the house. She was a wonderful woman. She was just pure herself. She knew from Aldous Huxley to Polly Moran, who used to take her teeth out and regale everybody with something like that. Bea Lillie, of course, was one of Fanny's best friends. Hanley and Fanny did not really socialize—just occasionally. He felt it best to keep the two apart.
DAVID:	You have been in some dramatic programs.
FRANK:	Fu Manchu
VEOLA:	I was Princess Nadji on *Fu Manchu—Chandu.* I beg your pardon. *Chandu the Magician*, that's right.
FRANK:	Poor kid, doesn't know.
DAVID:	Out in Portland, there is a Chandu fan, who has hours and hours of Chandu . . . .
VEOLA:	This was the period when Tom Collins did the juvenile and I was Princess Nadji.

DAVID: Frank and Veola . . . .

VEOLA: Thank you.

DAVID: This has been my moment of moments. I really
           have had a terrific time meeting you. You are the
           most gracious couple that we've had the experience
           of having at our convention. I hope the folks who
           have the opportunity to watch this tape are as
           thrilled with the experience as I have been. I'm
           happy to say that there are not hundreds, but
           thousands of people who still not just remember,
           but listen to and enjoy your talents.

VEOLA: I'm going to kiss you.

DAVID: Thank you.

FRANK: Thank you.

VEOLA: Well, that about wraps it up. I hope you have
           enjoyed this little portion of the convention which
           I could share with you. Thanks for tuning in.

Chapter 5
HILDEGARDE
(1906–2005)

Interview: February 24, 1989

One look at Hildegarde as she opened her apartment door to welcome my wife and I, and I could feel myself melting into a Walter Mitty-like daze. I had seen publicity photos of her and have listened to numerous broadcasts of *The Raleigh Room* that featured the singing voice of this wonderful chanteuse, who was always introduced as the "Incomparable Hildegarde." But all of those radio performances were aired during the early to mid-1940s, over forty years ago. Indeed, the lady who insisted that she would rather be interviewed in person than on the telephone was all of eighty-three years old at the time of our interview, just a year younger than Parker Fennelly was when I visited him at his home. The startling difference was that Parker looked and sounded his age, while our hostess had me daydreaming about Mae West, attired in her most seductive outfit. Her figure was svelte, her hair perfectly coiffed, and her face failed to reveal any sign of her true age.

And her voice. It had that same intriguing lilt to it that John Dunning describes in his 1989 landmark encyclopedia of old-time radio, *Tune in Yesterday*, as fooling various European nationals into thinking that she was born and raised in a neighboring European country.

Readers, who share the back-and-forth quizzing of this amazing woman as I did, might be interested in acquiring a copy of her long out-of-print book entitled, *Over 50—So What!*, in which she writes about the lifestyle that she was convinced would keep her fit and trim. Considering that she lived to the age of ninety-nine, and continued to give concerts into our mid-1990s, her prescription for life might be worth its price in gold.

David: It's February 24, 1989, and my wife, Susan, and I are delighted to be in the apartment of the incomparable Hildegarde, who never, ever needed an introduction. She's very kind, and is going to allow me to ask her several questions, and hopefully, will answer them in a comfortable way. Hildegarde, you have the reputation, of course, as being the "Milwaukee Chanteuse." Tell me about your background in Milwaukee. Is that really your hometown? Were you born in Milwaukee?

HILDEGARDE: No, I was not born in Milwaukee. I was born in a little town called Adell.

DAVID: You were not born in Milwaukee.

HILDEGARDE: No, I was raised in Milwaukee. I went to a parochial school in Milwaukee, and then I was at Marquette University. My major was music. I wanted to be a concert pianist. I had some fairly good teachers, but then I got into show business and I went into the popular field.

DAVID: How did you get into show business? What were some of your earlier . . . .

HILDEGARDE: Don't you know my life? Don't you know anything about me at all?

DAVID: I want you to tell it to the world. I want your voice telling it.

HILDEGARDE: I see. Well, anyway, it was in Milwaukee where I was going to school there—at Marquette. One afternoon, I was at the Palace Theater, and I saw an act which was called Jerry and Her Baby Grands. There were four white baby grands on the stage. The girls were dressed in colonial costumes. It was gorgeous, absolutely breathtaking. I sat there and I thought, *Oh, if I could only be one of those girls—to get out of Milwaukee.* So, I went backstage, and I met the woman who was the Directress. Her name was Jerry. I said, "I'd like to join." She said, "Well, let me hear you," and I played "Twelfth Street Rag," and then she said, "Do you sing?" I said, "Yes." I sang "Am I Blue," and she said, "Well, I have no opening at the moment, but I will let you know if there is." I remember I wore red at the time. So, I gave her my address and telephone number, and three weeks later, I received a telegram asking me if I would join her junior act in Springfield, Massachusetts. That meant the junior act played split weeks in Vaudeville. But the act that I saw at the Palace was always just a week, you know, a week in all the Palaces throughout the country. But the split weeks is the one that I joined, which was all right with me. I got into show business and out of Milwaukee (laughs), and to this day, I play "Twelfth Street Rag." I tell the audience, "Here's a piece of music that got me into show business and out of Milwaukee," and right into it I go and I play it real fast. Any more questions?

DAVID: I was going to ask you who were some of the people who influenced you in your early career, and you just mentioned one person . . . .

HILDEGARDE: Well, the woman—no. She didn't influence me. I was pretty good before I met her. I was a good pianist. I always wanted to be a great pianist. I was fairly good. I used to have trios and quartets and quintets. I organized them, and I went to the library, and I got music by the masters, and we sight-read these great, great concerti and all the wonderful music of the masters. But when I got into show business, that's when I started to develop as a performer, but it took many years. I was very bad in the beginning. I was just a pianist, and you know, did what I had to do. But later on, I wanted to become a singer and a performer and that's when . . . .

DAVID: You got into nightclubs or supper clubs?

HILDEGARDE: That didn't come right away. I was still in Vaudeville. After Jerry and Her Baby Grands, which lasted about a year, I was out of a job, and went to Chicago, and I met an agent, I remember. I said, "I'm available!" He said, "Good. Can you accompany an Irish tenor?" I said, "Sure, I can." So, I accompanied the Irish tenor—and I was on the road with him. When that finished, I got into another act, and that was Oklahoma Bob Albright. He had a big costume like a cowboy, and I had to dress as a cowgirl, all in white. I accompanied him, and we sang "My Blue Heaven." When that finished, I got with Tony DeMarco, the famous ballroom dancer.

DAVID: Tony and Sally?

HILDEGARDE: Yes, but with me it was Tony and Nina. Al Siegel was my other pianist. He discovered Ethel Merman. He was the one who taught me how to play rhythm, use the thumb. After that, I accompanied a very elegant woman called Edith Meiser from Vassar. She was a very elegant impressionist, and I sat and played the piano with her very demurely. She made me wear a black gown so I would not upstage her. I sat in the dark and I played the piano.

DAVID: That's not the same Edith Meiser who's well-known for Sherlock Holmes, is it? There's an Edith Meiser who has written Sherlock Holmes stories.

HILDEGARDE: No, no, you're wrong. This is a different person. She was in Broadway shows. Anyway, one time she was taking a bow, and then I went off the stage, and the electrician put a spotlight on me and I quickly bowed, and thought, *Oh, I got a spotlight.* And she called up and said, "Didn't I tell you not to put a spotlight on my piano player? See that doesn't happen again." Well, anyway, we see each other once in a great while. She's in her nineties now. I'd tell her about it, and she was so amused. I said, "Yes, yes, you were afraid I would upstage you." After that, I went to London and I started there . . . .

DAVID: Did you go to London on your own, or did you have an agent?

HILDEGARDE: Yeah—as a one-woman show, as a performer. Of course, I had an agent, who booked me. The band that saw me—Martinus Poulson saw me—in an audition, and he chose me out of several hundred girls. I opened in London, September 11, 1933, and I was a flop. I wasn't ready, and he said, "I got you here ten years too soon. You don't dress well. Spend your money on clothes, learn how to perform, and get a rapport with an audience." And ah, I was heart-broken. I got a job in Paris, and that's where I started to sort of refine my artistry.

DAVID: Now, up until this time, you talk about the piano. When did you develop that singing voice? You sound so much like a French singer. You don't sound like an American singer. Your voice sounds Continental.

HILDEGARDE: No, it does not.

DAVID: Yes, yes . . . .

HILDEGARDE: Everybody always thought I was from Europe. Well, you see, German was my first language, and I have a good ear for languages. I have a good tongue to pronounce correctly.

DAVID: It's lilting. Even when you speak, it's melodic.

HILDEGARDE: Oh, really? You're getting me very self-conscious.

DAVID: No, no, it's true, very true.

HILDEGARDE: Thank you. That's the way the voice is. It is rather unique, I suppose. Even when I go into a store like Saks, they don't know my face, but they say, "Ah, the voice—Hildegarde." I say, "Yes." (Laughs). Anyway, it was terrible in Paris. I was in Club Casanova. I got a job there. It was terrible. I wasn't good at all. But one night, the King of Sweden came in, and he flipped over me, and his favorite song was "Did You Ever See a Dream Walking," and then he came back and asked me to sing it again, and that sort of helped my career.

DAVID: The name Hildegarde—did you always have that as a professional name?

HILDEGARDE: NO! It started with Mother when I was two months, eight days old, when I was baptized "Hildegarde." That's my real baptismal name.

DAVID: Does Hildegarde have another name?

HILDEGARDE: Yes.

DAVID: Is it a secret?

HILDEGARDE: Don't let's confuse the issue.

HILDEGARDE: Okay, that shall remain a secret. No, it's not. My full name is Hildegarde Loretta Sell. S–E–L–L. That's it. Okay, Gus Edwards—I forgot to tell you about Gus Edwards. He discovered me in 1932, before I went to London. I was with him in a beautiful act called "Stars on Parade." It was gorgeous, and Eddie Garr was my leading man. His daughter today is Terri Garr, the film star. We became an item. Anyway, Gus Edwards said, "Are we just going to use the name Hildegarde by itself? It's very unique. You are unique. You have a strange—not strange—interesting personality." I didn't know what personality meant, but I said, "All right, suits me fine. Just call me Hildegarde."

DAVID: That stuck.

HILDEGARDE: Yes. And then later on, somebody suggested on my radio show, *The Raleigh Room*, that I should be called "The Incomparable," so that also has stuck.

DAVID: They both are appropriate.

HILDEGARDE: I think so. Do you remember *The Raleigh Room*? "Here she comes—the vivacious, the incomparable . . . .

DAVID: . . . Incomparable Hildegarde. Yes.

HILDEGARDE: . . . Harry Sosnick and his orchestra."

DAVID: *The Raleigh Room* was not your first radio program. Was *Ninety-nine Men and a Girl* your first radio experience?

HILDEGARDE: No, I think it was *Beat the Band*.

DAVID: You were with Weems?

HILDEGARDE: No, it was just called *Beat the Band*.

DAVID: Yeah, but who was the band leader? Was it Ted Weems?

HILDEGARDE: No, it was just from the radio station. I don't know who it was. But haven't you got one of those discs?

DAVID: Yeah, I do, but I thought the musical director was a man named Weems—Ted Weems.

HILDEGARDE: Doesn't it say in the program. Do you remember the program at all? Well, maybe the name will pop out that way. I don't remember that.

DAVID: But *Beat the Band* was your first radio performance?

HILDEGARDE: Yes, and then came *Ninety-nine Men and a Girl*. Or was it 100 men?

DAVID: *Ninety-nine Men and a Girl*. Could you talk about how you got the radio opportunities—a little bit about radio performing?

HILDEGARDE: These were offered to me. I was already a big success through the Savoy Plaza before the war. This was in New York, and oh, by the way, in London, John Royal heard about my success, and he brought me back to this country to do a sustaining show. That came first. Yes, that's right. I got $500 a program, and then I had many thirteen weeks. So, that was really my first appearance on radio in New York, and then came *Beat the Band*, and then came *Ninety-nine Men and a Girl* and *The Raleigh Room*.

DAVID: When you were on *Ninety-nine Men and a Girl*, that was the Raymond Paige . . . .

HILDEGARDE: Raymond Paige. Yes. That was offered to me because I was a success and people wanted to hear me. They couldn't come to the Plaza, so I was on the radio, you see, and that's how it was.

DAVID: Do you remember how many seasons that *Ninety-nine Men and a Girl* were on? Was that on more than one season, or . . . .

HILDEGARDE: I think two. 1939.

DAVID: Is that so?

HILDEGARDE: Well, I think maybe the one season then.

DAVID: And then you did these five-minute bits for US Rubber. Were they all done one after another, or were they done in . . . .

HILDEGARDE: No, they were done all together. Little commercials, you mean?

DAVID: Five-minute commercials with Dan Seymour and The Lyn Murray Orchestra, and you just came out and sang. That was just a one-time proposition.

HILDEGARDE: Gosh, you know a lot about me that I forgot (laughs). How do you get that all into your head?

DAVID: Only from the radio broadcasts—from the programs. After *Ninety-nine Men and a Girl*, you said you did not go directly into *The Raleigh Room*. Were there any other radio appearances after that, after the Raymond Paige series?

HILDEGARDE: No, then came *The Raleigh Room*. That was during the war.

DAVID: You were the star of that program.

HILDEGARDE: Um–hum.

DAVID: And that was on for several seasons at least, 1944,

1945, 1946. What kind of power, may I ask, does a star have in deciding who the guest will be, or is that all done by other people?

HILDEGARDE: Of course. I was the artist. I had nothing to do with that. My manager, Anna Sosenko, was the producer of *The Raleigh Room*. It was her creation. She and Herbert Moss, who was the director, chose the people to go on the show with me because they kept track of who was popular in Hollywood or here on Broadway, and then I had two great writers, Alan J. Lerner, who later on composed *My Fair Lady*, and Joseph Stein—*Fiddler on the Roof.* They were the writers of my show. They used to give me jokes. I wrote them all down.

DAVID: Based on some of the guests that you had on *The Raleigh Room*, could you talk about any interesting experiences that you had as a performer on that show? Were there always live audiences, or . . . .

HILDEGARDE: It was in Studio 8 H, my dear. That's when Toscanini had his symphonies. No, I don't remember everything, except I know once I had Tallulah Bankhead thirteen times, and I don't remember many things about all these great people like Cugat, Clifton. Tallulah Bankhead is the one person who never smoked in my presence. She never swore in my presence, because I was such a lady (laughs). She said, "I'll have to watch my speech in front of Hildegarde, darling, darling, darling." So I had Buddy Clark. Alec Templeton—you remember him?

DAVID: The blind pianist.

HILDEGARDE: Patsy Kelly, Irving Berlin. I have a photograph with him over there and shall I go on? Milton Berle, Taylor Caldwell the great writer, Walter Abel. Isn't it wonderful, and I can't recall anything except that we used to just come to the rehearsal. Everything was proper. We sat around the table. We read our scripts, and then we said goodbye.

DAVID: One rehearsal?

HILDEGARDE: The day before, and then we had another rehearsal on the day—like a preview. So, there was one rehearsal the day before, and then just before the program. Dress rehearsal, let's say. It was always very proper. Everything—hello, hello, hello, and when it was finished, it was good- bye, and that was it.

DAVID: No friendships? No socialization?

HILDEGARDE: No, that's right. That's true. Let's see—I want to mention some other names.

DAVID: Did you have any zany guests? Some radio stories talk about people who come on as guests and behave in an unpredictable way. Did you have any of that sort of thing?

HILDEGARDE: Well, Eddie Cantor was very quiet and nice. Although when I saw him in Paris, he always cut up a great deal. He grabbed me and put me on his shoulders. I still have a photograph of that. Of course there was Henny Youngman—he always was kidding. And Jan Murray—they were kidding, and there was Frances Faye. Those were comedians, and they were comedians even off the stage. I had Boris Karloff, Oscar Levant—remember such names?

DAVID: Oh yes, yes indeed.

HILDEGARDE: Georgie Jessel, Milton Cross, Burgess Meredith,

Patsy Kelly. Isn't it amazing? Vernon Duke, the great composer. Paulette Goddard. Remember Al Kelly that did the double talk? Willy Howard. It amazes me. Edward Everett Horton, Dorothy Kilgallen, Hattie Carnegie. Did you hear this?

DAVID: It's a *Who's Who* of the theater.

HILDEGARDE: I tell you, Herbert and Dorothy Fields. Sigmund Romberg. Well, should I stop? If you do. Perry Como. Those are all names that your people will hear and remember. Okay, that's about it.

DAVID: You were a guest star on programs during the war for the Armed Forces. I don't know if you remember a program called *Guest Star* . . . .

HILDEGARDE: Yes.

DAVID: . . . or *Here's to Vets?*

HILDEGARDE: Yes.

DAVID: But you were a guest on fifteen-minute segments of some of those programs. Do you recall doing any of those for the Armed Services?

HILDEGARDE: Surely, and on V-Day. Have you got a tape of my beautiful speech that night?

DAVID: No, I don't.

HILDEGARDE: Oh, I must find it and give it. I must say, I spoke very well. Oh, and even I cried when I heard it again, it was so impressive and so emotional, because that was the day peace was declared.

DAVID: Why did *The Raleigh Room* ever go off the air?

HILDEGARDE: I don't know.

DAVID: It was such a popular show.

HILDEGARDE: It was such a popular show. I guess television came in then and my sponsor—first it was Raleigh Cigarettes. That was Brown & Williamson. Then it became *The Penguin Room*. That was Cool Cigarettes, which was also Brown & Williamson sponsors. Then came *The Campbell Room*— Campbell Soups—see? And by that time, television took over, and I still say, damn it—excuse me (laughter)—that radio should come back. A program like I had—to bring the guests in. People can visualize the guests instead of seeing everything with your eyes. What about the ears and your imagination?

DAVID: Did those guests cost very much to bring on?

HILDEGARDE: I don't know. I never knew their salaries.

DAVID: Never knew what the economics of the shows were?

HILDEGARDE: No.

DAVID: You said you had Sosnick. You had a full orchestra.

HILDEGARDE: We had the full orchestra, the Director, the Producer, and myself.

DAVID: Who was your announcer? Do you know?

HILDEGARDE: I had Bud Collyer, Ed Herlihy, and several others. I can't remember now. So, I don't know what they got, but it wouldn't have been a great deal. I mean, maybe not even a thousand dollars a program, I don't think, or a person.

DAVID: When you left radio, did you go on TV at all?

HILDEGARDE: Not too much. A little bit, yes.

DAVID: Guest star, or . . . .

HILDEGARDE: I was on with Jack Paar. I was on with Merv Griffin. I was on with David Frost. I was on some panel shows. I never liked television. I was always self-conscious. I always thought, oh gosh, they'll see all the wrinkles (laughs).

DAVID: *What wrinkles?*

HILDEGARDE: And I'd get self-conscious about it. I'd say, "Don't come so far you see my fillings! (laughs)." But anyway, I'm going to be in Palm Springs in May. I have a big concert out there. My people are trying to get me on Carson and Pat Spayvak, which I dread, but I'll do it. Is that right, Spayvak?

DAVID: Close. It's Sajak.

HILDEGARDE: Sajak. Strange name. I suppose he's Bohemian, or something like that.

DAVID: You'll sit at the piano and sing?

HILDEGARDE: I don't know, maybe I will. Maybe just talk, but I know I'm going to be down there May 27th, in the Bob Hope Cultural Center. The theater is called McCallum. M-C-C-A-L-L-U-M, and I have my own production. It's called, "A Beautiful Review." It's a two-hour show. That's what I did in Carnegie Hall in 1986. It was called "Last Night When We Were Young." The song was written by Harold Arlen and E. Y. Harburg. I sing that in the show, too, but it's a gorgeous song. I do it very well, says she modestly. I really do. It's a song that has schmaltz for me. I like such songs. So you see the show must go on.

DAVID: You were always a romanticist.

HILDEGARDE: Oh, yes, I do beautiful, romantic songs.

DAVID: Don't slap my face, but let me ask you this: there are a lot of men that you were photographed with for those radio magazines. Was Hildegarde ever married? Were there any important men in Hildegarde's life?

HILDEGARDE: Yeah, plenty, plenty, plenty. I had four big romances and twelve times in love, but never married, no. It's just as well. I'm happy with my life the way it is. I have given my life to my work and my audience and the world, and I believe it's God's will, and there's nothing you can do about it.

DAVID: Are there people in the theatrical world, the radio world, the Broadway world, whom you're still close to as friends, or are most of your friends outside of that?

HILDEGARDE: They're all gone. I was never really very close to people in the theater, because I was always the star of something, and they came to me, and then it was goodbye. I was traveling on the road all the time. I traveled all my life since 1926, so I was here today, gone tomorrow. I met lots of men. I had affairs here and there. Goodbye, hello, another one, another one, another one. I was quite a swinger (laughs). All those broken hearts! (Laughs). Yeah, I did break a few hearts, and I'm sorry I did. I'm sorry I did. But my life is quite interesting.

DAVID: Better to have lived and loved . . . .

HILDEGARDE: That is so true.

DAVID: Because of the fame—who else came from Milwaukee? Jack Carson used to joke that he came from Milwaukee.

HILDEGARDE: Liberace, although Liberace really comes from West Bend, which is a suburb of Milwaukee.

DAVID: Is there a place in Milwaukee that has some of your memorabilia?

HILDEGARDE: Yes, Marquette University.

DAVID: So, if one were to go to Marquette, there would be an exhibit in some place?

HILDEGARDE: Yes, one hundred. I just told you. Don't you remember?

DAVID: Yeah, but you didn't tell me that on tape. You told me that earlier (laughs).

HILDEGARDE: Yeah.

DAVID: A hundred scrapbooks at Marquette.

HILDEGARDE: Those were the ones from the 1920s. Then, the ones from the 1930s and 1940s, Wyoming, and then the later ones, when I appeared in New York more often than that, went to Lincoln, here, right here in New York.

DAVID: You indicated, and again, this is before we put the tape on, you said something about—you had at one time, some of the discs of your own broadcasts— some of those large discs.

HILDEGARDE: Yes.

DAVID: Were they given to you by the sponsor, or were they just something that, because you were the featured artist, you walked home with those gifts?

HILDEGARDE: Well, you know what? I don't know where they came from. See, I used to live at The Plaza. When the radio show terminated, I guess the sponsor let me have all those discs, and then I moved from The Plaza with my gorgeous Steinway, and all my possessions went into a storage place because I was going to Europe. I was traveling all over the place, for heaven's sake, and I came back, and I got everything out and got this apartment built. I was waiting since 1950 to find an ideal place for me. A friend of mine, Helen Rich, lived downstairs. I used to say, "Oh, Helen, I wish I could have an apartment. I want one so badly." And she said, "I'll keep my eyes open." So luckily, this one was available on the 8th floor. So, then I took everything out of storage, including the big discs. I got here and I said, "Where am I going to put—what do I need them for?" And so out they went. I threw them away. How awful of me.

DAVID: Oh, my gosh—just thrown away.

HILDEGARDE: Just thrown away, my dear.

DAVID: All that radio history.

HILDEGARDE: Yeah. Well, I think little by little, I'm getting something back, but very little (laughs). All these wonderful people in this black book, they would have all been on those discs. Maybe this man has fifty-eight, but that's only fifty-eight. There were thirteen weeks in the program. That could have been the whole duration of *The Raleigh Room.*

DAVID: Could have been two seasons.

HILDEGARDE: Yes. Then I did another stupid thing. At The Plaza, when I was moving, the manager said, "You know, downstairs you have a lot of *Life* magazines. The Fire Department just noticed that. You've got to either take them or throw them away." So I said, "Oh, throw them away." Number one was in it. Oh, for heaven's sake! That's what you can do under duress.

DAVID: I was going to ask you about your future, but you just answered that by telling me about this appearance that you're doing in Palm Springs.

HILDEGARDE: Well, that's not the only thing in the future. I hope to have some concerts. I'd like to do lectures, or to do the one-woman show that I have: "Last Night When We Were Young," where I have a very handsome young man with me and a wonderful pianist. We three have a two-hour show together and I can have an orchestra, too, if I wish.

DAVID: Are you doing night club work or are you doing supper club work?

HILDEGARDE: I just closed at the Rainbow. You didn't come to see me.

DAVID: No, I didn't. I'm sorry.

HILDEGARDE: Rainbow and Stars. That's on the 65th floor.

DAVID: Right.

HILDEGARDE: I opened Friday, January 13, and the *New York Times* gave me a marvelous review, as well as *The Post*. That was just last month.

DAVID: Do you have people coming up to you after the performances who remember you when you were a radio performer?

HILDEGARDE: Yes. They all say, "We remember you from the Persian Room, and I still remember you wore this. Do you still wear the long gloves?" And I say, "Yes, I do." They say, "You brought us such memories." "I fell in love with my husband." Or "I fell in love with my wife before we got married at one of your programs." It was very sweet. People always come up to you and say remember me and how impressed they were. I'm glad I left an indelible impression on people after forty some years.

DAVID: Again, you are the incomparable romantic because your songs are always songs of love.

HILDEGARDE: Surely.

DAVID: There's none of that rock-n-roll garbage.

HILDEGARDE: No. I know, but I have some very "up" numbers, too. I was in legitimate shows. I was in *Follies*. In my act, I have a song that I did in *Follies* called "A Paris." The song I sang in Gus Edwards' review, it's "Zwei Herzen," that was in German, because he put me out as a little German immigrant.

HILDEGARDE: Gus Edwards is very famous for (sings) "School days, school days, dear old . . . ." and also, "By the light, of the silvery moon . . . ."

DAVID: When you worked for Gus Edwards, were you in

the review at the same time that some of the—not Jessel, but . . . .

HILDEGARDE: No, no. I was his latest protégé. Eddie Cantor, Georgie Jessel, Georgie Price . . . .

DAVID: Those people all came before you?

HILDEGARDE: Walter Winchell. They were all before me. I was his latest, and I joined him in 1932, and I was cast as a little immigrant girl, and had an ugly costume on. As I said, Eddie Garr was my leading man, and then I sang "Zwei Herzen," which is a beautiful waltz. I was in *Can-Can*. I did the lead in that, and then I'd sing also "Allez-vous-en." Then, I was in *Five O'Clock Girl* at the Goodspeed Opera House. I'd sing "Nevertheless" (sings) "Maybe I'm right, maybe I'm wrong . . . ."

DAVID: (joins in) "Maybe I'm right, maybe I'm wrong. Maybe I'm weak, maybe I'm strong." I'm doing a duet with Hildegarde! (Laughter).

HILDEGARDE: So, I've had a very good program. Very diversified. I sing, even accompany my very elegant young singer. The last time, it was Tony Cointreau, who was from the family of the Cointreau liquor people—after dinner drink. A very famous name. I played and said to him, "Tony, you know when I first went into show business, I was an accompanist. I accompanied____, and I mentioned the Irish tenor and the Oklahoma da, da, da, da." I said, "Now, I'm going to accompany you." And I go to the piano and I play "La Vie en Rose" for him. Then, we'd do it in French together. It was very lovely, a very interesting performance, I must say.

DAVID: Any more?

HILDEGARDE: You've exhausted me. Susan, do you have any questions you'd like to ask?

SUSAN: (Sneezes).

HILDEGARDE: Gesundheit!

SUSAN: Thank you. There's nothing I can think of.

HILDEGARDE: I used to paint. You see that painting there, that Saint Cecilia? I did that when I was eighteen. I have two more with lemons. I have Venice, St. Marks, and I have a . . . .

DAVID: You just reminded me of something. Parents are very proud of their children. How did your parents react to their daughter going on stage and becoming famous? Did they live long enough for them to see you as really a star?

HILDEGARDE: Well, that's a nice question. When I first got into show business with Jerry and Her Baby Grands in October 1926, when I had the opportunity, Mother said to Father, "We must let Hildegarde go. This is her chance—she's musical. She's ambitious." And Father said, "Well, no, I don't agree with you. Let her be a secretary or something." Mother said, "She goes!" And she went. And I got on the road and that's how I started, and Mother, bless her soul, was always my champion. And Father, who later on died of cancer, saw me the last few months of his life, when I appeared at The Riverside Theater in Milwaukee, and he sat in the box, sick. He saw me in *Gus Edwards Review.* He was thrilled and he cried. He said, "Well, you're right. You chose the right thing for her."

DAVID: That must have given you a thrill.

HILDEGARDE: It makes me sad to this day. So, Mother lived to see me as a very important star, when I was the queen of the Persian Room at The Plaza.

DAVID: Do you have brothers or sisters?

HILDEGARDE: I have two sisters, and also I was not only in the Persian Room, you know, these hotels; I appeared at The Roxie. I appeared at the Capitol here. I appeared in the Chicago Theater, all over in Detroit, big, big, big, big theaters with my Raleigh Room act.

DAVID: Right.

HILDEGARDE: I had Patsy Kelly sometimes. I had Basil Rathbone sometimes. It was a real production, so . . . .

DAVID: I hope I didn't bring a tear to your eye.

HILDEGARDE: That's all right. There was the question, and I answered it. It brought back sadness and . . . .

DAVID: You mentioned sisters.

HILDEGARDE: Oh, yes.

DAVID: I assume you have some nieces or nephews, then.

HILDEGARDE: No. You'd be amazed. Nothing. The line is finished. Germaine lives in Texas. She, in the last few years, she's been ailing and failing. She had open heart. The other sister lives in Venice, Florida. She has had cancer for about four, six years now, failing and ailing. I haven't seen them in four years. They don't want to see me. I guess because they don't look so good, or something. It's very sad. I feel terrible about it.

DAVID: Well, let's change the subject. Let's get you into something a little more cheerful.

HILDEGARDE: No, they were wonderful sisters. They were musical. At one time, we had a little trio. Germaine had played the violin, and Honey—we called her Honey—her name was Beatrice; she played the cello. No, the other way around. And I played the piano, and we played classics in our home in Milwaukee.

DAVID: You have been so gracious. I really appreciate this. I will take this tape home. Hopefully, nothing will happen to it. I will transfer it to reel-to-reel because that really is how I keep most of my tapes.

HILDEGARDE: I see.

DAVID: I'm going to share you, because what I hope I will be able to do will be to tell some of the people who collect radio programs, that I now have a very, very rare program that no one has ever heard.

HILDEGARDE: Right. That's true.

DAVID: That is Hildegarde talking about her own life.

HILDEGARDE: My radio career.

DAVID: Have you written a biography? Have you ever thought about . . . .

HILDEGARDE: Yes, in 1963. There was a book that came out called *Over Fifty—So What?* I like the So what part.

DAVID: I'd like to get a copy of that.

HILDEGARDE: It's in the libraries, yes.

DAVID: Susan, I'll have to add that to my want list. And the name of the book?

HILDEGARDE: *Over Fifty—So What?* It was written with Adele Fletcher. It's a good book. It's more about health, though, not too much about my life. Some of the life, yes, and there were some pictures of me with Jackie Gleason, and Irving Berlin, and Christian Dior. Nice pictures.

DAVID: Do you talk at all about your radio career in the book, or mostly about health habits?

HILDEGARDE: I think the radio was mentioned because I had photographs in the book with the radio people that were with me on the program.

DAVID: I will have to add that to my collection of books.

HILDEGARDE: Well, you'll find it someplace I think, in the library.

SUSAN: What is your secret to such vim and vigor?

HILDEGARDE: Have I got that?

SUSAN: You're doing something right. You've got a message for other people: how to stay youthful.

HILDEGARDE: Do you know how old I am? Eighty-three. But I've taken eighty-three, reversed it to thirty-eight, and add twenty.

SUSAN: (Laughs).

HILDEGARDE: Quickly, how old is that? Fifty-eight (laughter). No, I've been very strict with myself and my diets. I'm very disciplined. I'm a health food nut, within reason, of course. I take natural vitamins. I drink Mountain Valley Water. I'm Vice President at Large of the company. That's why I drink it. I also watch—no junk food, no salt, no white flour, no sugar. Very strict. Very strict. I watch the scale every day. I will not allow myself to have that middle-aged spread (laughter).

SUSAN: I beg your pardon.

HILDEGARDE: I look every day at that scale. If I'm up a little half a pound, I say, "Uh-uh. Got to do something about it." So, I'm very careful the next day. I take very good care of my skin, too. I have a certain regime that I use, and I do it religiously. I don't skip. I mustn't skip. If you have pretty skin, take care of it now.

SUSAN: It's too late (laughs).

HILDEGARDE: No! What are you, about a fast forty-two?

SUSAN: Well past.

HILDEGARDE: I didn't say past. I said fast.

SUSAN: Oh, fast.

DAVID: You have been so charming and so delightful. I will not keep you.

HILDEGARDE: Do you know what? There's going to be a snow storm now. Did you hear? I called the Weather Bureau. It said later this afternoon. Notice it's twenty-four hours later, as it is.

DAVID: May I take just a quick peek at some of your memorabilia? I want to . . . .

HILDEGARDE: Get a better picture of me. I was talking and they never turn out so good.

Chapter 6
MIRIAM WOLFF
(1922–2000)

TWO INTERVIEWS, NOVEMBER, 1998

My interview with Miriam Wolff, a most versatile and, I should add, extremely intelligent actress, had its origin in an unexpected meeting almost a decade earlier with Charles Michelson, the well-known syndicator, who played a major role in preserving so many Golden Age of radio series.

It all began at a Friends of Old-Time Radio (FOTR) convention sometime in the late 1980s. During a workshop presentation, Michelson mentioned that he had access to the scripts of one of my favorite programs, *The Witch's Tale*. That piece of information stayed with me for many years until 1998, when I arranged with Michelson to publish a collection of the scripts together with an introduction that would discuss the history of the program and its creator, writer, and actor, Alonzo Deen Cole.

In addition to having the opportunity to examines Cole's personal scrapbooks, my next most valuable source of information about the program came from one of its performers, Miriam Wolff, who at age twelve, played the role of Nancy, the more than hundred-year-old witch, who opened and closed each weekly program. At the time, Miriam was a regular member of the cast on the wonderful CBS weekly children's program, *Let's Pretend*, where her specialty, not coincidentally, was portraying wicked witches.

Miriam and I initially spoke informally at Friends of Old-Time Radio conventions. She was a cautious woman, who did not wish to waste her time on fools who merely wished to satisfy their own curiosity. But years later, once I had begun work on *The Witch's Tale* book, and once I had become a published author, as well as publisher, I contacted her at her home, and she graciously agreed to speak with me in an "on the record" telephone interview. Prior to finalizing the book's Introduction, I telephoned her a second time to double check some facts and make sure that I hadn't forgotten to ask her anything in the first interview. (The second interview appears below in an abridged format in order to avoid repetitious comments).

I last saw Miriam in 1999, when my wife and I were researching our guidebook to used bookstores in Canada. We visited with Miriam in her Toronto apartment, and lunched with her in a local restaurant. It was with great sadness that I learned a year later that one of the kindest, most giving veterans of old-time radio that I have ever had the pleasure of knowing had sadly passed away.

DAVID: How or why were you selected to play the part of Old Nancy?

MIRIAM: How did I get the job? Adelaide Fitz-Allen, who did the original Nancy, died. She was something like eighty-five years old, and I was twelve or thirteen. Nila Mack and Alonzo Deen Cole worked together in Vaudeville years before, doing one-night stands all over the country. She knew him, and she had heard that he was looking for someone, and I had been doing witches for her on *Let's Pretend.* They had auditioned about 600 actresses, and had different people doing it for about four weeks after Adelaide died. I decided to audition for it because I'd been listening to the show secretively. My mother wouldn't let me listen to it because she thought it was too scary for me. I had the radio under my pillow at 11:30 at night, and was scared stiff, but apparently, was able to imitate. I had been listening to Adelaide Fitz-Allen for a long time. Anyway, it was quite an experience. When he—Cole—came in, he said he was in a rush. He had to rehearse. He had to get the show on the air. Would I come back after the show was over, which was at midnight? I went over to NBC. I was a friend of Molly Picon. She was on *The Rudy Vallee Show*, and I spent a little time with her because I knew she was very nervous about the show. And then I walked back to WOR from NBC.

DAVID: At age twelve?

MIRIAM: Yeah (laughs). I always job-hunted on my own. I didn't take my mother with me at that age. It's amazing. I live in a suburb of New York, so I was born in the city, and I used to travel in the city without any qualms at all. I'm thinking about a twelve-year-old young lady traveling in New York at that hour (laughs). I had long curls, Buster Brown-type bangs, and a big sailor hat. I took my books with me because I went from school. I was going to Julia Richman High school, at that time. I was ahead of my years. I graduated high school when I was fourteen and a half. I was here in time to listen to the show. He put me up in the control room, a separate control room from where he was, and I listened to it and came down afterwards. It was unusual for a kid to be there at that hour anyway, and as a gag, because I had long curls and had my school books and a barrette and a hat, he said, "Okay, let's hear it." And when I did it, he said, "You're starting next week at $10 a show." And $10 a show was a lot of money to me at that time (laughs). He said, "I don't want anybody to know you're doing it, because that'll spoil the illusion." So, I never got any publicity on it.

DAVID: That's marvelous. In doing a little research, my sense tells me that the program first went on the air in 1934 and came off in 1938. At what point did you join the program?

MIRIAM: 1935.

DAVID: Very, very early in the program, then.

MIRIAM: Um-hum. I was on it for three years, and it started out with my just playing the witch, but we had a repertory company that was Alan Devitt . . . .

DAVID: Mark Smith.

MIRIAM: Mark Smith, Marie O'Flynn, Mr. Cole—Alonzo Deen Cole—and myself, and we played all the parts.

DAVID: I was going to ask you first what you remember about the personalities and the talents of Mr. Cole and Marie O 'Flynn.

MIRIAM: They were very talented. They were extremely neurotic people, but they were very talented (laughs).

DAVID: Do you know the name Charles Michelson?

MIRIAM: No.

DAVID: He may have known Mr. Cole because he used that phrase. He described him as a creative genius, but also a little strange. Is it possible for you to give me some examples or illustrate that comment?

MIRIAM: Well, yeah. We never started rehearsal on time. We were called for 3:30. That was just after school. I could get up there on time, and sometimes he'd show up at 7:00. The show went on the air at 11:30 at night, so it would end at midnight, and he would show up very late sometimes because he was still writing. And as a matter of fact, sometimes he was still writing when we went on the air (laughter). And if we were long, say five minutes or ten minutes long, he would cut us off, re-write an epilogue for Old Nancy, and we would continue the script next week, and he would write twenty-five minutes to fill in (laughs).

DAVID: I've just seen some of the original scripts. I think they were his scripts, because they had lines through them with numbers, so you could see he was timing it as he wrote and . . . .

MIRIAM: (laughing) Yes, he was timing it while we were on the air. When I saw the scripts, I thought he just read them back and said, "No, I've got to shorten this," but apparently, it was a last-minute. We worked on a ball mike. So, we were all working around the mike. I have a picture of it actually, somewhere (laughs). Now that I think of it really, I remember also that Marie, who was married to him, used to say—she was very sympathetic with me—she kept saying to him, "She's only a child. Don't scream at her." He never directed in a quiet voice.

DAVID: Why did it go off the air?

MIRIAM: I really don't know.

DAVID: Did you have a sponsor, or was it sustained?

MIRIAM: No, it was sustaining, always sustaining, and maybe that's why it went off the air. Maybe WOR felt they couldn't afford it any more. And incidentally, I think the way it was done was Alonzo Deen Cole had a package for which he was paid, and I think he paid the actors out of that. It was one of the reasons he was so stingy (laughs).

DAVID: Did the actors, Mr. Smith and Mr. Devitt, play in other companies as well?

MIRIAM: They played in other shows, you mean? Oh, yes. They were very popular radio actors.

DAVID: So they were not related just to this program?

MIRIAM: No, no.

DAVID: And the same with Marie O' Flynn?

MIRIAM: No, Marie O' Flynn actually worked only on *The Witch's Tale*. She had a very unusual voice. I don't know if you remember. It had sort of a quaver to it and she could play anything. But she played the ingénues always, and I played all the character parts on the show. Her voice was very distinctive, and I think that he didn't want her to do other shows.

DAVID: Was he involved in any other broadcasts, or was this his only baby?

MIRIAM: He did *Casey, Crime Photographer*. He wrote it.

DAVID: At the same time Staats Cotsworth was there?

MIRIAM: Yes, so Staats would know him.

DAVID: With regard to the scripts, some of the scripts by title appear to be adaptations of original works done by others. Were they all adaptations, or did he originate any of them?

MIRIAM: My feeling was that they were all originals. I mean that is what he led us to believe.

DAVID: Okay, because I just saw a script entitled "The Queen of Spades," and I always thought that was a Pushkin, but maybe not.

MIRIAM: No. They were all originals, as far as I know.

DAVID: In that case, my God, he had an imaginative mind.

MIRIAM: He had a very imaginative mind.

DAVID: He would have been an excellent writer for the pulps, because the pulp stories and his stories were very similar.

MIRIAM: Well, I remember once—this is just sort of an aside—when we were doing the show, there was a murder committed somewhere in New England. A chap was driving by a quiet road, and at that time, when you drove, you just drove very slowly, and there was a light on in a farm house there, and he was going to go in and ask some directions, I think. He heard these screams and these shots, and he took a gun and came in shooting, and it was because *Witch's Tale* was on the air.

DAVID: Oh, my God!

MIRIAM: And that's how real the thing was at that time. So, I mean it was a program that was extremely unusual. I can remember the rehearsals when I'd come in, and I was very young the first weeks that I was there. Mark Smith was huge. He must have been about six feet wide by about ten feet tall, as far as I was concerned. When he stood with you at the ball mike, he took up three-quarters of the space, and I used to play his mother quite regularly on the show (laughs). He was a wonderful actor. Alan Devitt was a dear man, but he had false teeth, and when he said all his lines in which he was supposed to be excited, the teeth started to come out and he'd clap them back in again with his right hand, and we'd go on with the scene. I was twelve years old—fourteen years old. I sat there at rehearsal listening to the story because I had been a fan, you know. I would come in on cue, but at that time, I was doing just the prologue and the epilogue, and I started to shiver. I was so scared, just sitting there and listening to them.

DAVID: In the studio?

MIRIAM: In the studio, with the scripts.

DAVID: Did you have many visitors at the studio, or was that verboten?

MIRIAM: No, no. He tried to keep it as private as possible. He would not give any publicity out on my being a kid because he didn't want to spoil the illusion, and as I say, he wanted to keep Marie O' Flynn off other shows because of her unusual voice. He wanted her associated only with *The Witch's Tale*.

DAVID: Apparently, the rehearsals were on the same day as the broadcast.

MIRIAM: Yes, well, he wrote 'til the last minute.

DAVID: Some broadcasts were done east coast and west coast. Were these done only once, or were they . . . .

MIRIAM: Only east coast. Oh, I see what you mean. They were rebroadcast. I think they were rebroadcast, yes.

DAVID: Were they done on record, or—you didn't actually go through the script a second time?

MIRIAM: No, I don't know how they did that if they rebroadcast, because we were on, as I say, we'd get off the air at midnight, so that would have been 8:00 in California. It's quite possible that they just broadcast it straight through on the network. I'm not sure. Roger Bower was the announcer on it, I remember.

DAVID: Sometimes, people talk about peculiar things happening in the middle of a broadcast either accidentally or pranks. Did that ever—did anything of that sort of thing ever occur on your broadcast?

MIRIAM: (laughs) Well, I performed a prank.

DAVID: While you were on the air?

MIRIAM: No. Marie was ill one week. I played the ingénue for the first time. I very rarely played ingénues. I had a phone call after the broadcast from someone who said, "I've fallen in love with your voice and I've got to meet you."

DAVID: (laughs) Yes.

MIRIAM: And I said, "I'm sorry, I'm busy. I can't meet you until after school." He said, "Oh, you teach as well." And I thought, oh, what the heck, so I said, "Oh, yes." And we made an arrangement to meet in front of the Astor Hotel, and we would know each other because we were both carrying straws, and I met him the next day. I came from school with my heavy briefcase (laughs) and my curls and my sailor hat, and I was carrying my straw, and he came over to me, and said, "Are you Miriam Wolff?" And I said, "Yes." And he said, "Come on, I'll buy you an ice cream soda." (Laughs) And we talked.

DAVID: That takes me to the question of fan mail. Was there much?

MIRIAM: Oh, there was a lot of fan mail. Oh, yes.

DAVID: It would all go to Mr. Cole?

MIRIAM: It would all go to Mr. Cole, yeah.

DAVID: Did he share it with the cast?

MIRIAM: Um, no. No. He was very strange. I mean, really very possessive about everything.

DAVID: How old was he at the time, or approximately how
            old was he and the other cast members?

MIRIAM: He was an old man to me (laughter).

DAVID: In his thirties, forties?

MIRIAM: He was in his thirties. I don't know how old he
            was. I really don't.

DAVID: Okay. Or any of the other cast members.

MIRIAM: If you go back to the days of Vaudeville, I would
            say he was about, oh, fifteen years older than I was,
            certainly not any more.

DAVID: Were you discovered by Nila Mack?

MIRIAM: Oh, no. I worked long before I worked on *Let's
            Pretend*. I did a little show called *The Uncle Gee
            Bee Kiddie Hour* (laughs), when radio first started.
            I started to work when I was four years old.

DAVID: Do I dare to ask you if, like Gypsy, your mother
            encouraged this, or was it your idea?

MIRIAM: I couldn't do it myself. I was four! (Laughs).

DAVID: Was it something you enjoyed doing, or something
            your mother wanted you to do?

MIRIAM: Something my mother wanted me to do and that I
            actually enjoyed to a degree. I mean, it was my
            whole life. I didn't know anything else. You do that
            to a kid and that's it, but I think it did a great deal
            of harm, I really do. The business itself, and the
            competition, and the auditions, and the nervousness,
            and all that I think are very unhealthy for kids. I

never was a child. A lot of the other child stars in radio kept their own personalities, because they played themselves. I always played character parts.

DAVID: Not only were you never a child, but you almost always seemed to be cast as a witch. Was that a peculiarity of your voice or was that . . . .

MIRIAM: Yes. I had a very heavy voice. I did a show called *Five Star Final.* I don't know if you ever heard of that?

DAVID: Yes.

MIRIAM: I played the newsboy. Alice Frost was on it. Clark Gable. It was on daily. It was a dramatized news show. I used to play the ingénues and some older women's parts, as well, in the show.

DAVID: While you were still ten or twelve years old?

MIRIAM: At that time, I was eight or nine. I had an unusual voice.

DAVID: I remember listening to *Let's Pretend* programs, particularly "Hansel and Gretel," where I wouldn't want to be anywhere in a house with that person (laughs).

MIRIAM: Well, thank you.

DAVID: The witch's laugh.

MIRIAM: Very funny.

DAVID: Even though I'm mainly concerned at this point about *The Witch's Tale*, as long as you did spend so much time with Nila Mack and *Let's Pretend*, are there any special memories of Nila Mack?

MIRIAM: Arthur Anderson is writing a book on *Let's Pretend.* He's almost finished.

DAVID: He attends our conventions every year.

MIRIAM: I've been to the convention twice. As a matter of fact, I couldn't come this year.

DAVID: What are your thoughts on the convention? May I inquire as an avid fan? We always wonder whether or not we're imposing on the guests. It's so great to have them there.

MIRIAM: It's wonderful to go and see everybody. It really is a thrill. I, personally, at this point, am not interested. Not, not interested, but I can't—I haven't got the energy to do all the things that are required of, you know, doing the broadcasts and the scripts and the rest, and particularly, Ron wanted me to do a *Witch's Tale.* They wanted to have a *Witch's Tale* evening last October, and he asked me, and I was thrilled. I thought it was a wonderful idea, but I can't do it. I'm not well enough to do it. So, that is my feeling about it. I certainly am pleased to see everybody, and the people there are marvelous. I mean, the fans are just—you come away with an ego that is not to be believed. It lasts for the next five years.

DAVID: (laughs) Well, I'm delighted to hear that, because without the folks who played in radio, it would really not be much of a convention.

MIRIAM: I think it's a great idea. I think that the people who were in radio are very pleased, really, to be a part of it because it's part of our lives, you know, and it's a medium that will never return in the same way. When I started, for example, there were no sponsors and it was revolutionary. Everything we did, any problems that came up, we had to solve on our own. It was all left to our imaginations, and the early days of radio were very exciting.

DAVID: You must have had some sound effects department on both . . . .

MIRIAM: The sound effects departments were marvelous, and the engineers, too. The engineers and the technical people were wonderful. Think of the timing, for example, the problem of timing a half-hour show or an hour show. You had to be on the second. Not just on the minute, but on the second. It made a nervous wreck out of you, but it was a discipline that nobody has now and I wish some of the actors today had it.

DAVID: Were there any special sound effects that were done either on *Witch's Tale* or *Let's Pretend* that stand out in terms of their imaginative quality?

MIRIAM: There wasn't anything that they couldn't improvise on. I mean, if you said to them, "Well, this is the sound of a monster—an ooey, gooey monster going through the mud," and they would do it! (laughs). You never turned around to look and see how they were doing it because you were too busy reading your script.

DAVID: Now, on the *Let's Pretend* programs, at least the tapes that I have, one has the impression that there is a live audience, that there are a bunch of kids in the audience.

MIRIAM: There was an audience. We always had an audience.

DAVID: Did that throw you off on *Let's Pretend*? How did you keep the audience quiet while you guys were involved in the drama?

MIRIAM: There was no question of keeping the audience quiet. They were spellbound. They were in awe of everything that was happening.

DAVID: And, of course, there you had Cream of Wheat, so you did have a sponsor.

MIRIAM: Long before Cream of Wheat, we had a studio audience, when we were working in the little studio on the 22nd floor of CBS at 485 Madison Avenue. We had an audience of about seventy-five to a hundred people, and there were times when there were very young children who were frightened and they had to go out of the studio in the middle of the broadcast. They'd cry, and the mother would put her hand over the face and lead them out. But usually they tried to keep the audience to at least four to five-year-olds so they knew they could control them. The kids were so excited about being at a show, and as I say, in awe of it that they just were part of the show. It was nice because we played to the audience. We were actors. We played to the audience, and we were taught the discipline.

DAVID: Never wore costumes?

MIRIAM: No, we never wore costumes.

DAVID: Where did you go professionally after *Let's Pretend* and *Witch's Tale*? How long did you stay in show business?

MIRIAM: I went to Hollywood. I did *Studio One* every week

with Fletcher Markle. At that time, it was sustaining, and then it turned commercial, and we went to Hollywood with it. I did a lot of radio shows, did theatre, directed, wrote, came to Canada in 1956. I married my husband in 1959, moved to Paris with our young son in 1961, and came back from Paris to Canada in 1980. During the period from 1956—I'm sorry, from 1965 to 1980, I organized a new method of teaching English by means of improvisation. I had the Sorbonne and the rest of the people there in education at it. I came back here and worked with the Gifted Children's Program, teaching them communication skills, and just recently, have been working at the University of Toronto with the multicultural medical students, teaching them communication skills by means of improvisation. It's my own method. You see, we do have something in common. We're both educators. That's fascinating.

DAVID: Yes. You don't miss the . . . .

MIRIAM: Well, I gave up working in theater when my son was born. I had been working for thirty-five years. I became ill and I was not able to do it, so what I'm doing on my own is sort of sneaking in work (laughs).

DAVID: But it sounds like a labor of love.

MIRIAM: I love it. I've written a book on phonics, and I use that in the improvisation.

DAVID: Nancy had a birthday every week. Did anyone ever question the fact that Nancy had a birthday every single week?

MIRIAM: No, no. Nancy was someone who was so sinister

that you never questioned anything that she did. "One hundred and ten-year-old I be today" (laughs). That made her very wise. She never was the same age. I asked Mr. Cole about that and I said, "You made a mistake. She's not 110. She should be 111." He said, "She forgets how old she is. She's eternal." (Laughter).

DAVID: That's a good answer. That's a very good answer.

MIRIAM: Oh, he was a character.

DAVID: Somebody told me that there was a magazine called *The Witch's Tale*. It must have been like a comic book at the time.

MIRIAM: I think there was. I think he did that. He made some extra money on it that way. He sent the stories in and they did the drawings.

DAVID: Before I say goodbye, do you have any problem at all if I were to share any of this conversation with your many fans?

MIRIAM: Oh, no.

DAVID: Thank you so very, very much.

MIRIAM: Thank you for calling.

DAVID: Bye-bye.

MIRIAM: Bye-bye.

I conducted this second interview with Miriam Wolff as a follow-up just prior to the publication of *The Witch's Tale.*

DAVID: Oh, I'm so glad I caught you home. This must be Miriam Ross, formerly Wolff.

MIRIAM: Oh, yes. This must be David.

DAVID: This is the man who's been following you for years. I hope you have just a couple of minutes that we can chat. When I saw you at the convention in October, I was rather discouraged. You recall we chatted briefly in the lobby of the hotel.

MIRIAM: Yeah, I remember.

DAVID: You asked me how the book was coming along. I told you that even though you were so nice to me a couple of years ago—you sent me some photographs—you chatted with me on the phone, answered lots of questions I was having. Well, let me put it this way, a small problem with Mr. Michelson in terms of getting . . . .

MIRIAM: Who is Mr. Michelson?

DAVID: Apparently he lives on the west coast. He says he was Alonzo Deen Cole's agent.

MIRIAM: Never heard of him.

DAVID: He sold or syndicated some of those programs overseas to Australia and to other parts of the world. He was apparently a friend of Alonzo Deen Cole's first wife, Marie.

MIRIAM: Marie O'Flynn. I didn't realize that he'd been married again.

DAVID: They were divorced, apparently, in the 1950s . . . .

MIRIAM: Oh, really?

DAVID: . . . and he married a woman named Dorothea, who lives in Glendale, California. She tells me that she married him around 1955. She is the person who actually had the scripts in her closet at home. I had no idea who she was or that she even existed.

MIRIAM: I had no idea who she was when you kept mentioning her in your letters. What ever happened to Marie O' Flynn, because she was the one . . . .

DAVID: I asked him that question. Take what I say with a grain of salt, because I'm just repeating what has been told to me, but his comment was, "She may have ended up in the nuthouse." And that's an expression—that's not my expression—it was his expression. He had the sense that she was somewhat . . . .

MIRIAM: She was a bit strange, but she was very down to earth, much more so than he was.

DAVID: He's described by his widow as being "quite a ladies man," a person who, anytime there was a party or something, he was the center of attention, and would just sit down on the floor and tell stories.

MIRIAM: How old was he when he died?

DAVID: Well, he died in 1971. I have his birth date some-where, but I don't have it right in front of me. You were born in 1922, according to the . . . .

MIRIAM: Right.

DAVID: . . . and your first appearance, because now I actually have every single one of the scripts.

MIRIAM: Wow! Wonderful.

DAVID: I spent—it's insane—I spent day after day, because I had to return the scripts. I didn't buy the scripts. I bought the right to reproduce a half-dozen or so in an anthology. My feeling is, my wife tells me, "No one's going to buy the book," but it's a labor of love. I don't think Arthur Anderson made any money or made much money on *Let's Pretend*. (Laughs).

MIRIAM: Tell your wife to mind her own business. She'll be very surprised.

DAVID: But it's such fun. Such fun. The only trouble with the program is that it was around. I hope you don't mind me saying this: the programs were broadcast from 1931 to 1938. Some of the other programs that are around—like *Let's Pretend*—whoever made the transcription discs for *Let's Pretend* must have used good quality transcriptions.

MIRIAM: No, I'll tell you what happened. Most of the *Let's Pretend* shows that you've got were done after tape came in. *Witch's Tale* was live. Any of the shows that were done live, including *Let's Pretend*, all they had on those—and I don't know where they got the tapes of them—were air checks, and they were done on huge, wax records. Those wax records were for the people in the studio to make sure that nobody had said a dirty word, or in case there was call back on it. Then, they were recorded over by the next program, so they were lost.

DAVID: Well, apparently there were some kept of *The Witch's Tale*.

MIRIAM: Wax.

DAVID: But they were poor quality.

MIRIAM: Well, they were all poor quality at that time. It was a live show. There was no technique of taping them. Tape was not in yet. They hadn't invented it yet.

DAVID: One of the things that Mrs. Cole gave me—not gave me—she didn't give it to me—she loaned me a copy of his scrapbook.

MIRIAM: Oh yes?

DAVID: In his scrapbook, he has copies of the playbills for when he performed for Schubert Theaters in the teens. He was in Vaudeville. His sister apparently was on the stage also. His wife tells me that his sister's name was Muriel, and they named the cigar after his sister. Interesting story if it's true. Even if it isn't true, it's an interesting story.

MIRIAM: (laughs) Interesting story, yeah. Isn't it great you've got all this? Now, what are you going to do with all of this information?

DAVID: Well, the first thing, after spending day after day at the copying machine—thank God my machine didn't break down—I now have copied approximately 330 scripts. That's the entire run of the program. He kept everything. That man was meticulous. Everything was kept in file folders, chronologically, so the first thing I am doing is to put together a log of each program date, title, and in most cases, he has casts. For example, I can tell you that your first performance as Nancy was on June 13, 1935.

MIRIAM: Really?

DAVID: Before you, let's see, Ms. Fitz-Allen, who was, I guess, the first Nancy.

MIRIAM: Adelaide Fitz-Allen.

DAVID: She passed away in February. He tried a couple of other people after her death.

MIRIAM: He auditioned quite a number of actresses.

DAVID: My notes say that three actresses actually played—when I say this, I'm taking this from the scripts, because he lists the people who were in the cast. The first person named after Mrs. Fitz-Allen passed away is someone called Barbara Winchester. I don't know if that name rings any bells.

MIRIAM: No.

DAVID: Then, a person named Holland—Ms. Holland. And then Ms. Lubowe. L-U-B-O-W-E. Winchester played it once. Holland played it two or three times. Lubowe played it two or three times, and then Miriam Wolff, and he spells your name on the script W-O-L-F-F.

MIRIAM: Good for him. He got my name right (laughs). Well, in all the books, it's spelled W-O-L-F-E. I'll tell you what happened. Have you got a minute? I'll tell you . . . .

DAVID: I've got lots of minutes.

MIRIAM: Okay, what happened with that was my legal name was W-O-L-F-F, and when I worked, I used W-O-L-F-F. When I did *Let's Pretend*, I thought I was using W-O-L-F-F, but when I went down to the CBS cashier, they put on my checks W-O-L-F-E, and I couldn't stop them. I kept complaining and I kept complaining, so I opened a bank account W-O-L-F-E, and my name became F-E after that (laughter). That's the story.

DAVID: That's funny, because I thought he was misspelling it on the scripts. Everywhere I see your name, it's always W-O-L-F-E.

MIRIAM: No, that was the correct name, because that was before AFTRA came in and just before Nila stopped giving us $3.50 in the palm of her hand, and they established a cashier at CBS, where we had to go pick up our checks. So there! [(Laughs).

DAVID: Well, I'm not going to keep you on for an hour or two, but first, would you be willing to write a brief Foreword or Preface? Something for the book?

MIRIAM: I've got to know a little more about the book first before I say yes or no, okay?

DAVID: I'll tell you exactly what I'm hoping to do. As you know, *The Witch's Tale* was one of the very earliest. I don't know of any creepy horror program that was broadcast prior to *The Witch's Tale*. I would like to write an introduction for the book, something like "Before *Tales of the Crypt*, before the slasher movies, before even *Lights Out, Suspense* and *The Shadow*, there was *The Witch's Tale*." I'll provide a little bit of history with regard to how it came to be broadcast, talk about Mr. Cole as the author, and talk a little bit about how the scripts were developed. Many of them came, apparently, from other sources, but he wrote most of them.

MIRIAM: He wrote most of them. They were mostly originals, yeah.

DAVID: I don't know how long the introduction will be yet. I haven't even outlined it, but I have some ideas. It will basically talk a little bit about old radio, a bit about the history of *The Witch's Tale*, and a short biography of Mr. Cole. At that point, I would introduce about—I was thinking about twelve, but thirteen sounds like a more mysterious number— try to select thirteen scripts to be reprinted in anthology form. Perhaps one from each year that the program was broadcast, and at the end of the book, have a log of the programs, and that's about it.

MIRIAM: What are you going to do with the pictures and the material that you have there?

DAVID: Well, there's a beautiful picture that you sent me of Nancy, of the witch as a little girl. If I can get that, I don't know how many of them, but if I can get a few of them in the book, I would like to try to do so.

MIRIAM: No, what I'm trying to say is, what are you going to do with the material though?

DAVID: I'm not sure I follow you.

MIRIAM: The stories that I told you about *The Witch's Tale*, and the background, and the people. It's just going to be a book of the scripts with an introduction by you.

DAVID: Yes, yes. I would try to use your material as part of the introduction. I wouldn't repeat anything in the introduction that you would put in your preface.

What I was hoping would be that you would talk about it on a first-hand basis—how you got involved in *The Witch's Tale*, and why you remember it fondly, and why you would like to share these scripts, hopefully, with today's audience. If I'm being dense, forgive me.

MIRIAM: No, you're not being dense. It's just that I don't want to write your book (laughs).

DAVID: No, no. That's why I'm not asking you to write pages and pages. I just thought . . . .

MIRIAM: I'm sorry, I'm very direct.

DAVID: No, no. I'm not asking you to write my book. I don't know of any other human being who exists on this earth . . . .

MIRIAM: Thank you, I'm very touched (laughs).

DAVID: . . . who knows as much about that program as you do. Mrs. Cole was twenty-one years younger than Alonzo Deen Cole. She tells me that she heard the program when she was twelve years old.

MIRIAM: Who's this—Dorothy?

DAVID: Dorothea, I guess, is her name. But she said she heard the program when she was twelve years old and she asked her mother, "Who would want to go home with a man like that?" And then she said a few years later, "Of course I went home with a man like that."

MIRIAM: Is she an actress?

DAVID: No, she has nothing at all to do with show business.

Apparently, he had no children by his first wife, and they had two children.

MIRIAM: Really?

DAVID: No, they had one child as husband and wife. She has a daughter and she has two grandchildren, who are his grandchildren.

MIRIAM: Oh, for goodness sakes.

DAVID: So, your name on the book, from my perspective, would be the honor, because . . . .

MIRIAM: Thank you. I really am very pleased that you're asking me, and I'm just being very wary because I am a professional writer.

DAVID: I appreciate that. I don't want you to feel like you have to write anything of any great length. I want you to be comfortable.

MIRIAM: What I was thinking of doing, actually, was something that was in the style of the script, as Nancy. I don't know what anecdotes you're going to use, but I would like to use a couple that I told you about.

DAVID: I would not repeat anything you said, believe me. That would be foolish.

MIRIAM: I didn't know whether you had it all prepared.

DAVID: No. I've got a lot of thoughts.

MIRIAM: You know what I'd like you to do so you don't waste your telephone time and the rest of it? Write out a sort of précis of what this whole thing is about, and give me, say, a first page of your

Introduction, and give me some idea of the material you're going to use, and then let me go from there, because otherwise, I can't plan on anything. Just show how you plan to present the material that I've given you, anything that you feel that you want. Well, I've forgotten most of the stuff I've told you, frankly. I know what's in my head, but I'd like to know what you're going to use of it, what you'd like to use of it. It's your book. Then, I would be happy to write a fun Introduction.

DAVID: Arthur Anderson wrote the book on *Let's Pretend*. That was his book. My feeling on this book is that I'm an editor, I'm not the author. The author of this book is Alonzo Deen Cole.

MIRIAM: Actually, it's an anthology of scripts, what you're doing.

DAVID: Right. I'm not the author of the book. The cover, the title of the book, will read *The Witch's Tale* by Alonzo Deen Cole. My name won't even go on the cover. It will be on the inside page as the Editor, and as the Editor, my sense is I'm not a talented writer in that respect. Believe it or not, my wife and I have published guides to used bookstores. That's the extent of our publishing.

MIRIAM: Oh, that's another thing I was going to ask you. Who's going to publish this?

DAVID: We are.

MIRIAM: Oh, you are?

DAVID: We are, because we've published before.

MIRIAM: Who's going to distribute it?

DAVID: My wife is going to distribute it. We've sold, believe it or not, 40,000 books since I retired as a Superintendent of Schools. We're thinking of doing a book on Canada—on the used bookstores of Canada.

MIRIAM: (Laughs).

DAVID: We wrote a book the year I retired in 1992. We haunt used bookstores. We wrote a guide to the used bookstores in New England. We printed 2,000 copies, thinking if we sold 1,000 we would break even.

MIRIAM: Yeah.

DAVID: We sold the 2,000 within six months, and that book has been reprinted several times and revised.

MIRIAM: What kind of presentation are you making on it? How is it bound?

DAVID: If you'd like, I'll send you a copy of one of our books, because one of our books . . . .

MIRIAM: How this is going to be bound?

DAVID: We'll do it the same way that we've done this book. It's going to be a trade paperback. We'll probably run about 1,500 copies. We're going to try to market to two markets.

MIRIAM: Is it going to be hard cover?

DAVID: No, it's going to be a trade paperback. We're going to sell it for $22.00. I think we're going to sell it for $22.00. We'll try to sell it for $22.00. It's going to cost me several thousand dollars just to get it printed.

MIRIAM: Yeah.

DAVID: But we're using the same marketing techniques that we used for our other books.

MIRIAM: Way?

DAVID: No, I appreciate . . . .

MIRIAM: I'm just trying to figure out what my part of it can be.

DAVID: Well, it can be as modest or as generous as you want to make it.

MIRIAM: What I was thinking, actually, was something extremely brief, particularly emphasizing his sacrosanct scripts. You couldn't touch them without his breaking into rages and firing you from the show if you changed a word in his script. I mean, I thought I would present it that way so that every word you read is important in this book, because this is the technique that he used. I may be on the wrong track.

DAVID: I feel like—I don't want to direct you.

MIRIAM: But if this is something that interests you, then I probably could do it that way, but I would like to do it with humor, and as I said, maybe at the end of it just say, "So draw up to the fire and gaze into the embers and look at your book and start shivering."

DAVID: That sounds frightening enough to me. (Laughter).

MIRIAM: I just said that off the top of my head. I hope I remember it, but, I mean, that's the kind of Introduction it would be.

DAVID: Again, I'll put something in the mail to you. If
            you'd like, I'll send you a copy of one of our books.

MIRIAM: I'd appreciate that. I'd like to, really, what I would
            enjoy, would be to have you write out your—now I
            can't think of the word . . . again, my Introduction
            was going to be more of that of a fan than that of
            the professional. That's fine. I just want to know
            exactly how to approach mine, you see? And it
            depends on what the book is.

DAVID: The book is an anthology. And if I had the power
            to tell you, my direction would be to say, "I was
            there. I, Miriam Wolff, was there. I remember."

MIRIAM: Well, I don't want to get into all that.

DAVID: Here's what it was like for young people, for old
            people, etc. I used to have a professor in college.
            When we would ask him how long a term paper
            should be, do you know what the typical
            response was? Like a woman's dress—long
            enough to cover the subject and short enough to
            make it interesting. That was his comment. So I
            didn't mean to make you blush, but that's what
            the man said.

MIRIAM: I'm too old to blush. Well, let me give this
            some thought, and I'll see what I can come up
            with. In the meantime, if you do have any part
            of the Introduction, I would be interested in
            seeing it.

DAVID: I don't really have much. As a matter of fact,
            almost everything is almost in outline form.

MIRIAM: Well, that's the word I was looking for. Send me
            the outline.

DAVID: Can I ask you a couple of questions while we're on the phone now?

MIRIAM: Sure.

DAVID: These are typed out in front of me. I'm not going to put anything in my part that repeats anything that you say. My comments here: you were born in 1922, and made your first appearance in 1935. At that time, you were thirteen years old.

MIRIAM: This is what I think would interest the audience. He, Cole, not only wrote at home until the last minute, he came into rehearsal three hours late, revised every word as we went along, and then when we were on the air, kept giving us notes to make changes in the script. When the script was overly long, he cut it and rewrote the epilogue in his own shaky handwriting. So, we continued it the next week, and we did a two-part version instead of a one-part version. Am I making sense?

DAVID: Yes, yes.

MIRIAM: You've got your mouth open?

DAVID: My mouth is wide open. I'm in awe (laughter). Did you do a show at Carnegie Hall?

MIRIAM: Not Carnegie Hall. It was on *The Star Spangled Theater.* It was years after the show had gone off the air. He called me back to do Nancy and a couple of other parts in *The Gypsy's Hand*, and even then, everything was very hush-hush about my playing the witch. So, he was very strange, Deen.

DAVID: Do people ever compare you to Ms. Fitz-Allen?

MIRIAM: Well, he did, and anytime I started to sound a little bit more like myself, he'd scream, but I mean scream, and Marie would say, "Oh, Deen, she's only a child and she's doing very well, so leave her." Eventually I did my own thing, but at the very beginning I was imitating her. He had, if you notice in the scripts, the dialog for Nancy is written in dialect, and she was from New England.

DAVID: Nancy Holcomb. You actually had a last name. Did you know that?

MIRIAM: I did? I didn't know that.

DAVID: In the first episodes, she was called "Nancy Holcomb. H–O–L–C–O–M–B.

MIRIAM: Isn't that great? That's another gag, because "Holcome" is a lot of bullshit.

DAVID: No, H–O–L–C–O–M–B.

MIRIAM: I know, but that was his way of saying it. That would be him (laughs).

DAVID: Marie O'Flynn was the only other female.

MIRIAM: Marie O'Flynn and I played all the women's parts, except occasionally, when it was absolutely impossible, or when he wanted someone special on the show, he'd call someone like Hester Sondergaard. They'd be on it occasionally, but we were the only regulars on the show, and I played the ingénue once when Marie O'Flynn was sick. This is the stuff I think you should use in your book, but I don't want to be the one to write it.

DAVID: All right, but I don't want to overdo, in terms of

marketing, the two groups we would try to market the book to would be: A. radio people, and B. people who perhaps have no interest in radio, but who are only interested in reading a bunch of horror stories. In other words, the horror market and the radio market.

MIRIAM: Yeah. Will the scripts hold up to that?

DAVID: I'm hoping so.

MIRIAM: Because I think most of the horror came from the performance.

DAVID: That's the gamble, because if they were short stories, there'd be no problem.

MIRIAM: This was one of the reasons we weren't allowed to change any words. He had a certain rhythm going that was there to frighten you.

DAVID: Right. The scripts actually are typed, but his handwriting is all over the place.

MIRIAM: He kept rewriting. Everything. And when he wrote the scripts to start with, he did them in longhand. And when he was doing them at home, I understood from Marie that he was hell to live with, because if he couldn't get something right, he would break into a rage and he would start throwing dishes. She had more broken dishes than any woman who was ever married.

DAVID: Maybe he's the reason she went into an institution if she did (laughter). There was also a period in September of 1935 when you had a sponsor. Martinson Coffee sponsored you for a while.

MIRIAM: Yeah, for a very short period. Didn't improve my salary at all.

DAVID: Did you have any contact with Mr. Cole after the program went off the air?

MIRIAM: Yes. I went up to visit him up in Scarsdale at their place just the one time that I went up there.

DAVID: Of course he did *Casey, Crime Photographer* after that.

MIRIAM: He used me on *Casey* one or two times.

DAVID: I thought I'd try to get in touch with Jackson Beck, who would not know him from *The Witch's Tale*, but would know him from Casey.

MIRIAM: From *Casey*, yeah. What was the name of the chap? Karl Swenson?

DAVID: Karl Swenson has passed. Staats Cotsworth played Casey.

MIRIAM: Staats Cotsworth, I'm sorry. Staats Cotsworth.

DAVID: He's gone.

MIRIAM: If you're just doing this as an anthology, except for your own personal curiosity, I don't know why you're looking for all these stories.

DAVID: Well, either to provide a little bit of color, or as you say, after a while, you become so deeply involved—people who do research for any project, it's like an iceberg—you may print only a small portion of what you learn, but you feel so much better because no matter what the reader has read, you know that you really know the people involved.

MIRIAM: Yeah. Well, leave them wanting more as they say (laughter).

DAVID: Always leave them that way. Okay, you've been very kind. I'm not going to keep you any longer.

MIRIAM: I'm very pleased that you're doing this.

DAVID: I'm so happy, that after having met you again and being so discouraged, that things just seemed to turn around shortly thereafter.

MIRIAM: If you have the scripts I'd be very curious to see them, all 350 of them.

DAVID: They were sent to me by FedEx in four large boxes. I've got to return the boxes to Mrs. Cole.

MIRIAM: Yeah, without the scripts (laughs)?

DAVID: No, no, with the scripts. That's why I made the photocopies of all the scripts.

MIRIAM: Yeah, now you have the right to . . . .

DAVID: What I did was to pay a royalty.

MIRIAM: To whom?

DAVID: To Mrs. Cole, based on the fact that we print between 1,000 to 1,500 copies. If we print any more than that, or if it goes into a second printing, then I'd have to go back to her.

MIRIAM: Did she specify the number of scripts you could use?

DAVID: I think in the cover letter we said somewhere

between a dozen—about a dozen. So, if I stretch it to thirteen, I'm not going to get into trouble.

MIRIAM: May I put my neck into this and give you some advice on what to choose?

DAVID: I'm always happy to hear you.

MIRIAM: I would say many of the scripts, on second reading, particularly if they're read by someone who is not an actor, your audience will not be actors. On the second reading of the script, if you find that it doesn't play, or that it lacks in any way, choose the ones that are the tightest. I think out of 100 to 300 you'll probably be able to find, if you're lucky, thirteen.

DAVID: My thinking was: A. to stay away from the classics. In other words, he did a radio adaptation of *Rappaccini's Daughter.* He did *Frankenstein.* He did *The Golem.* He did things like that. I would try to stay away from anything that was an adaptation, because people are familiar with those stories.

MIRIAM: Yeah. Unless they were awfully well-done, and then that way, it might be even more interesting.

DAVID: B. I would also stay away from the two-parters because they would be twice as long in terms of using the scripts. He actually did one three-parter.

MIRIAM: Well, this is what happened: we got on the air, and he discovered that we were going over. His timing was off, and so he had to rewrite every time. He had to draw the damn thing out and as a result . . . .

DAVID: You mean the two-parters were not originally planned as two-parters?

MIRIAM: No, they were planned as one script. That's what I was telling you. We'd be standing around the ball mike and he'd shove this legal pad in your face and say, "This is the epilogue. Change it. Read it." And you can hardly read his handwriting. You know from his scripts what his handwriting was like. I would do an epilogue, saying it was to be continued next week. He would go home and rewrite say five pages of script. The last five pages, he would stretch out into twenty-nine minutes.

DAVID: Wow. The man had talent.

MIRIAM: The man had a great deal of talent, but sometimes, it didn't work. That's why I'm saying to you, take a look and see which ones are the tightest, because a lot of them would not hold now.

DAVID: Okay. I hope that I can be the judge of that. I'm not sure that my talent is that good.

MIRIAM: Then don't write the book (laughter).

DAVID: I'm not writing the book; I'm editing the book.

MIRIAM: Don't edit it (laughs).

DAVID: Yes, Ma'am. Yes, Ma'am

MIRIAM: No, I'm being very cruel.

DAVID: No, I've been around. If I can't take it I shouldn't be here. If you can't take the heat, get out of the kitchen.

MIRIAM: No, really, I'm very pleased that you're doing this. I'm delighted.

DAVID: I used my David Siegel stationary. When I write to you again, I'll probably use our Book Hunter Press stationary. So, if you get something that says Book Hunter Press on it, don't think that it's a solicitation.

MIRIAM: All right, thank you.

DAVID: I'll include one of our books just so you can see.

MIRIAM: I would like very much for you to do that. Would you mark it, please, unsolicited gift, because I'm liable to be charged . . . .

DAVID: I'll put something on the envelope saying, "This is a gift."

MIRIAM: Just unsolicited gift.

DAVID: Unsolicited gift? Okay. I don't want you to pay for anything.

MIRIAM: No, it's just that it's silly . . . .

DAVID: I'll be happy to do that.

MIRIAM: Okay. Thank you very much.

DAVID: It has been wonderful speaking to you. We're going off, by the way. My wife and I are going off to China come March 14, so I will try to get this out to you before we leave, but if there's a period of time that we're not in contact, it doesn't mean that I've fallen off the face of the earth.

MIRIAM: Well, I hope not—especially not that particular face of the earth (laughs).

DAVID: Whenever you reach the point that you feel comfortable about putting something in writing, just . . . .

MIRIAM: I'll tell you something. I've been making notes, okay (laughs)?

DAVID: Go ahead. Yes, Ma'am. Yes, Ma'am.

MIRIAM: Which I don't usually do, but I got pretty excited about this, all right? It might not show in my voice, but that's my witch that comes out once in a while.

DAVID: Do you still have the cat? The black cat, Satan?

MIRIAM: Oh, incidentally, one of the things I want to put in the preface is that he played the cat. Alonzo Deen Cole played the cat.

DAVID: At the end of the program, it always says, "Nancy and the Cat were played by themselves," as though there was a Nancy and there was a cat.

MIRIAM: Well, he played the cat, and he timed his meows just about the same way he timed his script. Every sound was important. It established the mood of what he was doing and you can tell that best by listening to the tapes.

DAVID: The man was a genius.

MIRIAM: He really was something else. And he had a terrible, terrible temper (laughs).

DAVID: Well, my former mother-in-law would always tell me, "An artist can be forgiven anything." I always disagreed with her, but never publicly.

MIRIAM:	I don't agree (laughs). I like kindness. Even if I'm part witch, I like kindness.
DAVID:	Yes, well, it's nice.
MIRIAM:	Anyway, before I melt and your purse melts, thank you for calling.
DAVID:	Thank you for taking my call. I appreciate it.
MIRIAM:	All good luck, and if I don't speak with you before then, have a good trip.
DAVID:	Thank you so much.
MIRIAM:	Right.
DAVID:	Bye-bye.
MIRIAM:	Tell your wife it's going to be okay.
DAVID:	All right, I'll tell her.
MIRIAM:	Bye.
DAVID:	Bye-bye.

Chapter 7
DOROTHEA COLE
(1918–1999)

INTERVIEW: NOVEMBER, 1998

I am unaware of any interview that Alonzo Deen Cole, the man credited with having written, directed, and acted in every episode of the early radio horror series, *The Witch's Tale*, granted during his lifetime. Cole, who also wrote most of the *Casey Crime Photographer* series, as well as scripts for *The Shadow* and other popular series, died in 1971 at age seventy-three. Most of what we know about Cole's career is derived from the programs, advertisements, reviews, and other press clippings that fill the pages of several thick scrapbooks that he kept and which have been thoughtfully preserved initially by his widow and currently by his daughter.

Considering Cole's apparent affection for supernatural literature, I confess to having given some consideration to arranging an interview with him by means of a séance. Seconds later, coming to my senses, I instead reached out to two people who knew him: Miriam Wolff, the adolescent actress, who worked with him week after week for many years on *The Witch's Tale* program (see the previous interview), and the person who knew Cole more intimately during his final years, his second wife and widow, Dorothea.

Dorothea was twenty-one years Cole's junior and only one year younger than Miriam Wolff. During the interview that follows, she recalls the early years of their marriage, when Cole was still at his prime. She also shares memories of guests at house parties and of her husband's charming guests, particularly the women, by his storytelling skills. It is, however, Dorothea's story, so let her tell it.

DAVID: Hi. My name is David Siegel, and I'm calling you to thank you very, very much for making the scripts of Alonzo Deen Cole available to me and also to wish you a very, very, happy birthday.

DOROTHEA: Oh, well, thank you very much.

DAVID: The scripts arrived today. I called Mr. Michelson to let him know that they got here safely. I understand you're getting quite a bit of rain where you are.

DOROTHEA: Oh, yes, yes. Today was nice, but it's not gonna stay that way.

DAVID: Would it be okay—do you have a minute or two— is it possible that I might be able to ask you some questions about your husband?

DOROTHEA: Well, uh, yeah. Let me turn down the TV.

DAVID: Sure. I just hope this isn't a bad time for you.

DOROTHEA: Well, no, I'm going out in a little bit, but . . . .

DAVID: I'll try not to keep you on too long. Anytime you have to go, just let me know and I'll get off the telephone.

DOROTHEA: Sure.

DAVID: The reason I want to ask some questions is I have some literature, some of the books dealing with radio, but that's always very formal and very professional. He was born here, and he did work on this program and this program, but there are very few people that one can talk to who really knew him and can talk about him personally. The only other person I know of is Miriam Wolff. I don't know if you know Miriam Wolff, but she . . . .

DOROTHEA: The name is familiar.

DAVID: She was an actress, as a little girl actually. She played Nancy after the actress who played Nancy passed away.

DOROTHEA: Oh, oh yeah. I guess that's where I heard it. I was his second wife, you know.

DAVID:	I don't want to get into his personal life. Did you know him when he was active in radio, or did you meet him after *The Witch's Tale* and after *Casey, Crime Photographer*?
DOROTHEA:	I met him when he was doing *Casey, Crime Photographer.*
DAVID:	I see. Was that in New York?
DOROTHEA:	Yeah.
DAVID:	And I guess what I'm gonna try to do is ask you if you have any recollections of any of his experiences on the radio, or any of his feelings about his radio work. Did he direct, or just write?
DOROTHEA:	He directed, wrote, and acted in them.
DAVID:	In *Casey*, as well as the others?
DOROTHEA:	No, not in *Casey*. He just wrote that one.
DAVID:	I think there was an actor named Staats Cotsworth who was on *Casey*. Did you meet any of the actors who were in *Casey* and the other shows?
DOROTHEA:	Yeah, I met the whole . . . .
DAVID:	Jackson Beck is still around. I think Jackson Beck was one of the actors on *Casey*.
DOROTHEA:	Yeah, yeah. I have a picture of the whole bunch standing around the piano.
DAVID:	That was another question I was going to ask. If you have any photographs at all that you could either Xerox or possibly make available just on a loan basis that we might be able to use in the book.

DOROTHEA: Um, well, would you want any of *Casey* or just *The Witch's Tale*?

DAVID: *The Witch's Tale* is obviously preferable, because *The Witch's Tale* is the one that the book will be about.

DOROTHEA: Well, I think Charlie Michelson has pictures from *The Witch's Tale*.

DAVID: I have some that I got from Miriam Wolff, but I thought that Mr. Cole might have had some of his own.

DOROTHEA: Well, I don't know. Did Michelson show you any that he had, or . . . .

DAVID: We didn't get a chance to talk about that. We just talked about the scripts initially.

DOROTHEA: Oh, yeah. Well, he has some pictures, I know.

DAVID: Okay, well, I'll get back in touch with him on that, then.

DOROTHEA: Yeah.

DAVID: Were you involved in radio yourself as a performer or an actress?

DOROTHEA: Oh, no. I wasn't. I used to listen to *The Witch's Tale* when I was about twelve years old, and I used to listen to him.

DAVID: I see.

DOROTHEA: He was twenty-one years older than I was.

DAVID: Did it frighten you?

DOROTHEA: Yes. I used to say to my mother, "Oh, can you imagine going home to a man like that?"

DAVID: (laughs) And then you went home to a man like that.

DOROTHEA: Yeah, yeah, some years later. There we were, across a crowded room . . . .

DAVID: What kind of person was Mr. Cole? He had to have some imagination.

DOROTHEA: Oh, Lord. He had imagination, all right. He was very intelligent. He loved to read. He read all the time. He was very volatile. Quite a personality; temperament; very charming. All the ladies liked him.

DAVID: That's a positive attribute.

DOROTHEA: Yeah, yeah. I remember at a party one time, he was always the center of attention, you know. He was telling a story, and I said to some gal next to me, "Oh, I already heard that one." She said, "Well, I didn't (laughter).

DAVID: How to win friends and influence people.

DOROTHEA: Yeah. He'd sit down on the floor cross-legged, and everyone would gather around, and he'd go on all night and tell stories. In fact, with just the two of us, he could go on all night and tell stories.

DAVID: It's too bad you didn't have a tape recorder at the time.

DOROTHEA: Yeah, it really was. He would tell some stories.

DAVID: Were these stories he made up, or were these just stories he had heard?

DOROTHEA: No, they had happened in show business.

DAVID: Oh, well, do you remember any of them?

DOROTHEA: Oh, Lord, not too many.

DAVID: Any at all that you can recall that deal with radio personalities, or any of his experiences on the radio? I'd love to hear . . . .

DOROTHEA: Oh, gosh, I don't know, offhand. I can't think of any right now.

DAVID: I wonder whether or not, since you do have to go somewhere, if I might be able to call you back and maybe do a little brain surgery, so that the next time I call, you might have some of those stories on hand.

DOROTHEA: (laughs) That's a long time ago. He was the one that went through all that stuff. He met a lot of different people.

DAVID: Did he have any favorites, or people that he particularly liked and talked about a lot, or people that he didn't like?

DOROTHEA: Oh, yeah, no doubt. I'm trying to think. I don't know . . . .

DAVID: Who were his favorites?

DOROTHEA: Oh, gosh, I don't know. I'm drawing a blank.

DAVID: You're the clue to the past.

DOROTHEA: Golly.

DAVID: Today, the only people who would remember *The Witch's Tale* would either be people like myself, who listened to it as a child, or people who have copies of the old tapes. There are a few copies of the old tapes around.

DOROTHEA: Yeah.

DAVID: But it would be so interesting for people who read the book not just to read the stories—the scripts—but to get a kind of an insight on the person who wrote them. That's really why I'm calling you.

DOROTHEA: He did a compilation of—well, it's like a scrapbook. It might come in handy.

DAVID: Do you have that scrapbook?

DOROTHEA: Yeah, I do. It just dawned on me. I mean, the shows he was on when he was on the stage an . . . .

DAVID: Is it possible to borrow it? I would not keep it. I would just make Xerox copies and return it to you.

DOROTHEA: Well, you can do that. It's funny, I didn't think of that before, because it's really something that would be of use to you.

DAVID: It really would be very, very helpful.

DOROTHEA: Yeah.

DAVID: Can I give you an address that you can send it to, and I would be more than happy to pay you for the postage.

DOROTHEA: Sure, wait a second while I get a pen here.

DAVID: Oh, you are so kind.

DOROTHEA: Just a minute.

DAVID: Now that you mention it, I know Mr. Cole picked a winner when he picked you, because he picked a woman who's a quick thinker.

DOROTHEA: Oh, I don't know how quick it was, but finally it came to me.

DAVID: (He gives address) I won't keep it more than a couple of days. I will Xerox some pages from it and whatever postage you put on it I'll put that money in the envelope when I return the scrapbook to you so you will not have to lay out a penny for it.

DOROTHEA: Oh, that's okay. I wonder if I could insure it?

DAVID: Yes, I think that's a good idea because that's the kind of thing you certainly don't want. These things are not so much valuable in the sense of money as they are in the sense of history.

DOROTHEA: Oh, sure. I know. This would be very good because it really has a lot of stuff in it.

DAVID: It would have reviews. I was going to ask you if he was in any plays, if he was in any . . . .

DOROTHEA: Oh, sure. He went all over the country in the stock companies, and then he was in Vaudeville with his first wife, and then they did a radio series called *Darling and Dearie*.

DAVID: What's the name of that?

DOROTHEA: *Darling and Dearie*.

DAVID: Sounds like a soap opera.

DOROTHEA: Yeah, it was like a honeymoon couple, you know, like they're doing now . . . couples on TV.

DAVID: That's interesting. I never heard of that one.

DOROTHEA: They did that for awhile. I've got a picture of them—a really weird picture—funny.

DAVID: (laughs) Put that in the scrapbook and send that one along. I promise to take very good care of these. The scripts are going back to Mr. Michelson by the way; I'm not keeping them. I'm Xeroxing them, and hoping to pick about a dozen or so that we'll include in our book. By the way, I hope he told you this, but we are dedicating the book to Alonzo Deen Cole. In his memory, and you're going to get a special thanks to Dorothea Cole for making the scripts available.

DOROTHEA: Oh, that's nice.

DAVID: Obviously, we'll send you a copy of the book.

DOROTHEA: Oh, great.

DAVID: I don't know whether or not I've exhausted you, or whether or not you can think of anything else in terms of what he did after *Casey*?

DOROTHEA: Oh, he was writing different movie scripts. I think he sold a couple of them, but I don't think they even put them on. Then, we came out here, because he made a deal with somebody. They made a pilot of *The Witch's Tale* in New York.

DAVID: Right.

DOROTHEA: And we came out here. We thought they were going to put it on, and I think the guy dropped dead of a heart attack or something.

DAVID: Oh, my gosh . . . .

DOROTHEA: Yeah, so we were stuck out here and I've been here ever since. So, that was that. He was writing, you know, different things.

DAVID: Did he write or publish any books?

DOROTHEA: No, he never wrote a book.

DAVID: Magazine articles?

DOROTHEA: No.

DAVID: Just basically stories.

DOROTHEA: Yeah, just plays and scripts.

DAVID: He had a really fantastic imagination.

DOROTHEA: Yeah, he said one time he was writing in the middle of the night. He used to write in the night, when it was quiet and dark. I don't know what he was writing, but he said he scared himself.

DAVID: (laughs) He could have been as well-known as

Stephen King.

DOROTHEA: Oh, yeah, yeah.

DAVID: As a matter of fact, he was much more talented than Stephen King.

DOROTHEA: Yeah, well, he was the first one to start that stuff, you know, in radio.

DAVID: Did he ever tell you where he got the stories from? How his imagination developed in that manner?

DOROTHEA: Well, he would write a lot of things when he got ideas from different stories and books.

DAVID: He adopted them from other stories.

DOROTHEA: Not all of them, but some of them.

DAVID: Right.

DOROTHEA: He'd get an idea here and there. I don't know how he ever started it.

DAVID: Did he keep in touch with other radio personalities after he moved to California?

DOROTHEA: Not too much that I know of.

DAVID: Did he have any brothers or sisters who were in the business?

DOROTHEA: Yeah, his sister. She was a kid actress in St. Paul, Minnesota. In fact, Muriel Cigars were named after her.

DAVID: Oh, really?

DOROTHEA: Her name was Muriel, and the old guy who made the cigars was so infatuated with her that he named the cigar after her.

DAVID: There's a song about Muriel Cigars (laughs).

DOROTHEA: Yeah, well that was my sister-in-law.

DAVID: Is she still . . . .

DOROTHEA: No, she's deceased.

DAVID: I see. Was she on the radio, or just on the stage?

DOROTHEA: No, she was on the stage. She was a kid actress.

DAVID: Anyone else in the family?

DOROTHEA: No, I don't think so.

DAVID: Did he have any children?

DOROTHEA: One daughter, mine and his.

DAVID: Is she active in theatrical work at all?

DOROTHEA: No, no. Nope.

DAVID: What does she think of her father's work?

DOROTHEA: Oh, they were so much alike, they were fighting all the time.

DAVID: Sounds like my son and myself.

DOROTHEA: Really? (Laughs). Yeah, they were so much alike, I was always the referee.

DAVID: Does she write?

DOROTHEA: No, she doesn't write. I just wrote a poem. It just
             came off the top of my head. I saw an ad in a *TV
             Guide*—"Send in Your Poem," and I sat there and I
             wrote this thing. I think I'll send it in. I may win a
             thousand bucks.

DAVID: Why not? Why not? Just may be your lucky year
             (laughter). Well, look, I won't keep you any longer.
             You've been extremely pleasant. It's been really
             wonderful talking to you. I hope you don't forget
             that scrapbook, because that really sounds exiting.

DOROTHEA: Oh, I won't. I won't forget. I'll try to dig it out,
             and maybe send it out tomorrow.

DAVID: Oh, you're so sweet. I promise you that it will get
             back to you in one piece. Scout's Honor.

DOROTHEA: Okay, all right.

DAVID: It's going to be a while before this book is done.
             Books take a long time.

DOROTHEA: Yeah.

DAVID: But we are really hoping to get it out by the end of
             the year. It would just not be possible without your
             help, so I just felt I had to call you. I had to thank
             you, and I really hope that this is a wonderful year
             for you.

DOROTHEA: Well, thanks very much. I sure appreciate it.

DAVID: Well, it was swell talking to you.

DOROTHEA: Okay. I'll get it out to you.

DAVID: Thank you so very much.

DOROTHEA: You're welcome.

DAVID: Bye-bye.

DOROTHEA: Bye.

Chapter 8
ROBERT VAN DEVENTER
(1931–)

INTERVIEW: MARCH 22, 1999

Late 1990s, I learned that "Bobby Maguire," the teenage prodigy, who held his own against a panel of well-known adults on radio's *Twenty Questions*, was seeking audio copies of the programs in which he had appeared. In real life, Bobby was actually Robert "Bobby" Van Deventer, the son of the distinguished WOR news broadcaster, Fred Van Deventer, who adapted the popular parlor game, sometimes referred to as "animal, vegetable, or mineral" for radio.

One of the unanticipated benefits of having a large collection of vintage radio programs is that I can barter them for other radio programs or materials that I don't have. So, in a *quid pro quo*, I was able to send Bobby several copies of *Twenty Questions* in exchange for his granting me a telephone interview.

Some ten years after making that initial contact, I am so very pleased to say that Bobby, one year my senior, continues to be gracious, friendly, and warmhearted when he hears from me, as he did for this publication.

DAVID: This is Dave Siegel, old-time radio fanatic. I have the great pleasure of being able to speak with Robert Van Deventer, better known in the world of vintage radio as Bobby McGuire, teenage whiz-kid of Mutual's popular panel show, *Twenty Questions*. Today's date is Tuesday, March 22, 1999, and Bobby has graciously offered to share some memories of the program he was featured on.

BOBBY: Teenage whiz-kid. That's very interesting. I like that. I like that (laughter). It's so long ago that I was either a whiz-kid *or* teenage. It's pleasant to hear the words again.

DAVID: Well, your voice was very pleasant on the radio, and it certainly hasn't lost any of its tenor. I know you're writing a book about the program, and in the book you describe the inception of *Twenty*

Questions as a network program. Can you share some of those beginnings with us?

BOBBY: Yeah. I have in my hand my Boy Scout diary of 1945. I shall read the entire entry for Sunday, June 10. "Charles Stark played golf with us today, but it rained. We stayed up late, exams begin in the morning. We may have a new radio show." End of entry.

DAVID: How old were you when you wrote that?

BOBBY: I was not quite fourteen. I was thirteen.

DAVID: I wonder how many fourteen-year-olds today keep diaries, and how many of them are as serious as you were at that age?

BOBBY: (laughs) Well, I think it grew mainly because it was one of the items you could buy from the Boy Scout Quartermaster.

DAVID: I see.

BOBBY: And so, once you had it, you had to kind of use it. It cost 50¢.

DAVID: Terrible to leave it empty.

BOBBY: 50¢. Yeah. That particular diary does not mention the show again. I petered off in writing in it in the summertime, and didn't take it up again. There was no diary in 1946, so the inception of the show is strictly a matter of memory. I've always rued that, because I had the diary for 1945 and l947, and 1948 but not the important year, 1946. But anyway, that day was the day that's described in the piece that you read. To understand it, you really

have to know who my father was. Fred Van
Deventer, who had been a newsman almost all his
life, was on the news on WOR. He started in
Tipton, Indiana, when he was in high school, and
worked for the *Indianapolis Star*, where he knew
Earl Derr Biggers, who created Charlie Chan.
Then, he went on to Chicago, and knew Frank
Knox, who was the publisher of the *Chicago Daily
News*. He later became Secretary of the Navy, and
knew the prototype of the characters in the great
Hecht-McArthur play, *The Front Page*. He was the
Hildy Johnson type newsman, and when the
Depression came along, he had all kinds of difficulty
getting a job. He finally wound up, about 1935,
with the *Springfield Ohio News*. I think it's now the
Sun-News, or the *News-Sun*, and succeeded at one
of the copy desks there in the newsroom in the city
desk of Scotty Reston, who had been there for a
year or two, and moved on eventually, of course, to
the *Times*—the *New York Times*. It isn't quite true
to say that Dad took Reston's job, because Reston
was mainly a sports writer at that time, and Dad
was a regular telegraph editor. But anyway, that was
where he was when I was old enough to remember.
He went from there to the Associated Press Bureau
in Detroit. When he was there, somewhere along
the line, about 1940, 1941, he took an audition to
be a newscaster with WJR, the Goodwill Station.
This was owned by G. A. Richards, who owned a
string of stations around the country at that time,
and in 1942 went on the air, on WJR. My mother
woke my sister and me up early one morning. We
were ready to go to school, and here was Dad Van
Deventer in the news. We knew that there was
something in the wind—that he had taken the
audition—that he was getting the job, but we really
were surprised when we actually heard him. Then,
Elmer Davis, who was the great newscaster from

Iowa, later went to head The Office of War Information. WOR sort of created a vogue in New York, the success of the Midwestern voice. And on account of that, WOR in New York wanted someone like him. So, they got one of Dad's transcriptions and offered him the job, and he started in October, 1944 at WOR. So, between that time and that next June, which I just read the diary excerpt from, he got to know, obviously, people with WOR and Mutual. He had a feel for the place and knew where the bodies were and who to talk to, so that when this event came up that Sunday that you read about, it was agreed that he and Charles Stark would go ahead and talk to people to develop the show. So, that was the origin of the show. If you want me to describe that day, you're better off reading that twenty-page excerpt again.

DAVID: Well, that will be part of your book eventually, so folks who buy your book will have the pleasure of reading it.

BOBBY: Of course it's fictionalized, but the facts are accurate in that excerpt.

DAVID: You indicated that you and your family played this game of Animal, Vegetable, or Mineral and that was really the incentive for *Twenty Questions*. Why did they change the title from Animal, Vegetable, or Mineral to *Twenty Questions*?

BOBBY: (laughs) Let me explain that by just giving a brief summary of what happened that Sunday, because it was really a major coincidence that two people in the radio business, having Sunday afternoon dinner, were in fact having dinner in the house of a family that had always done quizzes and played parlor games, one of which was what we called

Animal, Vegetable or Mineral. It was in the back-and-forth during the course of that afternoon, that this is what you have to do to promote and produce and develop a radio program. During the course of this, someone mentioned Animal, Vegetable and Mineral, as well as other parlor games we had played, and Charles Stark himself was the one who said, "I can see it now. We'll have a panel of experts playing the game, and the master of ceremonies will be the one who answers the questions. He will have the subject for you to identify, and the panel of experts will guess." And this came to his mind and to ours, from other panel shows such as *Information Please*, and the *Quiz Kids*, although he was the one, certainly, who said it. So anyway, that's how it started. So, when they took it to New York and talked to Dave Driscoll, the head of news at WOR, and Norm Livingston, the head of programming, and it got talked up within the walls of 1440 Broadway, within a month or two it came back. Oh yes, people all played this. They all knew about it, but in the East, they called it *Twenty Questions*. This was news to us. We had never, first of all, heard the term "twenty questions," and secondly, we had never played with any limit on the number of questions. So, that's how the name came about. People in WOR at least, who had heard of the game, who had played the game, always referred to it as *Twenty Questions*. It's kind of like the difference, in its way, between what you call Coca-Cola in the Midwest and what you call it in the East. In the East, it's soda. In the West, it's pop (laughs). I guess that's the same kind of differentiation.

DAVID: Once the program was accepted, did Charlie Stark actually have a piece of the action?

BOBBY: He sued. What happened was, by—I'm guessing now, but I would say September—that was in June. They started talking it up in July. The momentum started to build probably in August, and since Stark was Dad's announcer, when we would go into WOR and see him, I would always say something like, "How's the *Twenty Questions* idea coming along?" He would always answer the same way. "We're still kicking it around." Well, finally Dad got fed up and he said, "We've kicked this around long enough. It's been weeks and months. If you don't do something by Monday or words to that effect, I'm going to go to Bill Fineschriber of Mutual on my own." Stark did nothing, so Dad went to Fineschriber, and from then on, Stark was out of it. Skipping ahead, on Saturday, February 2, when Dad did the 6:30 news and Stark, of course, knew that the show was going on that evening at 8:00, he said, "I'm suing Monday," and did. We settled. We didn't want to fight it out. It would have been a long-drawn-out process. I don't have any idea what the settlement was. We agreed that certainly he had suggested the idea of the panel. We couldn't get away from that. It was absolutely true. All along, in fact, we kind of hoped Stark would come back in, but no. He always stayed aloof, didn't want any part of it. At least he didn't take any part of it. So, anyway, that's what happened with Stark.

DAVID: I'm not going to ask you if it was a one-time settlement, or if he got a piece of the action.

BOBBY: No, it was a one-time settlement.

DAVID: I assume your dad actually owned the program?

BOBBY: Yes. When the show went on the air, Dad insisted with either Livingston or Fineschriber, and I frankly don't know which one it was. I think it was probably a collaboration, suggested and insisted, I should say, that however the contract was written, the actual rights to the show were going to belong to Fred and Florence Van Deventer. They agreed. Although I have copies of some of these, not the contracts themselves, but a lot of the correspondence that went back-and-forth, it certainly indicates that yes, they are the owners of the show. However, since the contract is in force, Mutual is actually in charge. Their ownership never really meant anything, except when it was time to renew the contract.

DAVID: I guess I'm getting a little ahead of myself now, but it sort of occurs to me that when we dealt with comedians like Jack Benny, or others who owned their programs, they got a single sum of money for the week, and from that sum of money, it was their responsibility to pay the cast. Is that the way it worked with your dad, or was everyone on salary?

BOBBY: No. It did later on, but not in the first contract. I don't believe that happened until the first television contract came up. I know with a couple of the television contracts, one with Mennen, one with Ronson, and one I believe with DuMont itself, they paid the whole nut, and out of that, Dad or the show paid everybody. But I don't remember which contract that applied to. I know it did not apply to the actual WOR Mutual, which is what we're primarily interested in.

DAVID: I know I've asked you this question before, but for the record, my sense was that if you were a listener of the program at the time, in the late 1940s, unless you had actually read materials put out by Mutual publicity regarding the program, if you were just an ordinary listener, and you heard the announcer talk about Fred Van Deventer, Bobby McGuire, Frances Rinard . . . .

BOBBY: Florence Rinard.

DAVID: Florence Rinard—I'm sorry—you would have thought they were three people who had nothing to do with one another once they left the station. That Fred was the newscaster, Bobby was a very pleasant, teenage young man, and Florence was a well-known musician. Then, of course, one discovers that Fred and Florence are husband-and-wife and Bobby is the young offspring. Was that accidental, or was that done with any kind of malice of forethought? Did your dad originally think it was going to be him and your mother and hopefully you?

BOBBY: What happened was . . . . no, originally, the panel was going to consist of Dad and three other people, one of whom would be a woman, one of whom would be a comedian in the sense of a wit, and the fourth of which I frankly don't remember.

DAVID: Turned out to be a teenager.

BOBBY: No.

DAVID: You were not on the first program?

BOBBY: Oh, no. Let me explain. When it was being developed over the fall of 1945, it was agreed, certainly, that Dad would be on the panel. He owned the show and it was his idea. He was the only famous one around, you see; famous, at least, in New York. Well, the female panel member was going to be Mary Margaret McBride, and she did two or three auditions right up into the fall, if not into the winter. I don't remember exactly which, but then sometime around December of 1945, she couldn't make it. It was a last-minute cancellation, and Mother was there, and they asked her to sit in for Mary Margaret. She did, and she did so well that Mary Margaret never came back again. This was nothing against Mary Margaret McBride, because she really didn't want to do it anyway. She couldn't fit it into her schedule at that time.

DAVID: Sheer coincidence.

BOBBY: I believe she was Martha Deane at that time, or maybe she had actually started using her own name. But anyway, she was out and Mother was in. Well, when that happened, they decided, almost perfunctorily, that she wouldn't be Mrs. Van Deventer any more than Mary Livingston was Mrs. Jack Benny. She would be a separate person. So, she simply decided to use her maiden name, which was of course pronounced "*Rye*nard," and not "Ray*nard*," but "Ray*nard*" sounded more erudite, so they decided she'd be Florence "Ray*nard*." A month later or so, in January, somebody, I think it was Fineschriber, decided it would be great to have a kid on the panel, mainly, I suppose, because of the success at that very time of *The Quiz Kids*. Well, they didn't have any idea where to get a kid, and they called—what's his name—Golenpaul?

DAVID: Yes, at *Information Please*.

BOBBY: It wasn't him, then. It was *The Quiz Kids*.

DAVID: Oh, Kelly.

BOBBY: Yes, well, he was the emcee. I don't mean him. Was it Cowan? Not Cowan. Yes, Cowan, I believe.

Anyway, the producer of *The Quiz Kids* said . . . well, they got them from certain places around the Chicago schools, and they had a whole thing set up to screen them, and that was too much work.

DAVID: Couldn't catch old Kupperman.

BOBBY: So, Dad said, "We'll bring Bob in to do an audition to see how a kid looks, see how the panel looks with a kid on it." I said, "Okay, I'd do it." At that same time, that same day, I think around the first week in January of 1946, they brought in Herb Polesie, whom someone had recommended as a possible Oscar Levant type. He had a dry voice and he was witty. He was a smart guy, actually.

DAVID: Had he done anything else on the radio, or was this his only . . . .

BOBBY: He was the producer of *It Pays to be Ignorant* and two or three other shows. His name appears several times in John Dunning's book. He was out of Hollywood, where he had produced movies for Bing Crosby in the late 1930s. He was kind of a well-known figure around radio, but not on the upper level. Not on the major Jack Benny, Bob Trout level. He was a well-known guy.

DAVID: Tom Howard would know him.

BOBBY: Yeah. At this same time, at the same audition, they finally found a guy, who they thought would be a good emcee—Bill Slater. They had tried Paul Wing, "Old Spelling Master," and they approached Fadiman, who didn't want any part of it. They approached Sigmund Spaeth, "The Tune Detective," and none of those guys did the job. Polesie and I and Slater all assembled with Dad and Mother at this audition the first week in January. The results of that were (laughter) rather copiously described in the twenty-page excerpt that I sent you. At that time, all three of us seemed like we were in. The live audition with the studio audience, the theater audience, was within two weeks, I don't remember exactly when. I agreed to do that, and then I would do the first show, and then after the first show, they would start scouting around like *The Quiz Kids* did to have a different teenager every week. And after the first show, they decided that was too much trouble. If I agreed, I would just stay on the panel, which is what happened.

DAVID: How did your last name come up? Where did they get McGuire?

BOBBY: Well, the same way my mother got Rinard. It was my grandmother's maiden name. I said, "If you're going to be Florence Rinard, I can be "Bobby McGuire." I suppose I could have used the maiden name of my other grandmother, but that was Roode, R-O-O-D-E. It didn't sound good at all (laughs).

DAVID: I see.

BOBBY: "Bobby McGuire" had a nice rhythm to it, so that's what it was.

DAVID: And once that audition show played, and the first program played, I guess they decided they weren't going to look elsewhere?

BOBBY: We had a little meeting on the stage after the show. We had agency people there. They all wanted transcriptions. There was no tape in those days, of course. Things looked good. It was upbeat.

DAVID: Was the first show sponsored, or was it . . . .

BOBBY: No. It was sustaining.

DAVID: Sustaining.

BOBBY: Mutual had come up with *Pageant Magazine* to provide the guests, provide the prizes, in return for which we would mention *Pageant* on the air and they would win a subscription if their subject was used.

DAVID: Do you happen to recall who the first guest was?

BOBBY: Yes. Guy Lombardo.

DAVID: Well, that was quite a guest.

BOBBY: I even remember some of the subjects that were on that first show.

DAVID: He didn't bring any of the Royal Canadians with him, did he?

BOBBY: What happened was he was our anniversary guest every year thereafter.

DAVID: He brought you good luck.

BOBBY: Yeah. Every February 2, or whatever show that he could fit in his schedule that was closest to February 2, he was our guest again.

DAVID: Okay, you said you remembered some of the questions?

BOBBY: One was Robert E. Lee. One was—they're fleeting now—I remember Robert E. Lee. I got that one. That's probably why I remember it. When I worked with a California packager for television who thought they might want to put *Twenty Questions* back on the air about 1958, I went to WOR to get them a transcription of radio shows, and I got the first show, and I heard it. That's probably why it's more vivid in my memory than simply fifty-five years, but then it was lost. Never got it back. Never knew what happened to it.

DAVID: Did WOR keep most of the discs or transcriptions? Did your dad take any or . . . .

BOBBY: They did until about ten years ago, the time of their anniversary that we mentioned in e-mail, whenever that was. The then Program Director told me that all of those transcriptions had been sent to the Library of Congress, or was it the Smithsonian? You know, I'm not sure which. I think it was the Library of Congress, and they didn't have any of them, but I never knew what was there. Of course, every show had to be recorded, because it was ad-libbed. There was no script, and usually, in fact, after the show, I would go up to one of the control rooms and the engineer would play it for me while Dad was doing his 11:00 news show. We would wait and go home together, and I would usually listen to the show.

DAVID: What day of the week was the program on?

BOBBY: Saturday. It was always Saturday.

DAVID: You didn't miss any school?

BOBBY: Saturday at 8:00.

DAVID: Okay, you started to talk about that meeting after that first program, which obviously decided that . . . .

BOBBY: Oh, standing around on the stage, we were talking
             to Fineschriber, and that's one scene I can still
             remember—the three of us standing there—Dad,
             me, and Fineschriber, and Dad said, "Shall we keep
             looking for teenagers?" And Fineschriber said, "No,
             let's just stick with Bob if he'll do it." And I said,
             "Well, I'll do it, but I gotta have certain Saturday
             nights off for Scouts and probably in the future for
             dates" (laughs). I never had a date in my life up to
             that time, you see.

DAVID: However, now you could tell your girls that you
             were a famous celebrity. You had something to offer.

BOBBY: In Princeton High School, it really didn't cut much
             ice.

DAVID: I see. Getting back to that unpleasant subject, or
             pleasant subject of money, is WOR or Mutual
             sponsoring the program before you got a sponsor? I
             don't imagine that the show brought in big dollars,
             but how, exactly, was that divided?

BOBBY: Oh, I can tell you that. I cannot tell you what the
             numbers were until Ronson came aboard in July. I
             think it was July. It might have been June. Once
             Ronson had come aboard, we split up the three
             salaries in such a way as to pay the lowest taxes.
             Included in that, you see, was Dad's news, so Dad,
             for *Twenty Questions*, I think was paid $50 because
             all of the news shows added up to whatever hundreds
             it was. The money that he would have been paid
             went on to my paycheck, and mine was just bout
             the same as Mother's. It seems to me it was about
             $350 a week.

DAVID: Did you get to keep any of it, or was that banked
             by Mom and Dad for you?

BOBBY: It was banked by Mom and Dad.

DAVID: Good! Can't trust these teenagers.

BOBBY: I got a war bond, then a savings bond a week, so in fact, I was making $37.50 a week.

DAVID: They didn't treat you like Jackie Cooper?

BOBBY: (Laughs).

DAVID: Tell me something about the guests that you had over the years. You really had some extremely well-known people on the show, some well-known comedians, politicians . . . .

BOBBY: Pardon?

DAVID: You had comedians, politicians, musicians, educators . . . .

BOBBY: We had a higher level of guests so far as academics, you might say, than most other shows that had guests. We had some movie stars and a lot of sports figures, but we also had deans, and college presidents, senators, and representatives.

DAVID: Were any of them embarrassed by the experience, or did they take everything in stride?

BOBBY: They were all good sports. I don't recall, in the early days at least, anybody who didn't realize it was like going in and playing basketball with the Knicks. You just do the best you can. Some of them were better than others. Some of the wits came out with some funny stuff, and some of them never said a word, but usually they were very interesting. They usually contributed something to the show, and some of them could really play the game. There were two that I remember that were especially good at the game. One was Ann Rutherford, and the other was Macdonald Carey, I believe, and he was on more than once and he was pretty good. There were others who could play, maybe not that well, but not badly, and there were some who were just totally at sea, but it was fun to hear them say so. So, they were pretty good.

DAVID: Now, on the occasions where you had to miss a program, either because of a Boy Scout commitment or illness, etc., who would step in for you?

BOBBY: Well, the first time it was a friend of mine in school, a guy named Paul Homrighausen, whose father was the Dean at Princeton's Theological Seminary. He was one of the brighter kids that I knew in school, and we practiced at my house two or three times so he was boned-up. He knew how to play. He didn't quite have the scoring spark. He just wasn't quite at home. I never did hear that show, but years later, and I mean forty years later, when we met one time by total accident in San Francisco, I asked him, "How did you do on that *Twenty Questions?*" He said, "Bob, I really messed up. I had a couple of them, but I was so tongue-tied I couldn't get them out. I didn't do the job." Anyway, that was the first one. Then, my sister took over for me three or four times. She came on as "Nancy McGuire," my sister. Nancy had all kinds of learning problems and didn't do much at all, but she didn't embarrass anybody. I never did hear any of the shows that she was on, but obviously, if she had completely messed up, Dad wouldn't have had her do it again. I went to Philmont Scout Ranch, which took me off of two shows in a row, and she did those, and then there were a couple of dates I had. I believe she did one of those and another one. I would have to strain my mind to remember who else filled in besides her.

DAVID: Toward the end, I guess, when you started college, or were getting ready to go to college, a fellow came in who seemed to take over for quite a while. Someone who I think you're still friendly with.

BOBBY: Oh, John McPhee.

DAVID: How did John McPhee get involved?

BOBBY: Well, what happened was, in my senior year in high school, I was not going to go to a college nearby. They wanted me to go to Amherst. We went up and looked at it. It looked all right. Then, between Christmas and New Year's of my senior year in high school, which was December 1948, we took a trip south and looked at three or four colleges, including Duke. I was overwhelmed by Duke, and we had lunch with the Dean of Admissions. He said, "Don't worry about getting in. You don't even have to take SATS." So, I applied to Duke, and I was accepted, and that was as far as college went. So, once that happened, I was summoned to New York by the President of Ronson, Mr. Harris, and in his apartment, he laid the law down. He said, "Look, I'm not going to continue to sponsor this show unless we get a replacement for the juvenile." I said, "All right, we will do it."

DAVID: How old were you at the time?

BOBBY: Well, I was seventeen.

DAVID:	And you're responsible for getting your own replacement?
BOBBY:	No, no. I was there because he was going to talk me out of going to Duke.
DAVID:	Oh, I see.
BOBBY:	I kind of left that out (laughs). I said, "I'm sorry, Mr. Harris. I'm going to Duke." He said, "Well, then, we've got to really break our backs to get a replacement." And they did. They held auditions of three or four kids each before each show, at least. I'm thinking April or May of 1948, at least three or four shows. I think they looked at fifteen different people from New York High School, all recommended by the principal. None was any good at all. They were all brains, probably all rocket scientists or brain surgeons now, but they couldn't play the game. Then we said, "We gotta find somebody." So, we started looking around Princeton, people that I knew, and the only guy that I knew that I thought had any chance at all was John McPhee. He was a year ahead of me in school, but we're the same age. He skipped a grade, and he was going to Princeton. He was known by my family, and his family was known. We all knew each other. John was one of my best friends, though not in my class. He wasn't in my gang. He was my best friend outside the gang, and I said, "I think John can do it." We had played in the halls of Princeton High, Johnny and I. He kind of cottoned to it. He likes a challenge. He was a great athlete, as well as the top scholar in his class. And at the time, he was at camp in Vermont, so we called the camp, probably mid-to-late August, because I was going to leave for Duke right after Labor Day. He flew in. He was on a canoe trip, and he hiked back to the camp,

got a ride to the airport, and flew into LaGuardia. I can still see him walking into the WOR newsroom, where we were going to meet.

DAVID: With a smile on his face, I hope.

BOBBY: Well, kind of a smile and a quizzical look. Like, what's going on here? We all had supper at Toffenetti's. You remember that restaurant?

DAVID: Okay, yes.

BOBBY: We had supper at Toffenetti's, and Dad laid the law down. He said, "Look, if you do this, it means every Saturday night unless there is some major occurrence." And John agreed. John agreed. He had already had an audition, and he could play almost as well as I could, and his name even sounded like mine—Johnny McPhee—Bobby McGuire. His voice was . . . .

DAVID: Two young Irishmen (laughter).

BOBBY: And he did it. He started that September.

DAVID: You did come back occasionally after that, did you not?

BOBBY: Well, yeah, when I was home on vacation, if they didn't have a guest, I might be the guest. There were also times when Johnny wanted the night off, and I was home on vacation, and I would sit in for him. So, I wasn't completely out of the show. When I came back from college, there was an interval there where we had a third juvenile, who lasted four or five months during which I was picking the subjects, actually. Then, I went back on, as I was twenty-three, the world's oldest living teenager (laughs).

DAVID: Did you guys get much fan mail?

BOBBY: Well, yes and no. You see, the fan mail almost always consisted of people sending in subjects. The result of that was we never saw it because they had the subjects that they were suggesting. We got over 130,000 letters a week, at one time. We hired a guy named Barney O'Donnell to handle the mail and the subjects that were being suggested.

DAVID: Well, that certainly showed your sponsor at the network that the people were listening. No doubt about that. So you're saying that most of the mail was simply people submitting questions, hoping to get a free Ronson, or whatever else was being offered?

BOBBY: Yeah, to hear their name mentioned on the air.

DAVID: No individual letters to Florence Rinard, or to yourself, your dad, or Herb?

BOBBY: No, for that reason. There was never a letter that I ever saw that didn't have a subject being suggested.

DAVID: Did all of these subjects come directly from those questions, or were some of them ringers that were decided just for that week?

BOBBY: They all came from the letters or cards. We emphasized we wanted cards because they were easy to file. They all came from them. However, how shall I put it—it wasn't that we went through the week's cards and from them picked the subjects; rather, we picked the subjects, and then Barney O'Donnell, the mailman, would see who had sent that subject in first. There was never a time when someone wanted to suggest a subject to play that had not been sent in by somebody.

DAVID: You're saying, for example, if somebody said Robert E. Lee, there might have been four people who said that?

BOBBY: 400,000 is more likely. We had a record of the first one of every subject submitted, so if we came up with a subject that had never been used, that had never been submitted, or never been thought of, and somebody decided we wanted to do that on next week's show, Barney would say, yes, that was first sent in by John Jones in 1946.

DAVID: I see. The file cards listed by topics: one file for Animal, one for Vegetable, and one for Mineral, one for human beings. How in the world did they do that?

BOBBY: They had roomfuls, roomfuls. They were all alphabetical by the first effective word in the phrase of whatever it was. There was cross-referencing, too.

DAVID: In addition to the four panelists, actually five panelists counting the guests, your dad, your mom, yourself, Herb, and a guest, and, of course, Bill Slater, how many other people were necessary to put this program together?

BOBBY: Well, there was the producer. His name was Gary Stevens.

DAVID: I'm looking at a list here of names who appeared in some of the references, and they identify a number of people. For example Charlotte Manson, they say, was the Ronson girl, whatever that means.

BOBBY: (laughs) During the Ronson years, we had two principal announcers. One was Frank Waldecker. He was the big voice who did the introductions and read the commercials on the male side. Charlotte was simply the female announcer.

DAVID: It's interesting you mention Lon Clark being on so many of the programs.

BOBBY: Well, Lon Clark was simply every Christmas our guest, the fifth member of the panel.

DAVID: But Charlotte and Lon worked together on the program that he did on a regular basis.

BOBBY: Oh, yes.

DAVID: She was his girl Friday.

BOBBY: People in radio, a lot of them knew each other all over the place. Lon Clark, for us, was our fifth panelist. Every Christmas, he was Santa Claus.

DAVID: Did you have Jay Jackson?

BOBBY: No, no. Jay came along much later. Jay succeeded Bill Slater as emcee the first broadcast of 1953, but Slater was being affected by Parkinson's, which later killed him, I believe. He simply couldn't continue, so Jay succeeded him.

DAVID: Other names listed, you mentioned Frank Waldecker, Gary Stevens . . . .

BOBBY: Gary Stevens was the producer. His job was to count the questions for Slater. He sat next to Slater and, too, got the guests. He used various connections to provide the guests, usually a week or two in advance.

DAVID: Jack Irish is another name listed.

BOBBY: Jack Irish was a WOR announcer who, on occasion, did some of the radio announcing, but not for Ronson. Waldecker only announced for Ronson. When Waldecker left the show, it could be that Jack Irish was one of those who took over, but there were others besides him. I believe Bruce Elliott, another WOR announcer, became the mystery voice. The mystery voice, who informed the listening audience what the subject was, was always a guy named Don Fredericks, whose real name was Frederick Stuthman. He was a Hollywood actor and succeeded in character parts rather well, long after the show was over. He was the mystery voice all the time I was on the show on the radio. But after that, when Ronson left the show, when we had television rather than radio, we had many other announcers. But on radio for Ronson, it was always Frank Waldecker and Charlotte.

DAVID: Now once the program, of course, went to TV and finally went off the air, I assume that your dad still retained ownership of the concept. Was there ever any effort to try to get that back on again in syndication or any other form?

BOBBY: Many. Too many to list. First, Dad and Mother, with our agent, whose name was George Elber, were selling the show throughout the rest of the 1950s. In 1958, Frank Cooper Associates actually did a run-through, but it never went on the air because the next day was the Dotto quiz scandals and Cooper was in the middle of that, so that whole thing was dropped. There were others in the 1960s, and then when Dad died in 1971, still another one came along, about 1973 I would say. A guy named Richard Rubin wanted to produce another show. They did a lot of work. They paid us money every year for the rights for almost ten years. Mother and I together after Dad had died, and then myself alone after Mother died. Somebody paid us for the rights to the show right up 'til about 1985, believe it or not (laughs). They didn't pay much, but they paid something.

DAVID: Well, that gave them the right, just in case.

BOBBY: There are all kinds of ancillary events, especially in Hollywood, so far as putting *Twenty Questions* as a TV show back on the air, including an attempt by Disney, without the rights. I threatened to sue, but then it turned out their pilot was such a dismal piece of junk they just buried it. That was the end of it.

DAVID: That's too bad. May I ask what you've done in the world? Have you been involved in the world of radio or TV since that program went off the air, or have you gone a different route entirely?

BOBBY: No. Only briefly in television in 1958, when I wrote questions for a couple of quiz shows. But except for that, I've never done anything but corporate, governmental writing. I've always been a writer.

DAVID: What have I failed to ask that I should have? I think I've run out of questions. I know you haven't run out of answers, but I've run out of questions.

BOBBY: (Laughs) Well, if something else comes to mind, don't hesitate to call again. The book I'm working on is a fictionalized account of a guy in Princeton High School, who is a quasi-celebrity in New York every Saturday night, and is advertised as the amazing fourteen-year-old schoolboy, but who, through five days a week in Princeton High School, has trouble getting a C average (laughs).

DAVID: That could not be biographical. I don't believe that. Not if you got into Duke.

BOBBY: (Laughs) Well, don't forget, I got into Duke because we had lunch with the Dean of Admissions and he was influenced by the specter of showbiz.

DAVID: It will do it every time.

BOBBY: Yes. I've so totally fictionalized the book that the characters are all different. I used my friends, changed their names, and then changed the characters.

DAVID: Is this going to appeal to juveniles, or is it going to appeal to adults?

BOBBY: Adults. I'm writing it for laughs, for fun.

DAVID: I hope you are writing it for money. It's nice to get some of that as well.

BOBBY: (Laughs) Well, you know what happened, Dave? I started this out strictly as a memoir, and I wrote 250 pages, and put it aside for a month or two, and sent excerpts to former acquaintances from Princeton High School. We all agreed that it was great as a memoir, but as a book it wasn't very interesting. So, I threw out that whole design and I revamped it more as a strictly humorous book.

DAVID: Do you have an agent?

BOBBY: No, I haven't even gotten that far. I don't even know how to get an agent. I published a novel some years ago, but that agent, whose name was Bertha Klausner, if she's still alive, would be one hundred years old. I kind of doubt if she's still in business (laughs).

DAVID: Okay, well, I won't give you any advice in that direction.

BOBBY: I think the thing to do is get a book somewhere that lists agents, but I frankly don't know how to go about it anymore.

DAVID: I'm sure there are. If I can come up with something, I'll send you an e-mail.

BOBBY: Okay.

DAVID: It's been a pleasure talking to you. You've been very, very, generous with your time. I really appreciate it. I apologize for any of the sound problems on those *Twenty Questions* programs that I sent to you. If you ever come up with a Francis Lederer one, I'd love to hear it.

BOBBY: That's just it. That's what I was going to say. I found it.

DAVID: Oh, wonderful.

BOBBY: I found it. I found Lederer. I will send you a tape. It was on the back end of a tape labeled as something else. I recorded it over *Break the Bank* or something, and forgot to change the title. I'll make you a dub and send it along.

DAVID: Thanks a lot. You're very, very generous. I appreciate that. You did indicate that you went to Newark once or twice.

BOBBY: I did what?

DAVID: You indicated that you've attended the Newark Old-Time Radio convention once or twice.

BOBBY: It was the year at that Holiday Inn outside Newark Airport.

DAVID: You know what you ought to think about doing, perhaps, would be to give Jay Hickerson, who runs that Newark convention—he's probably planning this one already—perhaps sometime in the future, you can get the folks who do the old-time radio conventions to do a *Twenty Questions* segment with some of the radio people who are still around. That could be a lot of fun and you, of course, would be the quizmaster.

BOBBY: That *would* be fun. The only problem is I don't think anybody's still around.

DAVID: Well, Jackson Beck, people like that are still around.

BOBBY: No, I mean who had a connection with the show.

DAVID: I agree with you there, but the show is certainly vintage radio.

BOBBY: I might be able to get McPhee to do it.

DAVID: Well, he and Charlotte Manson passed away a couple of years ago also.

BOBBY: Oh, he did. I didn't know that.

DAVID: She was not well.

BOBBY: I could inquire. The last I heard, Gary Stevens is still alive. He's eighty-some. He's remarkable. He sounds just like he did in 1948.

DAVID: What did Alexander King once say? My enemies are getting older?

BOBBY: (Laughs) Okay.

DAVID: Thank you very, very, much.

BOBBY: Very good, Dave. I'll be in touch.

DAVID: So long. I look forward to the Francis Lederer tape.

BOBBY: Okay.

DAVID: Bye-bye.

BOBBY: Goodbye.

Chapter 9

MARY SMALL

(1922–)

INTERVIEW: SEPTEMBER 24, 1999

What is it about female vocalists that, in some mysterious way, accounts for why five of the fifteen people who permitted me to interview them (Joan Merrill, Hildegarde, Mary Small, Ann DeMarco, and Peggy Moylan) fall into the same category of performers? Call it coincidence, kismet, or just luck, but I was able to capture reminisces of these five women.

I knew very little about Mary Small prior to the time that I made telephone contact with her. A fellow old-time radio buff, who collects audio of child performers such as Shirley Temple, Baby Rose Marie, and others, made me aware of Mary Small, who was featured in her own radio program, *Little Miss Bab-O's Surprise Party*.

The adult Mary assured me that her singing career continued well beyond her childhood, but I will leave the details for her to tell.

I'm happy to report that since my initial contact with Mary, I've been able to acquire several programs in which she sings. She does indeed have a beautiful voice that sounded very much like that of an adult.

DAVID: It is September 24, 1999, and I have the great privilege and pleasure of speaking with radio vocalist Mary Small, who entertained during radio's Golden Age. Mary, thank you very much for being willing to share with us.

MARY: I wish it were silver instead of gold. It's not so long ago if it's silver, right? Well, we'll take gold.

DAVID: It could be platinum.

MARY: Oh, I love that. That I like.

DAVID: Mary, tell us how you discovered that you had a singing voice. How did you get involved in music and singing? Where do you have your roots?

MARY: Well, I couldn't have discovered it, because I was that young I'm told. They didn't have tape or anything like that in those days, but I remember uncomfortably being awakened when I wasn't even talking. I was just crawling around, but I hummed a lot. I remember them waking me one night—I know it was dark—to ask me to sing for some company. I just did it because I was told to do it, but that was the beginning, and oh, a few months later when it wasn't wake-up time, midnight, I began to enjoy the singing. I think the reason I sang is because my father was a singer, and he couldn't see his way into the profession and so, as so many parents will, they do it through their children.

DAVID: So, your dad inspired you and encouraged you?

MARY: Yes, he certainly did. He pushed me. He was a theatrical father rather than what they call the mother. What do they say the mother is?

DAVID: Stage mother.

MARY: Yeah, he was a stage father, all right. I remember a song. He said, "You don't need friends. I'm your pal." Then, he went into a song. He was writing a musical, evidently in Baltimore, and the song was something you won't even remember. I was an infant. (Sings) "Pal of my cradle days, I - la da da - always. When I was a baby upon your knee . . . ." Real old, corny stuff, but I remember it (laughs).

DAVID: Some of that corny stuff is coming back. People enjoy it. There are a lot of records that . . . .

MARY: Bringing back the 1940s, but this is not the 1940s.

DAVID: The 1940s, 1930s, and even the 1920s, you can still buy an Al Jolson or an Eddie Cantor record.

MARY: Oh yeah, but what kind of fidelity do you suppose it's like? Can they make nice CDs out of them?

DAVID: The people who have the technical skill apparently are able to take the old records and clean them up.

MARY: I have a very large metal disc of myself on *The Rudy Vallee Hour*, when I was about nine or ten years old. The song was "Louisville Lady," and of course, the way they made the records then was with a specific kind of needle, which would not work with any other kind of needle, and I still have it, but I can't play it because I can't get a needle. I don't really care that much, but the song that this child sang was called "Louisville Lady," a very sexy song. I didn't understand what it was all about, but I'll never forget the title.

DAVID: Off the tape, I'll put you in touch with somebody who'll be able to take that record and make you a clean copy.

MARY: Oh, that's interesting. Now what can't you do?

DAVID: Well, I can't do it, but I know people who can.

MARY: Well, that's the same thing (laughs).

DAVID: Your home initially was Baltimore.

MARY: That's right, Baltimore, Maryland.

DAVID: And how did you get started on the radio? How did you make your first radio appearance, or where was it?

MARY: I was about six years old, and I remember in Baltimore we were listening to *Uncle Jack's Kiddie Hour*. Of course, who but my father said to my mother, "Fannie, you've got to get her on that show. She's better than all the others," which, incidentally, was a terrible philosophy, telling a child she's superior, you know, because I remember hearing someone I *loved* on that show, and I said, "Isn't she great." And she was. I don't know who she was, but my father said, "Oh, you're better." So, then I began to *think* I was better, which isn't good. A child should have humility. There are too many spoiled *brats*. Forgive me, but I had to get that in.

DAVID: But you should also have self-confidence, and maybe that's what your dad was trying to do.

MARY: When you love to sing, and you're born with it—I teach singing now and I have some people, who were born with it—some who were born a little bit with it, and so you go according to how much they have. But I never took singing lessons. My father sang to me eighteen hours a day. So, singing was what I did most of all, and I didn't even have friends. Finally, when I came to New York, which I'll tell you about soon, I went to a special school, where they were all theatrical and professional. There was a place called "The Mother's Room." Now, you know where I'm going. You know that I don't approve of children in show business.

DAVID: I'm letting you do the talking, Mary.

MARY: Well, come on, make me say something nice.

DAVID: Let's get back for just a moment to the kiddie show. Did you appear on that once, or were you on that on a regular basis?

MARY: I was on once, and I sang a song called "My Future
          Just Passed." I remember enjoying it. I remember
          doing it well and getting a lot of applause. Then,
          they called me the miniature Kate Smith. I wasn't
          fat, but I had a big voice.

DAVID: Did you involve yourself in any other Baltimore
          broadcasts?

MARY: At that point, my father—ever the enterprising,
          pushy daddy—called the Radio Editor of the
          Baltimore Sun at the time. His name was George
          Browning, and he's somewhere in the archives.
          He was a lovely, lovely man. My father, being very
          persuasive, got him to listen to me sing, and
          George Browning was impressed. I'm talking
          about myself, but since that little girl doesn't exist
          anymore . . . .

DAVID: That's why we're speaking, because we want to hear
          about yourself.

MARY: I know, but I hate to say, "Gee, I was great." I
          remember so much, and the money that I made
          and wasn't able to save—and wasn't given—
          reminds me I must have had something to have
          earned all of that. But George Browning called
          a man who was in town that week managing
          another famous name, Arthur Tracy, "The Street
          Singer."

DAVID: Yes.

MARY: He forced this manager, who did him a favor
          because, of course, he wanted a good write-up,
          and he let me sing for him, but I just realized that
          previous to that, there was a Gus Edwards. What
          was it? It was a contest—two thousand kids.

DAVID: Gus Edwards would travel around the country and audition children for his children's programs.

MARY: Oh, I didn't know that, but he was in Baltimore that particular week. This was before the other incident I just mentioned. I forgot the chronology, however, I sang (sings) "Just one more chance to prove it's you alone I care for . . . ." The very same key, the very same voice, and I won.

DAVID: That's a torch song.

MARY: Yeah, it sure is. I love it. I may do it on an album one day when I bring back some oldies. But when I went to New York with Gus Edwards, they turned me down. They said, "She's a freak. She's got a woman's voice and she's just a kid with little white socks and little chubby face and a Buster Brown haircut." You remember Baby Rose Marie?

DAVID: Baby Rose Marie grew up. She was on *The Dick Van Dyke Show.*

MARY: So did I. Wouldn't it be terrible if we didn't grow up? It would be great if we didn't grow up, actually.

DAVID: Baby Rose Marie did make a TV career for herself.

MARY: Yes, she went into acting. She had hurt her voice by doing a lot of Jimmy Durante, which required that growl. She developed nodules and had operations as it was told me. Our parents, not my mother so much, but her father—interesting about fathers and daughters if you talk to Sigmund Freud, which is a little late now, you'll find out about it. Theatrically it even gets worse. My father and Rose Marie's father kept us apart. We were kids about the same age, and we wanted to be together.

She was on the (sings) "Tasty's is tempting." She had Tasty Yeast and I had Bab-O. (Sings) "Shine little glow worm, glimmer, glimmer . . . ." Golly, you're making me remember things. I must have taken Sodium Pentothal or something.

DAVID: This is wonderful. You just keep it up.

MARY: She was on at 12:15, and that was called the Blue Network and the Red Network. WEAF was Red and WJZ was Blue. Now there's no more NBC, which was Red.

DAVID: Right.

MARY: She went on at 12:15, and finally one day, we went up to where we rehearsed separately with different pianists to Shapiro Bernstein. They had lots of the biggest hits. So, one day, we snuck into a room and started to play the piano and talk, and we enjoyed each other so much, so . . . .

DAVID: How old are the two of you at this time?

MARY: I knew you'd ask me that.

DAVID: I didn't ask you the date, so that won't date you today.

MARY: Today, it won't, but next week, it will. Well, we were under ten years old. I don't know who was older, but she was the greatest singer. I envied her. I felt she had the edge. But unfortunately, since I was the new kid in town, she went to California and did other things, and became an actress. I admit I am *not* an actress. I'm a singer. My voice was the same as a child as it is now, and it's kind of crazy. I would get—well, let me see—here I was about twelve years old, fifteen minutes, five nights a week at 7:15, getting proposals of marriage until they began to announce my age, but they still kept on.

DAVID: Was this before or after you appeared on the Rudy Vallee program?

MARY: Rudy Vallee introduced me to radio in New York.

DAVID: So this was after Rudy Vallee?

MARY: Yes.

DAVID: How did you get involved with Rudy Vallee, or how did he get involved with you?

MARY: The man who came in when Arthur Tracy was in town . . . .

DAVID: Was he your agent?

MARY: Arthur Tracy? No.

DAVID: No, no, this gentleman.

MARY: Yes, he became my agent and took me to New York and introduced me. This was *after* Gus Edwards. I got it mixed up before. At least if Gus Edwards rejected me, Rudy Vallee's people did not.

DAVID: So, your agent got you an audition with Rudy Vallee and Rudy put you on the air.

MARY: Right, exactly. That's how it happened. Then, I got my own radio show, which I just mentioned was fifteen minutes, five nights a week, which Frank Sinatra followed, and we knew each other pretty well. Me with my little white socks, he with his long pants, but he had just left the Tommy Dorsey Band and I came in at 11:00 with Walter Gross' Orchestra, a seventeen-piece *live* band. I rehearsed during the afternoon, and there was a commercial break of about sixty seconds, and Frank Sinatra came in at 11:15. He was billed as "the voice that is thrilling millions." The man who managed him also managed Dinah Shore, and the reason they made records and I didn't—many successful ones—was because at the age of sixteen, I got married to a songwriter. I insisted, being a dutiful, baby wife—well, maybe not baby wife. I wanted to be kind. I didn't want him to be Mr. Small, and so I sang all of his songs and didn't quite make it. Without a record, even then, when it was just beginning, you know, you didn't have a career. But I did play every presentation house in America in the United States. You know, there were four movies a day, let's say, at The Paramount, which I played.

DAVID: The Paramount, the Roxy . . . .

MARY: The Roxy, The Strand, and I forget, lots of benefits and Madison Square Garden. My God, 20,000 people in those days was a lot, you know. It's not like concerts today. What was I saying about the theater, when I was playing? There were four movies being shown, and between the movies and the Fox News—old fashioned, as I recall—they had Vaudeville. I would headline: "Radio's Little Child Singing Star," and I would get out there and belt songs like (sings) "I'm heading for the last roundup," which nobody knows now. Very big western song, and (sings) "I'm an old cow hand," which I saw on the Country Western Awards the other night.

DAVID: (Sings) "On the Rio Grande."

MARY: Oh, you remember that?

DAVID: Sure I do.

MARY: Good Lord! (Giggles) I think I may have told you everything that's ever happened to me.

DAVID: Not yet, not yet. Talk for a bit about what it was like in those days to perform on the radio. Were there live audiences? Were there many rehearsals?

MARY: No. There were lots of rehearsals. No live audiences. Very large orchestras, and I would come from school, rehearse—I had to go to a private school. It was called the Professional Children's School.

DAVID: You mentioned the last time we spoke that you and Milton Berle were . . . .

MARY: Yes, when I played The Palace Theater in Chicago, I had to take my schoolwork with me. The correspondence school. And he wanted to do my homework for me. He wanted to do a good deed. The big good deed was I flopped everything he ever did.

DAVID: Milton would be proud of that today, I'm sure.

MARY: (Laughs) I don't think he cares very much right now. He's kind of a happy—octogenarian is eight—he's in his nineties. What do you call that?

DAVID: I guess he's just a nineogenerian.

MARY: (Laughs) He's a funny fellow.

DAVID: Do you stay in touch, or have you been in touch with any of the people you worked with years ago? People like Rose Marie?

MARY: No, everybody's on the coast. I gave up my work after I went to London, because I had two children, and London was the beginning of big things for me. It would have been just great, but when you have two kids and you bring them with you, you can't get a nanny who will care, and I was so concerned about the kids. I was quite young, and I hate to say this, but my former husband wasn't exactly in the mood to be a nanny while I was singing on the stage. You see, he played the piano for me, so there was just nobody to connect the family and the profession.

DAVID: He was in the service during WW II, is that correct?

MARY: He was a sailor.

DAVID: Now, were you active at that time during the war?

MARY: Oh yes, I was. I played on Mark Warnow's program. *The Daughters of Uncle Sam* was the show I did with B.A. Rolfe, if you know who he was.

DAVID: He was a band leader, wasn't he?

MARY: Yes, and he had an all-girl band. I sang on his program for years.

DAVID: Chubby fellow, as I recall.

MARY: Big man. *The Daughters of Uncle Sam* we were called. Golly.

DAVID: Some of the people, who again according to the research or the material in John Dunning's book, that you worked with were people like Ben Bernie. You were a regular on his show, were you not?

MARY: That's right, I was.

DAVID: And what was it like to work with Ben Bernie?

MARY: Well, he liked little girls, and my mother had to be around me all the time. It's not nice to talk about the deceased, but what's happening today is even worse, I'm afraid. He scared me. You don't flirt with a little fifteen-year-old girl and say, "Hi, sweetie, aren't you cute," and all that kind of thing. So, you see, a child, particularly a girl in those days in the theater, there are two things to look at. You're suppressed because you cannot play with kids your own age, which is a natural desire, and you are watched over so carefully that you feel like you're doing something wrong, and you really want to go roller skating. When you played with Ben Bernie, do you recall—it was a half-hour show— did you do one song or two songs per program?

MARY: I did two songs. In those days, we had to do two shows because we had to repeat it at 12:00.

DAVID: East coast and west coast.

MARY: That's right. And you never felt that you were in good voice the second time.

DAVID: Do you remember any of the guest stars that he had on the show when you were performing with him?

MARY: He didn't have guest stars. It was only his own show, and a singer named Bobby Gibsonm and myself.

DAVID: Purely music? No comedy, no . . . .

MARY: Well, he was the comedy. He had a straight man.
            It was a very short show.

DAVID: Did he ever have Walter Winchell on his show?

MARY: Oh heck, no. They were enemies, but of course it
            wasn't real. It was just a press agent's dream.

DAVID: The Ben Bernie vs. Walter Winchell feud.

MARY: That's right. They loved feuding because it made
            good copy.

DAVID: You worked with Milton Cross also, I understand.

MARY: Yes, Milton Cross was my announcer many times
            when I had a very special program. He was one
            of the first people who held his ear when he
            spoke. You must see old-fashioned pictures of
            that. It sort of gives you a sounding board. There
            are lots of singers who do that, which is a bad
            thing to do. It gives you a dependency to hear
            your tone.

DAVID: What memories do you have of Mr. Cross, a
            very distinguished voice for the Metropolitan
            Opera?

MARY: A very lovely, wonderful, humble gentleman, not
            often in our business.

DAVID: I understand you worked with Bud Collyer?

MARY: Bud Collyer was my announcer when I had *The
            Little Miss Bab-O Program.* Oh yes, Bud was fun.
            He was a real great, great guy.

DAVID: I'm looking for little anecdotes. Harry Babbitt was someone else that you worked with.

MARY: Yes. Now, let me think. Harry Babbitt. What was the name of the orchestra?

DAVID: I thought Babbitt at one time was with Kay Kyser.

MARY: Kay Kyser. I couldn't think of the name. You're making me go way, way, way back in my memory book. Good Lord. I want very much to do a talk show at night with memories. Not like Joe Franklin; no records, just telling wonderful incidents like when I was with Julie Wilson in London. I walked into a restaurant. I didn't know where I was going or who was there. I said, "My name is Mary Small, and I'm an American." There was such a guffaw of laughter, and then it was Ziggy's—that was the name of the restaurant—and he said, "There's an American here—Julie Wilson." Julie Wilson was a big star in London at the time. Took it by storm. She said, "When you announced you're an American, how could you imagine not being one with your accent in London?" (Laughs).

DAVID: Couldn't fool them, huh?

MARY: I didn't try to, but I was stupid to say I'm an American. They thought I was trying to be funny, but I just wanted to be accepted. I don't know what it was.

DAVID: Did you work with Kay Kyser at all, or sing with his band?

MARY: No, I didn't sing with his band.

DAVID: What are some of the other bands that you sang

with? Popular bands?

MARY: Well, here's an interesting point about bands. When people who don't remember me now—naturally, it's so long ago—ask me, "What band were you with?" I was making thousands of dollars a week, and I was the star, and the band played for me, such as Walter Gross.

DAVID: What you're saying is, you were not a band singer; the band accompanied you. You didn't accompany the band.

MARY: Rosemary Clooney was a band singer, and Helen Forrest, who sadly passed away recently, and Kitty Kallen was a very good friend of mine. She sang with Jack Teagarden. All these names are unknown today.

DAVID: Kitty Kallen was well-known. She also sang with Harry James.

MARY: That's right, but Teagarden I don't think is, except for jazz musicians.

DAVID: Trombone Teagarden?

MARY: Right! You *are* amazing. I've never known anybody who remembers as much as I do about our business.

DAVID: We're probably the same age, Mary.

MARY: Oh, I'm much younger. I'm a good twenty-five years younger (laughs).

DAVID: I'm sure you are. Someone said you worked with Pick and Pat. Do you remember that?

MARY: Pick and Pat were like *Amos 'n Andy*. They had their own show, and I was a singer on that show. Benny Rubin. Did you ever hear of him?

DAVID: Oh, yes.

MARY: I was with him. Gordon MacRae was a guest on my fifteen-minute radio show. Oh, listen to this: Perry Como. They were trying all these new, young singers out. I was well-known, and they tried them on my show. Perry Como in the 1940s came over to me with his pipe. He had just left Ted Weems, whose name you know.

DAVID: *The Whistler.*

MARY: Right (laughs). He said to me, "Mary, I really have been a fan of yours for a couple of years." This was Perry Como, in those days.

DAVID: After he left barbering. He was a barber, you know.

MARY: No, this I did not know.

DAVID: On Long Island . . . .

MARY: He was a great singer, just a great, great, singer and a sweet man. Lots of nice people in this business. But I can't think of any memories that would startle you right now, except I say to mothers—and I don't have to say to fathers, because usually it's the mothers; it's rarely the fathers—people say, "Why don't you model your child? Why don't you put the child on *Star Search*?" I don't want to sound or introduce a tragic note. We won't mention names, but we know about the pageants and what can happen when parents live through their children. I think I did, or did I not tell you how the

Professional Children's School had a special room called the "Mother's Room?"

DAVID: Tell us about it.

MARY: Well, the mothers are in there, and here's what they would say: "We're auditioning today." *We.* Mothers of prodigies say "*we.*" (Laughs). Now, doesn't that explain that they're living through their children?

DAVID: Vicarious living, yes.

MARY: Right, and, tremendous competition and jealousy. "Did your daughter do a commercial?" "No, not today." "Well, mine did." I'm exaggerating, but it was not that far.

DAVID: Does the program *Three for the Money* ring any bells?

MARY: Two for the Show. Vaguely, because I can't remember when it was.

DAVID: A quiz program, again with Bud Collyer— Mutual . . . .

MARY: Yes, I did it. Good Lord, I worked a lot. Why don't I have a million dollars today?

DAVID: Well, you probably invested it in the wrong stock.

MARY: Well, I didn't have any of it. They took it away. I was a child anyway. My ex-husband wrote the music recently for *The Addams Family*, and he's no longer Mr. Small. Now, if people don't know me, I say, "I was married to Vic Mizzy. He wrote *The Addams Family*. I think that's a bit of irony that would make a good novel, don't you? (Laughs).

DAVID: Absolutely.

MARY: Now, I don't think you can ask me anything else. I'm all squeezed out of info.

DAVID: Well, let me try. Let me try. Can you recall any embarrassing situations that occurred, not necessarily to you, but during the radio program while the program went on live?

MARY: Well, I tried to whistle and this came out (blowing sounds).

DAVID: Not live, I hope.

MARY: Live, yeah. That comes to mind immediately. That was the only time I was embarrassed. Nothing terrible . . . .

DAVID: What about your fellow performers during a live broadcast? Anything . . . .

MARY: When I was a little girl, they were always very careful around me, so there was never any . . . .

DAVID: When I say embarrassing, I don't mean of an off-color nature; I mean people who sometimes goof, people drop a script or mispronounce a word . . . .

MARY: No, no.

DAVID: Everything went perfectly, then? Smoothly?

MARY: When you're prepared and you love it. I didn't love the life, but I loved the singing. I loved the applause, and I'd say to my mother, "Wasn't the applause a little less than the last show?" She'd go insane, because I'd always asked that. But that is the beginning of the terrible life of rejection when you grow older, you know?

DAVID: Let's see—I'm looking at the write-up here and it says—don't get angry at me . . . .

MARY: Is that what it says? Don't get angry?

DAVID: It says from 1933 to 1934, you were on *Little Miss Bab-O's Surprise Party* with guests Lucille Manners, Ernest Charles, etc.

MARY: I don't remember them, but Frances Langford, Eddie Albert, and a lot of other big names were my guests.

DAVID: Was he married to Margo at the time, or did that come later?

MARY: No, that came later.

DAVID: Eddie Albert had a radio program called *The Honeymooners* at one time, I think.

MARY: I don't remember that, but it was Grace and Eddie Albert first, as I recall. But my *Little Miss Bab-O Show*—I was dressed in the most horrific, awful, if you've ever seen the can of Bab-O. I looked like the can in a green satin outfit, a direct copy of the costume on the can (laughs).

DAVID: You worked with Ray Bloch, as well.

MARY: Yeah. CBS. He was a big wheel there.

DAVID: What do you recall about Ray Bloch?

MARY: Well, about the best band leader I ever worked with—in complete command—a consummate musician. Let me close with this. I would like very, very much, as I told you earlier, to do a talk show. I don't care where it is, tri-state, Connecticut, I know I could grab an audience. If I've entertained anyone during our conversation, that's the program I would call *Music and Small Talk*.

DAVID: You've entertained me, Mary, and I thank you very much for your time.

MARY: Well, you know everything.

DAVID: You are a sweetheart.

MARY: Next time I want to find out something, I'm going to call you, my friend.

DAVID: I will see you in October.

MARY: You got it.

DAVID: When someone walks over to you at the convention and taps you on the back and gives you a kiss on your cheek, don't slap his face. It'll be me.

MARY: No, I'll give you a kiss right back.

DAVID: Okay.

MARY: Thanks for calling.

DAVID: My pleasure.

MARY: Bye now.

DAVID: Bye-bye.

Chapter 10
ANNE DEMARCO
(1923-2004)

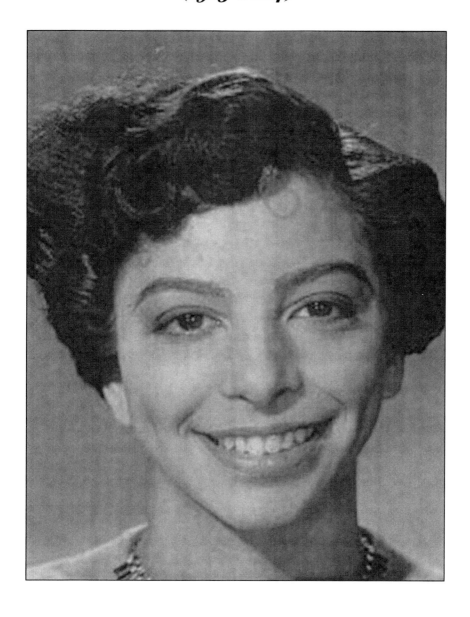

INTERVIEW: OCTOBER 6, 1999

Few sister singing groups could rival the popularity or fame of The Andrews Sisters. A good argument could also be made that if one takes into consideration accolades, record sales, guest appearances, and other measures of popularity and success, The Boswell Sisters and The Pickens Sisters deserve equal recognition.

On the chance that no one has as yet researched the phenomena of sister singing groups who performed during the 1920s to 1950s, I invite readers who have a special interest in the subject to investigate the wonderful series of radio broadcasts conducted by Richard Lamparski entitled, *Whatever Became of?* Among the hundreds of people interviewed on that program (see Chapter 2 of this book for a list of the radio personalities interviewed by Lamparksi) you can find Maxine Andrews of The Andrews Sisters, Patti Pickens of The Pickens Sisters, and Connee and Vet Boswell of The Boswell Sisters.

To that list should be added several other well-known sister singing groups, including The King Sisters, The Lane Sisters, The Dinning Sisters, The McGuire Sisters, and of course, The DeMarco Sisters.

It was a pleasure to speak with Anne DeMarco, one of the nicest radio people I've had the good fortune to be able to interview.

DAVID: Today is Wednesday, October 6, 1999, and I have the great pleasure of speaking with Anne DeMarco of the famous The DeMarco Sisters singing group. Anne, when did you and your sisters first begin singing together?

ANNE: We began singing together, the three of us. We were two, four and six years old. We were a trio.

DAVID: What caused you to sing together? Did you do it on your own, or was it your parents?

ANNE: No, my father, he was a singer, and he played the banjo and guitar and all, but didn't read a note of music. By the way, none of us ever did, either.

DAVID: Well, I understand Irving Berlin didn't either (laughs).

ANNE: Right, and that's who helped put us on *The Fred Allen Show*.

DAVID: Irving Berlin.

ANNE: Irving Berlin, yes.

DAVID: Now, you started to sing when you were two, four, and five did you say, or six?

ANNE: Two, four and six. We were two years apart.

ANNE: Two, four and six.

DAVID: Right.

DAVID: And you just sang at home, or did you start . . . .

ANNE: Our father taught us harmony. The first song he taught us was (sings) "When it's springtime in the Rockies, I'll be coming back to you," and he taught us each our parts, and we listened. To be sure we'd be on key, he had a Coca-Cola bottle.

DAVID: Right.

ANNE: And he'd blow in it, and he'd be sure we ended up on the same key we started with, and we always did.

DAVID: How long did you do that before you started singing with other people?

ANNE: Professionally? We were, oh, let's see, I think seven, nine, and eleven years old. My father took the trio to New York City. We went on an excursion ticket.

Somebody offered to pay for us. We were poor, you know? And we get there, and it was a weekend excursion, and we went to Radio City Music Hall, and there were all these people in the lobby, and my father said, "Sing." We were kids. We started to sing. (Sings) "The Object of my Affection," in three-part harmony.

DAVID: This is in the lobby of the Music Hall?

ANNE: The lobby of NBC that was right across the street.

DAVID: Radio City.

ANNE: Right, and a man started saying, "Get these kids upstairs!" And we went upstairs. The man made us sing—whoever he was—and then he says, "Come back in a month." And we said, "We gotta go back by Monday." The excursion was only for the weekend, you know.

DAVID: Where were you folks from?

ANNE: Rome, New York.

DAVID: Upstate.

ANNE: Upstate, right.

DAVID: Near Utica, right?

ANNE: Near Utica. Fifteen miles, that's right. So, then we went back to Rome, and then—wait a minute— then somebody said to us, "How about *The Paul Whiteman Hour*?" They had *The Paul Whiteman Show.* Do you remember Paul Whiteman?

DAVID: Oh, yes, yes. Pops.

ANNE: Right. They put us on *The Paul Whiteman Show*, the three of us.

DAVID: Do you remember what year that was?

ANNE: Yes, in the late 1930s.

DAVID: So you sang on *The Paul Whiteman Show*. That was your first radio appearance?

ANNE: The first radio appearance. From there, we went on Fred Allen's *Town Hall Tonight,* the three of us.

DAVID: Directly from Whiteman?

ANNE: Yes. Directly from Whiteman. Then, they said, "Well, give them the $250, and my father said, "How many months?" And they said, "The night." I swear to God, I'm not lying.

DAVID: Your father must have been thrilled.

ANNE: Oh, yeah. After that, we did *The Fred Allen Show*. That was the night that Stuart Canin was on—the twelve-year-old that played the violin—and that's what started the feud with Jack Benny.

DAVID: "The Bee."

ANNE: "The Bee," right, right, and that's the date we were on. We did everything from *Pick 'n Pat* to *Hobby Lobby* to *Show Boat*. We did all of these shows.

DAVID: The first time you appeared on *The Fred Allen Show*, was it a single appearance?

ANNE: Just as a guest.

DAVID: You weren't regulars to begin with?

ANNE: No, no.

DAVID: Then you guested on other shows?

ANNE: Right, and in 1945, we did the *The Fred Allen Show.*

DAVID: So you started . . . .

ANNE: I want to tell you how. By now, we were five. The other two were born.

DAVID: Oh, my gosh.

ANNE: Arlene and Terri.

DAVID: Aha!

ANNE: Now, we're five sisters.

DAVID: And you're all singing together.

ANNE: And my father taught us barbershop harmony, and he liked The Merry Macs. He said they do a thing with—he didn't know how to say whatever it is—I still don't know. Then, he taught us to sing in modern fifths, or something like that.

DAVID: Um–hum.

ANNE: And he took us to New York again. No, no. We stayed in Brooklyn at some relative's house, a distant relative. My Aunt Bea and Uncle Joe. They weren't really my Aunt Bea and Uncle Joe, but we called them that.

DAVID: They were family.

ANNE: Right. They were family, and so my father took us to New York again. Meanwhile, my father was suffering from a very bad liver ailment.

DAVID: Right.

ANNE: He said, "Dear God. I just want to live to see my five kids make good, and then I'll be happy to pass away." He drew a beautiful picture of Jesus. I'll never forget this as long as I live. And to make a long story short, he took us to the Brill Building. We were going to get free music or something.

DAVID: The Brill Building. Isn't that the place where ASCAP works?

ANNE: I don't remember, but I know that's where Irving Berlin's office was.

DAVID: Right, right.

ANNE: In the Brill Building. So, we're there to get music, or whatever. I forget. We always said we knew we were good. This is an awful thing to say, but we knew how good we were. Five little kids.

DAVID: Uh–huh. Adorable little kids.

ANNE: I don't know about that.

DAVID: Adorable. I've seen pictures. Adorable.

ANNE: Aw, thank you. So, we said, "Anybody that's important, we'll start to sing." So, I swear to God, this is the truth, this guy with a brown jacket and tan leather pants came in with sunglasses in the elevator.

DAVID: Yes.

ANNE: We didn't know who he was, and we wouldn't have recognized him anyway, so we said, (sings) "Put on your old grey bonnet," just to sing like that in harmony. He said, "Oh, my God, come with me. My name is Gordon Jenkins."

DAVID: Oh, my gosh.

ANNE: And he took us to Irving Berlin's office, and he said, "Irving, you gotta hear these kids. You won't believe it." And we did a little of that, and he said, "Oh, my goodness." And he says, "We gotta do *something*." He was so nice, and we always called him "Mr. Berlin." We were so impressed and everything, and then he says to us, he says, "Kids, where do you rehearse or anything like that?" We had no arranger or anything at the time, but this lady did want to arrange for us. Her name was Grace Shannon. She arranged for—what was the name of that big singer—the one that came out of the Army? A big singer, he had just gotten out of the Army, or something. I forget the name.

DAVID: Baritone crooner?

ANNE: Yeah, a crooner. Aw, doggone it. Johnny some-thing—Johnny Desmond. She was going to arrange for us—for nothing. She just thought we were so good. And Irving Berlin said, "Where are you going to rehearse?" And we said, "I guess Nola Studios, and he said, "No, you rehearse in one of my offices. Why pay Nola Studios? Isn't that great?

DAVID: Wonderful.

ANNE:	So, we did that, and oh, I forgot to tell you, the three of us singing?
DAVID:	Right.
ANNE:	Somebody told Babe Ruth about us. You know, the baseball player.
DAVID:	Yeah.
ANNE:	We were such dumb kids. We were like six, eight, and ten years old, the trio now.
DAVID:	George Herman Ruth.
ANNE:	I've got a tape of us singing with Babe Ruth.
DAVID:	Wow.
ANNE:	An audio.
DAVID:	Uh–huh.
ANNE:	Video, excuse me, a video. So, they said that we were Babe Ruth's protégés. Anyway, he did a Vitaphone movie for Warner, and he put us in the picture. They called us The Bambinos, Babe's protégés, right? And I said, "Here they are, The Three DeMarcos." And we sang, the three of us, all dressed up in baseball suits. I can bring that to show you when I see you, if you want to see it.
DAVID:	That's wonderful. That's terrific.
ANNE:	And we sang (sings) "It Happened on the Beach" in three part harmony with me playing guitar. And he said, "Over the ether." In those days, they said "over the ether."

DAVID: Your dad must have been so proud of you.

ANNE: He certainly was. Then, to get back to the five of us, Irving Berlin said, "I want to put them in *Annie Get Your Gun* with Ethel Merman." He went all the way to Albany to see Governor Lehman, who was the governor at the time. I mean, this can be attested to. You can't ask Irving Berlin.

DAVID: I believe you.

ANNE: He said, "I've got five kids that are so great." He made us learn (sings) "Doin' What Comes Natur'lly."

DAVID: I remember that very well.

ANNE: That's right from *Annie Get Your Gun*, and Ethel Merman, and everybody. What Mr. Berlin told us, first of all, he said, "It's a pleasure to meet you. I've enjoyed hearing your songs, but we have a thing in New York that I can't do anything about called the Geharing Society. G-E-H-A-R-I-N-G.

DAVID: Child Labor Law.

ANNE: He said, "If I gave permission for *these* children to sing in *Annie Get Your Gun*, *every* mother and her child would be around, and that's against the child—I don't know if you're old enough or young enough to remember the Child Labor Laws?

DAVID: Yes.

ANNE: But that's what it was. So, we couldn't, and he felt so bad, he went to Albany to plead with the governor, and that was that. Then, they talked about Al Goodman, who was the orchestra leader on *Fred Allen.*

DAVID: Right.

ANNE: And Berlin introduced us to Al Goodman, and Al Goodman called Fred Allen and said, "They want me to hear these five kids," but The Merry Macs were signed by William Morris.

DAVID: Big agency. Did you have any . . . .

ANNE: We had no agency.

DAVID: No agent.

ANNE: We had a manager that picked us up—Johnny O'Conner—who was a drunk, but anyway, he called Fred Allen and said, "I want to audition these five kids that Irving Berlin's raving about." And Fred Allen said to Al Goodman, "If these kids are any good, then you book 'em. I'll leave it up to you. You're the Musical Director."

DAVID: What happened to The Merry Macs?

ANNE: They didn't get the show.

DAVID: They lost it?

ANNE: Well, they thought they were going to be on because they were William Morris, and so was *The Fred Allen Show.* We were with nobody.

DAVID: They were not related to one another, were they?

ANNE: No.

DAVID: They were just a group that got together.

ANNE: Two of them, I think, were brothers. They were very, very good. That's the reason my father patterned us after them.

DAVID: Right.

ANNE: Anyway, to make a long story short, we auditioned for—you got a minute?

DAVID: I've got lots of minutes.

ANNE: Okay, my father said, when we went to audition—my father was really sick—so the five of us went to New York by ourselves. It took us 50¢ back and forth on the subway, a nickel apiece.

DAVID: Those were the days.

ANNE: Those *were* the days, right?

DAVID: A nickel beer and a nickel subway.

ANNE: My father said to us, "If you get *The Fred Allen Show*, call me up and say, 'Burn the mattress.'"

DAVID: (Laughs).

ANNE: Now, I gotta tell you what "burn the mattress" means. My father said that in Italy, where he was born, there was this man that always used to play the lottery. He told his wife, "I got a hunch, Angelina, if I put our life savings on the lottery, I have a feeling on 9-9-9-9 that we can just start all over again. If you see me coming home in a carriage, 'burn the mattress.' We'll start life anew, right?"

DAVID: Right.

ANNE: So, the guy goes to the lottery—the old Italian
              guy—and 9-9-9-8 comes out. He faints and falls
              down on the ground. So, the neighbors knew
              where he lived. Some neighbors that lived near
              him said, "Poor Jacomino. Oh, my God, he's
              fainted. Let's take him home." So, they put him
              in the carriage, and the carriage is coming up the
              walk, right? And the wife saw it and she burned
              the mattress!

DAVID: Oh, boy.

ANNE: In other words, she thought him coming home in
              a carriage he won the lottery, which he didn't. You
              got that? He came home in the carriage because he
              passed out because he *lost* the lottery.

DAVID: (Laughs) Poor fellow. No mattress that night.

ANNE: So, when we auditioned for *The Fred Allen Show*,
              and they said, "Kids, you got the job." So, we
              called my father, and we said, "Burn the mattress."
              He said, "Oh, don't say . . . ." "No, burn the
              mattress." And we got that, and we were on for
              four years, from 1945 to 1949.

DAVID: Did you actually have a contract, or was it a week-
              to-week situation?

ANNE: No, I don't remember if we had a contract or not.
              We went to MCA. You know how? Basil Rathbone.
              Remember him?

DAVID: Oh, yes, Sherlock Holmes.

ANNE: Sherlock Holmes. He sent a note to MCA, and

said, "For God's sake, help these talented kids," and they signed us with MCA.

DAVID: Now, you're represented well.

ANNE: Now, we're represented well. We played the Copa with Dean Martin and Jerry Lewis in 1951.

DAVID: How old are you this time?

ANNE: Oh, I don't remember; young.

DAVID: Teenagers still?

ANNE: Right, and we were singing (sings) "I'm late, I'm late, for a very important date" from *Alice in Wonderland,* or whatever it was. Unbeknownst to us, Joe Pasternak was in the audience, and he put us in a movie with Esther Williams called *Skirts Ahoy.*

DAVID: Marvelous.

ANNE: God bless him.

DAVID: Absolutely. Was that the only movie you were in, or were you in others?

ANNE: That was the only movie, yes.

DAVID: That was good enough, though. You were in a fine cast. Metro-Goldwyn-Mayer.

ANNE: In other words, we weren't even part of the picture. We were too young to even be Waves, at the time.

DAVID: But you were in the picture.

ANNE: We were in the picture. We sang (sings) "What good is a gal without a guy?" The "Navy Hymn," and quite a few things we did in there. We acted a little bit. e weren't actresses. Matter of fact, the director said, "Come in and say 'We're The Williams Sisters.'" So, we all came in with our suitcases with the recruiting thing, and we said, "We're The Williams Sisters," and he went, "Gee, you come in like a GD Vaudeville act (laughter). We weren't actresses. Then, we went (whispers) "We're The Williams Sisters." Now, he says, "I can't hear you at all." Sidney Lanfield was the director, but we were one take with all the songs we did. He was proud of us for that.

DAVID: Uh–huh.

ANNE: That's all. What else we did? We did *The Ed Sullivan Show* twenty-six times. Ed Sullivan. We used to call him "Uncle Ed," and his wife, "Aunt Sylvia." He'd take us to his apartment. I've got tapes of us on *Ed Sullivan*—video.

DAVID: What did you girls do for school while you were performing?

ANNE: We still went to school.

DAVID: Went to school every day?

ANNE: Still went to school, except that my two younger sisters went to professional school. We were taken good care of. Don't I sound intelligent (laughs)?

DAVID: You sound very intelligent. I'm impressed.

ANNE: Oh, I didn't say it to impress you. Anyway, to make a long story short, we went from there to *The Fred*

Allen Show. Oh, I forgot to tell you this: when we first started singing as the five of us—now this you *won't* remember, but *I* do—my sister, Arlene, who was the youngest, was ten years old. We were ten, twelve, fourteen, sixteen, and eighteen, right?

DAVID: Right.

ANNE: We made jazz recordings for Majestic Records. I wish I could get a hold of them. Jimmy Walker, who was the Mayor of New York at the time, or former Mayor, he wasn't the Mayor then.

DAVID: Beau James.

ANNE: Bud Freeman on saxophone, Billy Butterfield on trumpet, Ray McKinley on drums. I don't know who on piano—Teddy Wilson. It was a great jazz thing. I mean, Bud Freeman was so popular that when he died, his obituary was in *Time* magazine. So, he must have been somebody. I've got tapes of us singing (sings) "Chico Chico." Just kids, but all perfect harmony. That's what we did, too. Then came *The Fred Allen Show* in 1945. Up to that, it's been good. Then, we played the Copa with Sinatra. I'll bring you a picture of us and Sinatra when I see you Saturday.

DAVID: Right.

ANNE: And we played the Copa with him and he loved us. He had a crush on my sister, Gloria, who has since passed away.

DAVID: Sounds like you had a very exciting time.

ANNE: Oh, yes. It was good. And now, my husband and I sing. We entertain at all the nursing homes and they love us. We sing all the old songs.

DAVID: What kind of memories do you have of Fred Allen as a personality?

ANNE: He was very, very nice. We called him "Mr." Allen. He used to bring us Spruce Gum from Maine. We'd go to church with him every Sunday, to Saint Malachy's Church, with him and Portland. Humphrey Bogart took us to dinner. Ray Milland took us out to dinner. Charles Boyer played poker with us on the train. I think I told you that story.

DAVID: Yeah, he won $500 and paid it back to you.

ANNE: He gave it back, and when I got back to the hotel, they said, "Well, I only lost $30 and you lost . . . ." And I said, "Forget it. We're getting $100 a piece, the five of us."

DAVID: How about the others in the cast, Kenny Delmar, Minerva Pious , Parker Fennelly?

ANNE: Mrs. Delmar was very nice. Minerva Pious, everybody loved us. Matter of fact, when we started out *The Fred Allen Show*, they had to put a box out for my sister to reach the mike. That's when he said, "It isn't so-and-so kiddies." You heard it when we'd say, "Mister Allen, Mister Allen?"

DAVID: "Mr. Allen, Mr. Allllllll-ennnn . . . ."

ANNE: It isn't so-and-so kiddies. Let's see, 1955 with Sinatra. Then, we played a club. My sister met Keefe Brasselle, the actor, who has since passed away.

DAVID: He played Eddie Cantor.

ANNE: There was an argument. She left us, and said, "Screw you all."

DAVID: Oh, my gosh. That's a shame.

ANNE: Oh, yeah. He broke up the act. We tried to get another lead. We found Julie Stone, who was great. You know, Kirby Stone's wife? And we had a job booked in Las Vegas. We were on the train, and she didn't show up, and we found out she had a miscarriage. We were sued and we lost. They had their own Kangaroo court. They said, "Mouth your records." Well, we don't have that many records to mouth, you know?

DAVID: Right.

ANNE: But we *did* record for Decca. Do you know who sent us to Decca? Bing Crosby. He was on *The Fred Allen Show*, and he says, "Meet—not Milt Gable. We met him later, but it was someone else who was in charge of Decca, and he said, "Help these kids."

DAVID: Did you ever meet or work with any of the other sister groups like The Andrews Sisters?

ANNE: Oh, yes. As a matter of fact, The Andrews Sisters came to see us at the Copa, and we were such a big hit. We were embarrassed, because they were our idols, and we didn't like to show off in front of them.

DAVID: How about The Dinning Sisters?

ANNE: The Dinning Sisters were at our house in Brooklyn. My mother made macaroni for all of them.

DAVID: And The Boswells?

ANNE: The Boswells I never met, *but* I got in touch
            with—what was her name?

DAVID: Connee?

ANNE: No, not Connee. Oh, I forget. Anyway, I called her
            one time, and she called me back. She said, "Oh, I
            just *love* the way you kids sing. Of course, by now,
            they were much older. I think a couple of them
            had gone. Anyway, she used to call all the time,
            and if I wasn't home, she'd talk with Jimmy on the
            phone. She'd never get off. She lived in Poughkeepsie.
            I forget her name. It was an unusual name.

DAVID: I've got it somewhere, but I don't have it nearby.

ANNE: I'm not too young either.

DAVID: There were The Pickens Sisters also.

ANNE: Yeah.

DAVID: They were probably before your time.

ANNE: That was *way* before my time, but I remember the
            name The Pickens Sisters. I remember Jane Pickens
            used to do (sings) "Look at us, we're walking" on
            the telethon with Dennis James, who has also
            passed away too.

DAVID: I guess things started to die down when—in the
            1950s?

ANNE: Yes.

DAVID: Slowed down a bit?

ANNE: Right.

DAVID: That was when your sister left the group.

ANNE: Right. In 1958, I think.

DAVID: What are your best memories about radio? Anything different about radio than TV or anything more exciting or less exciting?

ANNE: I got a funny thing. One time we did *The Irish Hour*—the trio—and we're just sitting down, waiting for the—and they say, "Now here they are . . . The Mahoney Sisters," and we're looking to see who the hell The Mahoney Sisters are, and the guy says, "That's you!"

DAVID: That's you. DeMarco becomes Mahoney.

ANNE: Yeah, right.

DAVID: Italian becomes Irish.

ANNE: There's another group on. Another sister act? Honest to God . . . .

DAVID: It's been a lot of fun talking to you.

ANNE: Aw, same here.

DAVID: You have wonderful memories, and I look forward . . . .

ANNE: Thank you. Maybe we'll make some new ones.

DAVID: If someone walks over to you on Saturday—it's not this Saturday; it's the 20th or 21st, I'm not sure.

ANNE: I think it's the 23rd.

DAVID: It's just the week before Halloween.

ANNE: Are you good looking?

DAVID: Well, my wife doesn't think so, but I think so.

ANNE: (Laughs).

DAVID: At any rate, if someone walks over to you and gives you a very, very gentle peck on the check, you'll know it's me.

ANNE: All right.

DAVID: Tell your husband not to punch me in the nose.

ANNE: I'll tell him not to punch you in the nose.

DAVID: Okay, great speaking with you.

ANNE: All right, sweetheart, take it easy. And love to Mrs.—what is it—Siegel?

DAVID: Yes.

ANNE: I've got my caller ID here. I could have called you.

DAVID: All right. I'm sorry I couldn't send the whole tape. At least, you got some of it.

ANNE: Oh, yeah. I have some tapes here from *Fred Allen*, but I don't have them all. You know who has them?

DAVID: The Boston Library has them. Portland gave them, or left them to the Boston Library.

ANNE: And you know who else has the Kate Smith shows?

DAVID: Who has those?

ANNE: They sent me a tape and charged me $22 a piece, which was well worth it, with us on with Kate Smith—Boston University.

DAVID: That's wonderful. Are they on cassettes or on open reel?

ANNE: Video cassettes.

DAVID: Oh, video.

ANNE: I can bring that down when we get together. I do want to bring you the video with Babe Ruth.

DAVID: Okay.

ANNE: One more thing I'll leave you with real fast. He did that thing where he's supposed to say "ball one," right? And he kept saying "ball none," I swear. Would you believe it? When we were behind him, when he was doing that, they made us leave and go to lunch. When we came back, he was still doing it. You can see us there sometimes, and sometimes not. David, a pleasure.

DAVID: Great talking to you.

ANNE: Same here.

DAVID: Bye-bye.

ANNE: Thank you. Bye-bye.

Chapter 11
JANET (CANTOR) GARI
(1922–)

INTERVIEW: NOVEMBER 1, 1999

R eaders, who have attended any of the Friends of Old-Time Radio conventions during the past four or five years, are not likely to have missed an opportunity to visit the dealer room featuring a table covered with Eddie Cantor memorabilia. One of the two people behind the table is usually Brian Gari, the grandson of "old banjo eyes" himself, a gentleman, who not only reveres the memory of his grandfather, but who also heads the Eddie Cantor Appreciation Society. However, with all due respect to the memory of Eddie Cantor, I must confess that I've always found the smiling face of Eddie's youngest daughter, Janet, the proud mother of Brian Gari and the second person behind the table, to be the attraction.

Janet is not only a good luck charm for her son, but someone whose memories of growing up with Ida and four sisters must be told, and indeed has been told, in her own book, *Don't Wear Silver in the Winter: Remembering My Mother.*

Janet unhesitatingly consented to put up with my many questions regarding "life with the Cantors," or "how I was influenced by the Golden Age of radio."(The previous quotes are mine, not hers). Read on, my friends.

DAVID:	My name is David Siegel. Today is November 11, 1999, and I have the distinct pleasure of speaking with the youngest of Eddie Cantor's very, very famous five young daughters.
JANET:	I'm not so young anymore.
DAVID:	Well, we're all as young as we want to be.
JANET:	That's true.
DAVID:	Janet, thanks very much for giving me this opportunity to speak to you. How did you like the tape that I sent to you?

JANET: Oh, very interesting. Very interesting.

DAVID: Sound okay?

JANET: Yeah.

DAVID: Good, good. At what point do you recall first realizing that your dad was a well-known entertainer?

JANET: Um, well, I guess always, because people were always, oh, God, even as a kid at parties, they'd say, "Imitate your father," which, of course, I didn't do at all. I was shy and I was very upset by that, and so, I gathered he must be something to imitate. I had seen him in movies and I just *loved* him in movies, but, you know, it was not the same person that I saw at home.

DAVID: I always wondered how a person, this is true not just of you, but I guess the children of any well-known performer, how does one react to the normal person that you see on an everyday basis, who is such a giant outside of the home?

JANET: Well, at home, I think, he was like everybody else's father. I mean he was funny the way other people's fathers with a good sense of humor are funny, and he was a very affectionate father, and taught us all our sense of values, and yet, seeing him perform, well, of course I didn't see him on the stage until I was about fourteen, and then I saw him do *Banjo Eyes*, and I realized how he became a star. I mean I never saw such electricity in my life. The waves of *love* between him and the audience were incredible. That was very, very impressive to me. But, again, it was, well, there I was proud of him as my father, like "gee, look what Daddy's doing. That's great." In movies, it was like a separate character. It was somebody that, I don't know, was cute and fun, and I just enjoyed the movies, but as I say, at home he was, I guess, like anybody else's father.

DAVID: Did you and your sisters ever talk about your dad's celebrity?

JANET: Together?

DAVID: With one another, yes.

JANET: Well, yes, as a matter of fact. We had a very strict rule in our house that we had dinner at 6:30 on the dot every night, and *no* one was allowed to go out to dinner because that was the only time he knew he'd get us all together. He would go through all kinds of routines that he was going to do on the radio or whatever, and we would give opinions. He had a very volatile temper, and he had a valet named Maurice, who had his own family. He didn't live with us, but he took care of everything for him. One night, he was *so* mad at us because we all disagreed with something he was going to do on the air.

DAVID: How dare you?

JANET: Yeah. And he said, "Well, I can see everybody in this house is against me, and I'm going to a hotel." And he marched out of the room and started to go upstairs, and he said, "Well, as soon as I can get Maurice to pack for me!" So, he couldn't leave, but it's like the kid who wants to run away, but he can't cross the street (laughs).

DAVID: I see. I understand that you and or your sisters were friendly with some other celebrity children. The Marx Brothers were one.

JANET: Well, Miriam Marx was my best friend in high school.

DAVID: Was this in California or New York?

JANET: In California. I was born here and we lived here until I was nine, and then we moved out to California. You have to excuse my cold. I really have a bad cold.

DAVID: I'm very grateful that with that, you are still willing to talk to me.

JANET: Oh, *nothing* stops me from talking.

DAVID: Your dad, at one time, I understand, suffered from pleurisy.

JANET: Yes. Yes. As a matter of fact, he had to close a show he was in, a Ziegfeld show. Ziegfeld didn't believe him, and he offered to be examined by Ziegfeld's doctor. He was, and the doctor said, "This man cannot go on." He was taped up and he was in *agony.* That, apparently, ran in his family. Although we don't know too much about his family, we are trying to find out now.

DAVID: Did he use the five of you young ladies as a gag before he went on the radio, or did that start as a radio routine?

JANET: I found out at the Old-Time Radio Convention who the culprit was, when David Brown said he wrote that article, "The Cantor Home for Girls." I said, "Ah-HA! Now I know who made our lives miserable!" Because from then on, he picked up on that and used us as props. Now I *know* that—I mean, it affected us all very badly—but I *know* that had any of us had the sense to say, "This is giving people a terrible impression of us," he would have switched gears, because he loved us. But it never occurred to him, and we never said anything.

DAVID: All five of you were bothered by it?

JANET: Oh, terribly, terribly. We had the lowest self-esteem in the world, because people thought if he's trying to marry us all off, we must be awful.

DAVID: Did you get a chance to listen to your dad's program on a weekly basis?

JANET: On *Chase and Sanborn*?

DAVID: Yes.

JANET: Oh yeah, I was allowed to stay up late.

DAVID: He was on *Texaco* for a while also, wasn't he?

JANET: Um-hum. Oh yes, I heard all his radio shows.

DAVID: Did any of you attend the actual broadcasts?

JANET: Yes, very often.

DAVID: How did the programs differ? How did attendance at the programs differ in terms of . . . .

JANET: I think it was all pretty much the same format. It was definitely a variety show.

DAVID: But as you saw it and listened to it at home, when people see radio in person sometimes, they're disillusioned because they're imagining something else when they're at home listening to it.

JANET:	Well, that's very hard to say because what I would be imagining would be what I knew anyway. I can't tell you how it would feel as a total stranger.
DAVID:	Which of your dad's performances did you and your sisters find more entertaining—his films, or his radio, or his personal appearances?
JANET:	Well, I *loved* him in films, and seeing him in *Banjo Eyes* on stage was one of the most thrilling things I've ever seen.
DAVID:	Was that an original, or was that . . . .
JANET:	It was based on *Three Men on a Horse*.
DAVID:	I'm wondering whether if that was the original *Banjo Eyes*, or was that a revival?
JANET:	No, no. *Banjo Eyes* was an original, as I say, based on *Three Men on a Horse*.
DAVID:	I'm just wondering whether or not—I thought he had done that earlier and then had revived it later on.
JANET:	No, no, no. That was in 1942, I believe.
DAVID:	Oh, okay, my mistake then. I may be thinking of *Kid Boots*, or one of the others.
JANET:	Oh, no, that was a movie, but I mean *Banjo Eyes* on the stage was in 1942.
DAVID:	Your dad gets tremendous credit for having come up with the idea of The March of Dimes.
JANET:	Um-hum.

DAVID: How close was your dad to Franklin Delano Roosevelt, and how did the idea of The March of Dimes come about, do you know?

JANET: Well, he was good friends with him, and President Roosevelt had called him into his office to ask if he had any ideas about raising money to find a vaccine, and he said, "I wonder if you could find me a number of wealthy men to give a million dollars a year?" And he said, "No, I think we would be better off taking it to the people." At that time, there was a very popular newsreel called *The March of Time*, and he said, "Why don't we call it The March of Dimes?" And let *everyone* contribute, and the money started *pouring* in. My father did live to see a vaccine developed, which was one of the highlights of his life.

DAVID: I wonder whether or not the organization today still remembers Eddie Cantor as the person who was so responsible for their success?

JANET: Well, we had a meeting with them, and they were sort of lukewarm about it. In fact, nothing much came of it. They were going to do something about it. I don't know what, but we never did hear from them.

DAVID: I had mentioned to your son the idea of having a postage stamp devoted to Eddie Cantor, and . . . .

JANET: Ah. We've tried and tried. I can't get over the fact they did all those postage stamps of all the old-time celebrities and he was not included.

DAVID: That was disappointing to me, as well.

JANET: Yes, we tried.

DAVID: Can you share your impressions of some of your dad's show business friends? And who was your dad closest to in show business?

JANET: Well, of course George Jessel was like a younger brother to him. He came over all the time, almost every night. He came over to play cards with him, and George Jessel was much funnier at home than he was in public. My father tried. He used to say, "Georgie, you do things in questionable taste." He said, "The things you say at a stag dinner you cannot say in a mixed audience." And yet, in a living room, George was *hilarious*. My father used to laugh 'til the tears poured down his face.

DAVID: Was he close to any of the other comedians like either Burns and Allen or Jolson?

JANET: Well, Burns and Allen, yes, they came over.

DAVID: Jack Benny?

JANET: Yeah. I think that's about it. Oh, and Block and Sully, of course. They did hang out with the New York crowd. I mean, we never got to know any Hollywood celebrities.

DAVID: Were any of your sisters more affected by your dad's celebrity show business career than the others, or were they about equal?

JANET: Oh, Margie was his right-hand person. I mean, Margie was part of him. *Everything* went through Margie. Margie was the oldest. She was our born leader, and she was definitely part of his life. I mean he would come home from making a movie, and he'd come in the door, "Marge?" He'd kiss mother on the way, but it was Margie he had to talk to because she was like his other half, business-wise.

DAVID: I'm just thinking about that song, "Margie."

JANET: Oh no, the song just happened. It wasn't written.

DAVID: Just an accident?

JANET: Yeah.

DAVID: Let's see—how did your mom react to your dad's career? Ida became almost as much of a gag as the daughters. Did that bother your mom?

JANET: No, I don't think so. I mean, actually, they met when they were thirteen. She did fall in love with him because of his sense of humor. Mother was very funny herself and very hip. And she was much more old-fashioned than he was. She was very Victorian in her views, but she was very sophisticated in her comedic views. She could share with him everything he was doing. She would enjoy it a lot. I remember so many times when they'd be going out to get yet another award. They'd be all dressed up, and they'd come to say goodnight, and he'd poke her in the ribs and say, "Hey, Ida. What do you think about this couple from the Lower East Side?"

DAVID: Themselves, he was talking about.

JANET: Yes.

DAVID: Right. I've got a number of books here by your dad, and I'm wondering if there are any that I don't have. I have a book called *My Life is in Your Hands*.

JANET: Yes, well, that's being reissued.

DAVID: All right. I have *As I Remember Them.*

JANET: Um-hum.

DAVID: *The Way I See It, Take My Life,* and *Caught Short.* Are there any others that I don't have or don't know about?

JANET: I believe it's *The Way I See It* and *My Life Is in Your Hands* are coming out as a double book. They're being reissued. I don't know about any others.

DAVID: I just wondered if I was missing any books that your dad had written, or are those the only ones?

JANET: I don't think so.

DAVID: And I have three books that are written about your dad, and I wonder if I'm missing any there? One is called *Eddie Cantor: A Life in Show Business* by Gregory Koseluk.

JANET: Yes, that was excellent.

DAVID: The other is *Eddie Cantor: A Bio-bibliography* by James Fisher.

JANET: That was good, too.

DAVID: And the last one is *Banjo Eyes* by Goldman.

JANET: That was trash.

DAVID: Now, are there any others I'm not aware of?

JANET: No.

DAVID: Those are the three written by others about your dad.

JANET: Right.

DAVID: You like the two, but you don't like the third one.

JANET: It's not even a question of not liking it. It is absolute *trash*.

DAVID: Okay, I don't think I'll pursue that one any further.

JANET: Right.

DAVID: Tell me a little bit about your sisters. You mentioned Margie.

JANET: My mother would have trouble calling us by the right names. She'd go through everybody's name to get to the one she wanted, like she would go, "Margie, er . . . ." And she'd finally land on the right one. *But*, she did know us all, and so did my father.

DAVID: Now, Natalie was the next oldest?

JANET: Yeah. Well now, Margie mother dubbed "The Jewel." Natalie was "The Brick." Edna was "The Creative One." Marilyn was "The Shriyer," and I was "The Baby."

DAVID: You were always the baby. Did you ever wonder what it would have been like if there was a boy in that family?

JANET: I think he would have been *demolished*.

DAVID: You're joking.

JANET: No, I mean it. I think my father's personality would simply have crushed him out of this world. I mean, here he had five daughters, who worshipped him. I think a son wouldn't have had a chance.

DAVID: I see. How about the sisters? Did you girls ever want to have a brother?

JANET: No. We never thought about it one way or the other.

DAVID: You are kind of active these days in show business. Can you tell me a little bit about some of your activities?

JANET: Well, I'm a composer/lyricist. I worked with Harry Ruby's daughter, Toby, for many years. She did the lyrics and I did the music, and our partnership broke up several years ago. Now, Toby's gone, and so, I do my own lyrics, and I did a show called *Such a Pretty Face* with book writer Jeffrey Geddes. Not a *single* producer or agent came to see it, which is very unfortunate, and I've sent it around to a number of regional theaters. It actually comes back *unopened*. So, it isn't even as if anyone's turning it down; they don't even listen to it. And then, I just did the review called *It's a Nice Place to Live but I Wouldn't Want to Visit*. We had *packed* houses. The audiences *adored* it. Again, not *one* producer or agent came. I'm now trying to find a packager because, in the first place, I can't afford to keep producing it, and it would be great for conventions, or cruises, or small dinner theaters, anything. It's an hour's entertainment. That's all it is, entertainment. I would just like somebody to pick it up. I'm perfectly happy to give it away and just take writer's royalties, but I don't know where to find someone.

DAVID: Would it make a difference if you had an active agent working with you or for you?

JANET: Oh, it sure would.

DAVID: But you can't get one to work for you.

JANET: I can't find an agent either.

DAVID: That just doesn't seem to make any sense.

JANET: Oh, nothing in show business makes sense.

DAVID: Speaking of show business—and how soon we all forget—are any of your dad's friends around who might have been able to give you some help in that direction?

JANET: Oh, I don't think so.

DAVID: All gone.

JANET: Yeah.

DAVID: All right. I'm thinking about Brian, who's active, of course, in The Eddie Cantor Appreciation Society, in keeping the records, the tapes, and the CDs going.

JANET: Yes, well, Brian, you know, works on his own career, too. He's a wonderful composer/lyricist. He has albums out of his own things. In fact, he's coming out with one next month. Also, he has started writing a show about my father. He's negotiating right now for a book writer. I think it'll be marvelous. The eight songs that I've heard are *so* fabulous that I couldn't get over them, because he's writing it from the point of view of the man. Yes, of course, it will discuss his career, but everything he's written so far has been personal. It's been either from things my father told him, or I have told him, or things that he observed himself. They're very, very, personal songs, and they're either *extremely* touching or very funny.

DAVID: Are they going to include any of the songs that he did not write, but that your father is famous for singing?

JANET: Well, he and I were discussing that the other night and I was saying—I mean, he wrote a comedy song in the style of my father, which was fine. I was saying that I *think* he may *have* to include at least two signature songs, which would be "Whoopie" and "I'd Love to Spend This Hour with You."

DAVID: Not "If You Knew Susie?"

JANET: Pardon me?

DAVID: Not "If You Knew Susie Like I Know Susie?"

JANET: No, I don't think he needs to include everything my father ever did, because, as I say, it's still about a man.

DAVID: Right.

JANET: Well, I don't know what'll happen, but I just know that what he's written, Brian is one terrific musician.

DAVID: Do you recall what your father's reaction was to the movie, *The Eddie Cantor Story*?

JANET: Well, he was bitterly disappointed, as we all were.

DAVID: What was the blame? Was it Keefe Brasselle, or . . . .

JANET: He just took over, and I can't *imagine* what kind of contract he had with them, but just took over and ruined everything. Sidney Skolsky wrote the script. That's not the script he started out with. And Warner Brothers didn't want to include any of the movie companies, so his Goldwyn movies and everything else went unmentioned. Then, they said that he never did a charitable thing until he had a heart attack, which was *ridiculous.* He was doing humanitarian things all his life. hen, of course, none of us could *stand* Keefe Brasselle.

DAVID: How did they ever select him to do the . . . .

JANET: I *can't* imagine. I mean, the idea that he went around the house popping his eyes was so insane to me because my father did that on the stage, not at home.

DAVID: What memories do you have of people who worked with your dad, like Jimmy Wallington, or Harry Von Zell?

JANET: Well, I was very young, and I just thought they were all wonderful. I loved them all. I was a kid and I just thought everybody was such fun and so nice.

DAVID: Harry Einstein?

JANET: Oh, wow. I mean there was one terrific guy because he was very well-educated and a very interesting man.

DAVID: Parkyakarkus.

JANET: Yeah.

DAVID: Bobby Breen?

JANET: Well, Bobby Breen I found totally obnoxious as a kid, and then, I knew him later on, when we went to high school together. I really felt Bobby was very foolish not to go on with an acting career, because he really was a good actor. Many young actors like Roddy McDowell made the transition into being adult actors. I thought Bobby should have done that, but he didn't.

DAVID: What happened to him? He's in Florida now, I understand.

JANET: He books condos down there.

DAVID: He's not given up show business entirely?

JANET: Well, no, I mean he's booking condos.

DAVID: I'm sorry. When you said booking, I lost that.

JANET: Yeah, he's very successful down there.

DAVID: But in a different aspect.

JANET: Yeah, he's not performing.

DAVID: David Rubinoff.

JANET: I don't know what happened to him. I mean, he was a really good musician.

DAVID: But he never really spoke on the radio. That was someone else imitating him.

JANET: Right.

DAVID: Reed, I think. Alan Reed.

JANET: Right.

DAVID: Let's see, Dinah Shore and Deanna Durbin.

JANET: Dinah Shore was one of the nicest people I ever knew. She was a true friend and a *lovely* woman. She was very close to Margie, and when Margie died at the age of forty-four, she came down and just sat with my folks day in and day out. She lived up the hill from us and she just was there for them and broken-hearted.

DAVID: Deanna Durbin?

JANET: Deanna Durbin, when I met her, I was a kid, and she was, I think, just a little older than I was, but she was so *terribly, terribly* shy. I'm sorry that I never really got to meet her, and I wanted to because I admired her so much. But she kept in her dressing room, and she came out only when she had to perform. She was really *desperately* shy.

DAVID: She's living, I think, in France now.

JANET: Oh, yeah. She gave up show business, and she's happy as a Lark.

DAVID: Bert Gordon, "the Mad Russian."

JANET: My sister, Marilyn, was telling me about him the other night. I didn't know, but when he was very, very ill, my father very quietly paid all his hospital bills without his knowing it.

DAVID: Kind, kind person. Veola Vonn name ring any bells?

JANET: Who?

DAVID: Veola Vonn.

JANET: No, who's that?

DAVID: I thought she played one of the "Chippies" on your father's show. Always played romantic roles or attractive women. At one time, she was the wife of Hanley Stafford. I don't know if you remember Hanley Stafford. He played . . . .

JANET: Yes, of course I do, but I don't know who that is.

DAVID: Okay, well, I had met her a few years ago, and she told me that she played on your dad's show.

JANET: It's quite possible.

DAVID: Okay, do you recall any conversations that your dad may have had about any of his various *sponsors*?

JANET: About his sponsors?

DAVID: Yeah.

JANET: Well, he had conflicts with sponsors. He was very definite about his feelings when he gave a public speech about Father Coughlin. He said something about he didn't see how a man of the cloth could be preaching hate. He was taken off the air for two years. It was Jack Benny who got him back on. Later on, when he introduced Sammy Davis Jr. when he was part of The Will Maston Trio—this was on *Colgate*—Sammy Davis had done one of his *marvelous* dances. My father took out a handkerchief and mopped Sammy's brow and put it back in his pocket, in his own pocket. He got so much hate mail, and so did Sammy Davis, and so did the sponsor. Sammy Davis' agent called him and said, "I guess that's the end of you on *The Cantor Show*. So, he called up my father and he said, "I will understand if you want to cancel." And my father said, "*Cancel?* I've booked you for the next three shows!" And his sponsor did object, and he said, "Okay, he doesn't go on, I don't go on." That was the end of that.

DAVID: That's not the first time that he has been known to put out a hand to African-Americans.

JANET: Oh, absolutely. I mean, well, first of all, Bert Williams was his mentor in the "Follies." I mean, this was a man who was, as my father said, so far superior to *him*, that he learned everything from him, and he learned the difference, then, in what makes someone superior. It certainly isn't the color of your skin. It's what you are as a person, and that's how all of us grew up with no prejudice whatsoever, because we knew there were a lot of people who were much more superior than we were.

DAVID: Do you remember the name Thelma Carpenter?

JANET: Yes. When he hired her as a singer, and they said, "Well, she's going to play your maid, isn't she?" He said, "No. She's going to play my singer. She's not my maid. She's my singer."

DAVID: Right.

JANET: And that was the end of that.

DAVID: Dinah Shore didn't play his maid.

JANET: That's right. That's what he said. And so why should Thelma Carpenter?

DAVID: You lost one of your sisters. Are the other three still around?

JANET: Well, I lost two.

DAVID: Two?

JANET: I lost Margie in 1959 and Natalie just two years ago.

DAVID: Oh, I'm sorry to hear that.

JANET: Yes, it was very, very tragic. She was married to Robert Clary, the little Frenchman, for thirty-two years, and they had a wonderful marriage. She had been married before. She had a son by that marriage, but she and Robert had a really *wonderful* marriage, and she was my favorite sister. I will always miss her *terribly*.

DAVID: How are your other two sisters doing?

JANET: Well, Edna lived in Malibu for forty years, and she *never* should have moved into Beverly Hills. She moved in when Natalie first got sick, and she's been very unhappy there since. She's okay, but she's really not very happy. Marilyn, on the other hand, wrote the original story for *Love, Sidney*, which was called *Sidney Shorr*. It was a two-hour movie that became a series, and she has a new series now, which looks as if it *may* get on.

DAVID: So, it looks like all the Cantor children were involved in show business.

JANET: Well, Margie was, through my father. Natalie wasn't at all, except being married to Robert. Edna is also writing a novel, but nothing to do with show business.

DAVID: Was one of your sisters married to Sidney Skolsky?

JANET: No.

DAVID: I don't know where I got that idea. I thought he was related to someone in the family, or close to someone in the family.

JANET: No!

DAVID: Well, scratch that one.

JANET: Right.

DAVID: Okay, shows you how ignorant one can be.

JANET: Pardon me?

DAVID: It shows you how ignorant a person like myself can be. Sorry about that.

JANET: I mean, I've heard, you know, such *insane* rumors like affairs that my father was supposed to have had. One of the people they named was Dinah Shore. Well, that was so hilarious to me, not only because she was a friend of the family, but because Dinah Shore went for big hunks like George Montgomery and those big gorgeous guys. She wouldn't have looked twice at my father.

DAVID: Somehow, I suspect that your dad was pretty loyal to Ida.

JANET: Well, he loved my mother *very, very* much. He really did. He respected her so much that I mean, God forbid any of us should answer her back when we were kids. "Now you apologize to your mother this *minute!*" And yes, she was his best friend. No question about it.

DAVID: Would you talk a little bit about your dad after he became ill and when he was not able to work on a regular basis. How badly did that bother him?

JANET: Well, I'm sure it bothered him a lot, because he did try to do a number of personal appearances, but the medication he was taking for his heart made his speech slurred. But he was writing articles and sending them in, and he even, the week he died, sent away for his absentee ballot because he was always part of the world.

DAVID: And always a Democrat.

JANET: Yep.

DAVID: Always a Democrat.

JANET: Oh yes, a very loyal Democrat.

DAVID: Okay, I'm sure there are a lot of questions that I'm sorry I didn't ask you unless you'd like to contribute some things without being asked. I'm almost at the end of the half-hour tape.

JANET: Well, I can't think of anything in particular. I am fascinated at all the things that my son Brian is bringing out, because I keep saying, "Brian, do you have some supernatural connection to him that we don't know about?" I don't know where he gets all of his material.

DAVID: Well, I don't know whether you are planning to share the tape that I sent to you with him, but I've been collecting Eddie Cantor radio programs for years and years and years, and I've enjoyed listening to them over and over again. They're just as funny the second time around and the third time around.

JANET: Oh, that's very nice.

DAVID: Your dad has given me a great deal of pleasure, and it's been wonderful speaking with you. Thank you so much for being willing to talk.

JANET: Well, thank you so much for calling me. Bye-bye.

DAVID: Bye-bye.

Chapter 12
PAT HOSLEY
(1920–)

INTERVIEW: DECEMBER 6, 1998

The very first time that my wife (and sometimes partner in crime) Susan was brave enough to attend a Friends of Old-Time Radio convention with me, she recognized Pat Hosley, one of the guests, as someone she had known for years under a different name. In addition to having been a radio actress, Pat has had a successful second life as the author of children's books and as the founder of Kids to Kids International, a non-profit group that sends student-created picture books and educational supplies to children around the world, mostly in developing countries.

In her hometown, Pat and her husband, a former town supervisor, are known as the Kibbees, and very few think of her as a radio personality. I considered myself rather fortunate to have been able to speak with two prominent radio personalities, who actually resided within minutes of my home (Parker Fennelly, who was the first interview in this book, and now Pat Hosley).

Pat was kind enough to share memories of her work on a number of soap operas, as well as *The Aldrich Family* program, and if you happen to be a trained "googler," you'll find her listed in the cast of many important radio programs. I invite you to become acquainted with Pat Hosley. You'll learn that her creative life did not end with the advent of television.

DAVID: This is David Siegel. This is Saturday, December 6, 1998, and I am very fortunate to have sitting in our kitchen in Yorktown Heights, New York, Patricia Hosley. Am I pronouncing that right, Pat?

PAT: You are. You are. It's so good to hear it.

DAVID: Patricia is a veteran of the Golden Age of radio, and I am fortunate in that she has agreed to sit with me this afternoon and chat a bit about her career as a radio actress. Let me begin by asking you how you got started as a radio actress. When did this happen, and how?

PAT: It happened many years ago, I'd say, 1943, and 1944, and 1945 were the years when I was in New York City. When I said I was glad to hear you say my name, Patricia Hosley, that is because that *is* my maiden name. Now, I'm married, and my name is Pat Kibbe. That's the name I use as an author of children's books, which I am at this point. I became an actress when I left Southwick, Massachusetts. I lived on a farm in Massachusetts. I should have gone on to college. I had a scholarship, but I went to a summer theater the summer before I graduated from high school. I met a wonderful man there, and got a job in the summer theater, washing dishes for all the actors, actually, but I loved the acting part of it so much that I decided that instead of accepting the scholarship and going to Wellesley or some wonderful college, I went to New York, and I went to The American Academy of Dramatic Arts. When I graduated, I started making the rounds, and I wanted to be an actress. Actually, in those days, we didn't think that radio was really acting—at least *I* didn't. I accidentally got into radio. A school friend of mine knew Elaine Carrington, who was very famous writing a lot of soap operas. At that particular time, she had written a Broadway show and they were casting it. My friend from back on the farm told me that I should call her and possibly get a reading. He knew I was interested in the theater. I did call her, and she was kind enough to ask me to come up to her penthouse and to meet me. When I got there, she told me that I was much too young; there were no parts for me. She asked me if I had ever done any radio. I said no, but at that time, I had done a part in a show where I used a high squeaky voice in the theater, so I just did a little part for her that I'd done, and left her, and went back to my apartment, and told some of my actor friends that I had met Elaine Carrington. The next day, the telephone rang. I answered it, and the voice said, "Pat Hosley?" I said "Yeeees?" And the voice said, "This is Mrs. Carrington." She had sort of an affected voice, very deep and grand. I wasn't sure it was her. In fact, I was sure it was my girlfriend whom I'd told about the visit, imitating her, so when she said, "This is Mrs. Carrington," I said, "Yeeees?" like that. She said, "I'm calling to tell you that I have written a part for you on *Rosemary*. I said, "Yeeees?" And then, I began to giggle, and she said, "This really *is* Mrs. Carrington. I've written a part for you, and it's called Bird Brain, and be at a certain studio at CBS at a certain time, and then, of course, I realized who it really was and hung up. In a couple of days, I went to the studio and did the part, and it was perfect for me because she had written a part just like the part I had had in the school show. That's the way it started.

DAVID: That's a wonderful story.

PAT: I *love* it!

DAVID: Soap operas, of course, were always a continuation. They would go fifteen minutes each day for weeks and weeks. Do you recall how long you were on that particular show?

PAT: Oh, I was in and out, and I would never have too many consecutive times on it, because it was a young girl's voice. She (raises voice) talks like this, "I've never met a soldier before. It's got me all . . . ." (giggles hysterically), so they didn't dare bring it on too much.

DAVID: That became your specialty, because I have a sense, based on what I heard at the convention, that you really specialized in children's voices.

PAT: Well, young voices, but I *was* young at the time, and it was just my voice, which I guess I sort of still have. Anyway, that's what started me in radio, but I was still looking for jobs in the theater. I did get jobs in the theater, but I also got married, and I married the boy I went to high school with. He was, at the time, just getting out of the Merchant Marines. War was over, and he decided to go to college and then law school. I was delighted, because that meant that I could get into radio and theater. So, we stayed right in New York.

DAVID: I checked your dossier before this visit. The two Bibles of the Golden Age of radio, the John Dunning book, and Buxton and Owen, credit you with appearing on two major programs, *Frank Merriwell* and *The Brighter Day*. They don't list you under any of the others, and that's their mistake. Tell us a little bit about the two that they credit you for—*Frank Merriwell* and *The Brighter Day*, and then we'll talk about some of those other shows.

PAT: All right. The *Frank Merriwell* show was at NBC. It was a wonderful show and by that time, when I got on the *Frank Merriwell* show, I was pretty much into radio.

DAVID: You were a continuing character on that show.

PAT: Yes, I was somebody's girlfriend. I recall—I think it was . . . .

DAVID: Elsie Bellwood was the title that was given to you.

PAT: Right, and we did that Saturday mornings at NBC, and it was wonderful. But in the same time era, I was doing *Archie Andrews* at NBC in the morning. The most important step for me in radio, *I* think, was my husband started college. I was looking for work, and we lived in this little ground floor apartment in the Murray Hill District in a brownstone. It was wonderful, except neither one of us had any money, so I used to try to get into radio, mostly for the money rather than count on the theater all the time. I wrote postcards, and that's when they were penny postcards. I wrote to all the different shows and directors that I thought might be able to use me, or that I'd be right for. So I did write to Mr. Vail at Young and Rubicam for a part, or at least an audition on *The Aldrich Family.* Lester Vail was a wonderful, wonderful person and a great director and everything, but he was a little—how can I say—he didn't really concentrate, or didn't have time to focus. Evidently when he received my postcard, he just saw it in front of him. What I put on the postcard was that I had just finished a part. I had had a Broadway show, *On the Town*, where I did one of the little girls on the subway. I mentioned that I had been in the theater, because Lester loved the theater. Although I was twenty at the time, I said I had a very young voice, and I thought I would be very right for *The Aldrich Family.* Just when he was reading my postcard, the telephone rang and it was another producer saying that he was going to have a show with John Robert Powers, the famous model agency owner. He needed a young person with a teenaged voice who had a little stage experience, because it might be a Broadway show. As the producer was saying what he needed to Mr. Vail, Lester just saw my name on the postcard, and he said, "Oh, here's somebody—Pat Hosley." He gave

my answering machine the radio's number and
then hung up and called me. That job turned out
to be five fifteen-minute radio shows a week and
also half-hour shows, and eventually I had a few
television shows at DuMont, *The John Robert
Powers Charm School* they called it.

DAVID: What was the name of the radio program?

PAT: The name of the radio program was *The John
Robert Powers Charm School.*

DAVID: That's fascinating.

PAT: Peggy Allenby, who was a dear, dear friend and
wonderful actress, was on it, and Ken Lynch,
who was another wonderful actor and myself. Ken
was sort of in charge of all the exercise classes of
this charm school, and dear Peggy was in charge of
all the beauty and poise. She would talk about
that. I happened to be the little mail clerk, and the
person that would have to do the exercises or ask
the questions. It was wonderful, because we worked
together for fifteen minutes every day, and then,
I believe, we followed with half-hour shows. It
was unbelievable. That wonderful program put
my husband through college and law school and
let us stay in New York.

DAVID: Was that still in the 1940s or the 1950s?

PAT: 1940s. 1946, 1947, I believe it was.

DAVID: That's a program that is not well-known among
those people who collect old radio programs.

PAT: I know, and I'd love to find anything to do with
that, because, as I said, I was on every day. Then, it

was just the beginning of early television down at DuMont, and we were down doing those shows. But Mr. Powers wasn't an actor to begin with, and he did and said a lot of strange things without meaning to. Of course, it was *live* television. I don't know. I'll try to think of some of the things he said which were just so crazy, but it was a wonderful period for me. I think it was on at least a year. The whole continual thing, it was wonderful. Then, eventually, Lester Vail did hire me for *The Aldrich Family*.

DAVID: Who was playing Henry at the time you were on *The Aldrich Family*?

PAT: Oh, Ezra Stone always was playing him.

DAVID: I remember we chatted about that briefly at the convention, and when I checked the listing for casts for *The Aldrich Family*, I see all kinds of names. And again, our friends Buxton and Owen don't seem to have found . . . .

PAT: My name. I played Gladys, his girlfriend, and I was on for oh, many years, really. Joe Scibetta, Ed Duerr, Lester Vail were the directors. I worked for all of those.

DAVID: You gave me the dates. I could probably check some of the programs and find one where you were actually on it.

PAT: All right. I'm not certain right now, but I can go home and figure out the dates, because Norman Tokar and Ed Jurist were the writers at the time and so sharp, I remember. Ed and Norman took and wrote the television show, *The Aldrich Family*, which I was on, and then they started a special television show called *Young Mr. Bobbin*, which starred Jackie Kelk. I played his girlfriend on that. I can remember going to Washington, D.C. for a parade with Norm Tokar and with Ed Jurist. I don't know if that was for *The Young Mister Bobbin* television show, or *The Aldrich Family*, but all that happened in the same period when I was on the radio show. I always worked with Ezra Stone and with Jackie Kelk.

DAVID: Who played—was House Jameson the father at that time?

PAT: House Jameson, and I didn't know anyone who replaced either one of those. I know in the television version, we had lots of different people on it. I don't recall ever doing an *Aldrich Family* without Katharine Raht who played the mother, and House Jameson, Ezra Stone, and Jackie Kelk.

DAVID: Henry got into a lot of trouble. Henry's forte was always getting into trouble and getting out at the very last minute.

PAT: Yes, he was so sweet, and in the *Archie Andrews* show, he was always sort of like that also.

DAVID: Were you on that with Bob Hastings?

PAT: Oh, yes. Bob and I are very close friends, and Rosemary Rice, who was at the convention also.

DAVID: *Brighter Day.* I actually found a photograph of you. It's not a very good one.

PAT: Oh, my gosh! Oh, we had such a wonderful time with this. Jack Lemmon did his first radio show on *Brighter Day*, and I got to be a friend of Jack

Lemmon's. Maggie Draper just called me three days ago. She's in New York. She's writing. What I think would be *wonderful* if we—and Jay Meredith is a dear friend of mine, Maggie Draper, Jay Meredith, and I were all on *Brighter Day* together. We have kept our friendship all these years, and we meet at least once a year and have lunch together. Now, Maggie is in New York writing a book. Jay's daughter lives right here in Connecticut, and she comes and visits her quite often. We'll have to do a *Brighter Day* script at the next . . . .

DAVID: Well, you'll have to let Jay Hickerson know that.

PAT: It really would be so wonderful.

DAVID: Have any of you kept any of the scripts?

PAT: I don't think so. Here I am also in this picture. Here's Maggie . . . .

DAVID: It's a Xerox, but you can still see who it is.

PAT: Oh, golly. Oh, this is lovely. Ah, it's just *wonderful.*

DAVID: How did you get selected for *Brighter Day*? Is that the program that you were on the longest? If you can think of a continuing show that you were on for an extended period of time, which one would you say lasted the longest?

PAT: I really can't. There were so many. Most of them were, as I said, with my voice, I never had a leading lady role. I never did the bad guys. Whenever I would get a part, it would always be with a little bit of comedy in it, or things like that.

DAVID: Casting Director looking for young child . . . .

PAT: No, not looking for a young child so much as the good friend for a little comedy relief, and that sort of thing. I will have to go home and sort of think about all the wonderful times I can remember. I was always very busy. I can remember being in a show where—I'm sure many have told you this— where you'd be at CBS and you'd have the elevator waiting and you'd go down and get it. A cab would be waiting, and you'd go to Rockefeller Plaza, and then you'd have an elevator waiting, and you'd run up, and they'd open the door, and you'd get a script, and go right on. It was wonderful.

DAVID: You, too, were a part of that rat race, where you actually were on two or three shows on the same day in different studios.

PAT: I wasn't as busy as people like Bud Collyer, who is a dear friend of mine. He was always so wonderful and so busy, but we did do a lot of catching of taxis and running to another studio on the other side of town. It was wonderful because radio was alive, and early television had that aliveness, which none of it seems to have now. The very fact that it was instant and you were there and you were doing it just had some sort of excitement and truth to it that was lost after everything became recorded.

DAVID: Did you have an agent, or did you do all of your job-hunting on your own? Or once you were known, people just called you?

PAT: I think, really, I didn't even know they had agents in radio. I think in the theater I worked with Sarah Enright, who was a wonderful person. I had several different agents. In television, I did get an agent or two, but with radio I think it was more or less . . . .

DAVID: Word of mouth?

PAT: Word of mouth. The directors you would work
            with would like you and thought of you for different
            parts. I can remember doing a lot of *My True
            Story's, Whispering Streets*, and quite a few of those
            morning shows on ABC.

DAVID: Was there a time that Bette Davis was on
            Whispering Streets?

PAT: I don't remember that. No, I don't.

DAVID: Was that a continuing show, or a different drama?

PAT: It was a different drama each time. Your mentioning
            of a star like Bette Davis: I can remember doing
            some of *The Theater Guild* shows.

DAVID: Homer Pickett?

PAT: I don't remember whether he directed, but he
            must have, I guess. This show I did—and I've got
            to think of the name . . . .

DAVID: I have a list of *Theater Guild* shows, if it helps you
            revive your memory.

PAT: Yes. When I went back to the conference, it just
            seemed as though it was yesterday instead of how
            many years? Fifty years, or more. I just felt young
            and as though I could just go and do tomorrow. As
            a matter of fact, my dear friend Abby Lewis, who
            just passed on at Thanksgiving, when we were at
            the conference this last time, she mentioned to me
            and gave me the names of some agents, because
            everything now is agents. She said I should really
            get back and do some more voiceovers.

DAVID: You'd have a great voice for cartoons and commercials.

PAT: I did a lot of commercials. I did voiceovers for the Cocoa Puff commercials for years. All the commercials—Listerine, Maxwell House—and especially in the beginning of television, because I blended right out of radio into television. I started working in television in 1946 and 1947.

DAVID: Not too many of those kinescopes around these days. Fortunately, there are radio programs that still survive, but not very much of the early TV.

PAT: Well, those kinescopes I did give to the museum. The ones I had up in my attic all those years.

DAVID: Check your attic and see if you got everything.

PAT: And those great big records.

DAVID: Transcriptions. I would have killed for some of those.

PAT: *School of the Air* and *We the People*, or something.

DAVID: Milo—*We the People*—Milo something or other . . . .

PAT: I don't even remember the name now of . . . .

DAVID: *We the People Speak.*

PAT: It was a wonderful, wonderful era. It just seemed when I was back this October that it never ended; it was still there. For the first time, and I really have to say this, I really loved all those people that are collectors and that do have an interest in all this radio sort of era. Because I realized how important it really was and how much good was in it. I think when you compare the different media and the way we're going now, radio, and television, and now the internet, you see that we're getting further and further away from the real truth about everything. Do you understand what I'm saying?

DAVID: Being a child of radio, I certainly do. Radio presented more than innocence. It really presented something that was . . . .

PAT: It was so real. It was you listening. It was you doing it. It was just a part of you.

DAVID: Was this the first radio convention you attended, or have you been to radio conventions before?

PAT: Quite a few years ago, and even three or four years ago, but I never got myself so involved in it. I think it was because of—I don't know—my life has been in wonderful, different eras, I guess. In radio, and then from that, getting over to television, and then from television, becoming a writer. I'm an author of children's books.

DAVID: Speaking of writing, did you or other cast members get involved at all with the people who actually wrote the scripts to any of the soap operas, or any of the other continuing programs that you appeared on?

PAT: Not really, no, except with *The Aldrich Family*. I felt Ed Jurist and Norm Tokar were my friends. We went to parties together. We were sort of a family, that part of *The Aldrich Family*. This was during that period when television was just getting its feet on the ground.

DAVID: Was Clifford Goldsmith around at that time?

PAT: No. Maybe he was, but I didn't know him the way
             I knew Norman and Ed. But it's strange because
             my life, I think, with radio was wonderful because
             I started having my *family*, and it didn't matter.
             You could be very, very pregnant and still be doing
             your radio shows. With television, it was wonderful
             in a way because I did work with directors, who
             knew I was having my family. I did have five
             children, so they got used to me being pregnant.
             When they called me for a job, they'd say, "Tell
             me, are you pregnant?" And I'd say, "Which do
             you want? (giggles)." I had many calls for one
             show, *General Hospital.* It was supposed to be a
             teenager in the hospital in the bed. I, at the time in
             real life, was about nine months pregnant, but my
             director friend said, "That's all right. I want you.
             I'll put one of those movie magazines in front of
             your stomach. You don't have to get out of the
             bed or anything, so everything's great." But I think
             secretly he was hoping that I would give birth
             during the show on *General Hospital.*

DAVID: That would have been dramatic.

PAT: And then I did another on *The FBI* in "Peace and
             War" when it was on television, and I had to play a
             young unwed mother. It was about blackmail
             babies or something.

DAVID: Did you ever play *The FBI* on radio?

PAT: Yes, I did just a few times, I believe. As I said, my
             voice and whatever I did the best wasn't with the
             crime and with all those big, deep shows, although
             I seemed to do a lot of them on television. I was
             on *The Honeymooners.* I worked for Jackie Gleason.

Everything just seemed to blend in right from radio into television, and when I had my family, I went back to college. I went to the New School For Social Research, and still go there to this wonderful writing class. I began writing about my children and having some books published.

DAVID: People often talk about live radio and some of the funny things that happened if someone forgets a line or goofs in some way. Do you have any memories of any embarrassing moments, either for yourself or for some of your fellow actors in any of the shows that you were on?

PAT: Oh, gosh, I'm sure if I went home and thought and then came back, I would have many stories for you.

DAVID: We'll have a Chapter 2. This will have to be like a serial—continued next week . . . .

PAT: (laughs) Oh, yes.

DAVID: We'll get you back. We'll drag you back here.

PAT: Oh, I would *love* it.

DAVID: Rehearsal time—was there much time devoted to rehearsal?

PAT: Yes. Actually, yes and no. It depended upon the people you were rehearsing with, because we had so many fine actors. It was such a wonderful experience. As I finally learned, radio actors are the same as any other type actor, whether it's television or on stage. If you're an actor, you act. They were marvelous, marvelous people that I worked with and friends. You got into some of the rehearsals and you wouldn't start fooling around or talking and laughing. It wasn't casual at all, especially with some people in *The Theater Guild*. Then, there were other directors and other casts, who were so used to their parts, who were very, very casual, and yet always gave a wonderful performance. Sometimes, you worked with directors, who were pretty rough to work with and who were more interested in cutting and getting the show on. When I was on *The John Robert Powers Show*, because Mr. Powers was not a great actor, a lot of time would be spent with him and what he had to say in the beginning and the end of the program. Sometimes, we'd get on the air and he would go beyond his timing, and the director would have to come out, and while we were doing the show, the director would grab pages and start cutting and put it back in front of you. You had to be awake and alive. It was really sometimes very difficult, but most of the shows were fun, and with *The Aldrich Family*, when everyone knew one another and really loved one another, you'd do the show, but we'd have to come back to repeat the show.

DAVID: For the west coast.

PAT: Yes. Some would go out for dinner, and I would go back to my little apartment. I would go back to the studio, and sometimes people would be late and sometimes not as careful with their readings.

DAVID: There are several stories about people who were perfectly sober for the east coast broadcast and a little less so for the west coast broadcast. Do you have any recollections of that happening? Not to yourself, of course, but to others in the cast.

PAT: I certainly have, but I would never tell you that (laughs)!

DAVID: Okay, we won't put you under duress, but that did occur?

PAT: Yes.

DAVID: Oh, you're being very discreet.

PAT: Yes.

DAVID: There was a time, also, when a lot of radio moved from the east coast to the west coast. Were you ever tempted to move with and join some of the broadcasts that were done in Los Angeles, or did you always stay in New York?

PAT: No, I stayed in New York primarily because, as I said, I was there in the beginning with theater. I always hoped to continue more in that than I ever had a chance to. Then, my husband graduated from law school, and we did move to the suburbs and begin our family. I always stayed right in the city. Now really, I'm still in the same suburb, and I would like to get back to the city. I would *love* to get back and do voiceovers and things. Maybe you'll be the start of all this now.

DAVID: Let's hope so. Let's see what happens. We'll talk about your writing career and your educational career, your new life. On the air bloopers you don't want to talk about, or do you want to go back and see if you can remember some of those? You didn't move to the west coast. Did any of the programs that you were involved in move west without you?

PAT: Well actually, no. I think everything sort of just began with television. You sort of slipped into that, and the radio and actors did leave for the west coast. I was very busy in television, so I just didn't notice or realize what was happening to radio.

DAVID: Radio is still going, of course, but what we call the Golden Age of radio officially died sometime in 1960. They say the last programs that were broadcast were *Gunsmoke* and *Suspense* and a few shows like that. *The Big Show* with Tallulah Bankhead was one of the last major radio programs. I wonder whether or not people who were active in radio as you were, could see the handwriting on the wall? In other words, see fewer and fewer radio assignments as more and more people were watching TV.

PAT: I think that, because I did think of myself as an actor physically, too, and not just in the radio part of it, I think I was very excited about television. So, I really didn't have a concern about everything sort of petering out in radio. I was immersed . . . .

DAVID: How about some of your colleagues who were not TV kinds of people? For example, Ezra. You could listen to Ezra on the radio and think of him as a teenager, but if you saw Ezra, he just couldn't play that part on TV. You wouldn't think of Ezra Stone in terms of a TV persona.

PAT: Right. Well, you would, really—well, not as Henry Aldrich, certainly—but Ezra was a fine actor, and I think if he had wanted to, he could have become more of an actor.

DAVID: He became a director on TV.

PAT: Yes, when TV started, he took his talent and became a director.

DAVID: I was wondering about the psyche of the person. I
            don't know if you ever knew a person named Anne
            Elstner . . . .

PAT: Yes, I did.

DAVID: . . .who played—was it *Stella Dallas*?

PAT: I don't know what she played, but I know what
            you're getting at. Actually, it was the same when
            sound came to movies, wasn't it? I mean, certain
            stars who looked—and so now the radio people
            with wonderful voices didn't look that good with
            the body that went with the voice. They just didn't
            match.

DAVID: I guess that's what I'm getting at, whether or not
            you knew of any situation that might have hurt
            careers.

PAT: Well, I don't know, because I think if you're an
            actor, you can do all of these different media
            things. You train yourself to.

DAVID: One of my friends, who is particularly a *Frank
            Merriwell* fan, asked me to inquire whether or not
            you had any memory of the writer of that program
            or any of the particular history of the *Frank
            Merriwell* show. That was a very popular program.
            It starred Frank Merriwell, often in the teens, as a
            popular pulp magazine character.

PAT: Magazine, yes. I remember Hal Studer, the actor,
            who was also on that, and Fred Weihe, who is a very
            dear friend of mine and was a very great director
            on NBC. He directed part of it, I believe. I'm
            trying to think of the other NBC directors, but I
            don't recall working with any specific writer

because they rarely were there when the actual show was done, that I recall.

DAVID: How soon before the actual show did you get a script with any of the programs, the soaps, or the serious dramas?

PAT: Oh, just when you walked into the studio.

DAVID: For rehearsal?

PAT: For rehearsal, yes.

DAVID: And did rehearsal take place on the same day as broadcast, or was that a couple days earlier?

PAT: Oh, no. The rehearsal took place the same day of the show, unless it was a big show. I'm trying to think, because I'm getting confused with the early television shows, but the actual radio shows you just go in and read it once, and then you get up at the mike and have your dress rehearsal, and you'd be on the air. It usually wasn't more than an hour and a half or so that you'd be in the studio, or two hours.

DAVID: The soaps were all done without an audience. Henry Aldrich on *The Aldrich Family* was done with an audience wasn't it?

PAT: *The Aldrich Family* was done with an audience. I believe so, yes, for part of it, because it was at NBC, wasn't it?

DAVID: You hear a lot of the audience if you listen to the shows.

PAT: Yes, of course it had the audience. I'm trying to think of some of the shows that I . . . .

DAVID: *Theater Guild* would have an audience.

PAT: Uh–huh. I did some shows with Bob Hope. NBC had a series of specials on Saturday night. They had stars come in. I'll have to just go home and think and think for you and come back with all these wonderful names.

DAVID: Did you have to dress differently when the audience was there than you would have if you had done it before just your colleagues?

PAT: No, I don't think so. I never did. I think you just dress, but people did dress for the shows. Thinking back, everyone always looked very well-dressed, but casual. Not quite as much like, I shouldn't say, like an actor. The actors that are in the theater dress and look a little different than the radio actors did. I mean, this is what I am recalling.

Later, Pat has a very different career. After taking a class called "Writing Books for Children," she began writing as "Pat Kibbe," and she published *Mrs. Kiddy and the Moonbooms* with Macmillan. Her children's books became very big hits, and she began touring around the country, talking about writing to kids in schools. In 1986, she read a newspaper article called "Children on the Border," which was about refugee children on the border between Thailand and Cambodia. She began publishing books featuring kids making picture books for other kids. Those books led to her long involvement with the United Nations and Kids to Kids International.

Chapter 13
SANDRA MICHAEL
(1906–2003)

INTERVIEW: FEBRUARY 8, 2000

A phone call from a lady who introduced herself as the niece of the well-known author of the daytime dramas, *Against the Storm* and *Lone Journey*, immediately got my attention. The niece, Greta Michaelson, had plans to meet with her aunt for the purpose of converting the story line of the scripts into what she hoped might be a successful novel. Since she had only heard about these scripts, but was too young to have actually heard a broadcast, her reason for contacting me was obviously to obtain audio copies of both series. Even though the two dramas were broadcast during the daytime, they were purposefully not referred to as "soaps." For the most part, they were viewed as a "step above" soaps, and both series received many kudos.

Never one to lose an opportunity to exchange an hour or two of broadcasts for the chance to actually speak to someone who had created or participated in one of the broadcasts, I inquired if she would be kind enough to provide me with her aunt's phone number. She did, and the text of what ensued follows. The interview actually begins a few minutes after I made phone contact with Ms. Michael. Before turning my trusty tape recorder on, I had to let her know the purpose of my call and that the contact had been initiated by her niece.

During the course of the interview, Ms. Michael rather modestly described "how it all happened" and how an immigrant child who came to America speaking no English grew up to become a successful writer.

When Ms. Michael expressed extreme curiosity regarding how I had acquired audio copies of the programs she had written, I started to wonder why so many of the talented people who contributed so much to the entertainment of the American public appeared to have so few, if any, copies of their own work.

DAVID: It is Tuesday, February 8, the year is 2000, and I have the great pleasure of speaking with one of radio's great pioneers, the author and creator of such distinguished daytime dramatic series as *Against the Storm* and *Lone Journey*, Ms. Sandra

Michael. Thank you very much, Ms. Michael, for being willing to speak with me.

SANDRA: It's a pleasure for me and a privilege. I would like to add that in both of those programs, I had collaboration from my brother, Hans Christian Gunner Michaelson, and my sister, Gerda Michaelson. Gunner was also known as "Peter." The programs where they have contributed a lot should show their names. It wasn't always done. I could *not* have done all of those shows without their help. They happen to be far, far, better, finer, more imaginative writers than I am.

DAVID: One of the questions that I was going to ask—I have so many questions to ask—and I just hope that you'll be patient. I understand that you were born in Denmark.

SANDRA: Yes.

DAVID: How old were you when you came to the United States?

SANDRA: I hadn't been to school.

DAVID: So, you were preschool when you came to this country. Were you able to speak English when you came here?

SANDRA: Well, my mother and father spoke English because they had gone to Danish schools of course, and that's where they learned English. But no, I could not speak English. When we were first here, I had to ask my mother to translate what my little playmates were saying.

DAVID: I see. And your brother, Gunner, was he younger or older than you?

SANDRA: First born.

DAVID: So, he was a bit older. When you came over here, you couldn't speak English. You learned English in Milwaukee, Wisconsin?

SANDRA: No, no, no. It was Lewiston, Montana.

DAVID: Oh, okay. I'm getting things mixed up. I almost put my foot in my mouth. I was going to start this introduction by referring to you and your programs as soap operas, and then I read something in one of the reference books that said you became very angry when people called *Against the Storm* a soap opera, because you felt it was much more than that. I want to get to that a little later.

SANDRA: On the chronological steps that we've gone through, I would really prefer if we could stay more to the programs themselves. I tell you why: because I am trying to write a little sketch about the family life to precede all the letters.

DAVID: That's fine. I wanted to be very, very light on that. I'm just curious about how you learned English and how you started to learn how to write professionally.

SANDRA: I've always been interested in recording feelings, I guess. We moved to Chicago. My father, by the way, was an architect, and the reasons for our coming to the United States, that's a story *all* by itself, but has nothing to do at the moment with what we're talking about. But when we lived in Chicago, sometimes we went to Lincoln Park to the zoo. I remember watching the lions walking back and forth in their cages, walking back and forth, back and forth, with their great, beautiful paws and that swinging of their heads. I felt so sorry for them that I took my composition book at home. You know the lined composition books that children used to have in schools? I wrote the story of the lion from the lion's point of view, because I thought it was so *outrageous* that we stood there and stared at these beautiful lions. That's about the first thing I ever wrote, I think, when I was about twelve years old.

DAVID: But as you grew into adolescence, clearly, your writing became much more professional.

SANDRA: I wrote in school of course, always, and in college. I had the unbelievable privilege of being in Thornton Wilder's creative writing class in Chicago.

DAVID: Oh, my gosh.

SANDRA: He gave me enormous support and encouragement.

DAVID: Before or after *Our Town*?

SANDRA: Before.

DAVID: What a thrill that must have been.

SANDRA: It was. It was. He was a wonderful person and a *great* teacher, an inspirer.

DAVID: Did you write short stories, essays, do newspaper work?

SANDRA: Mostly essays in school.

DAVID: Then, this becomes a profession for you?

SANDRA: When I had my first job in radio.

DAVID: Was radio your first writing work professionally?

SANDRA: Yes.

DAVID: Was that in the Midwest, or was that on the coast?

SANDRA: That was in Milwaukee. Now, we get back to where you started.

DAVID: I don't know whether I'm cheating here or not, but is that where you met a gentleman named Gibbs?

SANDRA: (Laughs). Yes, indeed. He was my boss at the radio station.

DAVID: So, you got the job. Again, forgive me if I step on anything I shouldn't. You head me in the right direction. As a writer, you could have gone to a newspaper; you could have gone anywhere; but you went to a radio station to look for work and he hired you.

SANDRA: Well, the reason for that was that my brother, Gunner, was a journalist in Milwaukee. The paper and the radio station were connected, and he heard that there was a job open at the radio station. I was at the University of Chicago at the time, and he wrote and told me about it. I took the Toonerville Trolley to Milwaukee. There used to be a line between Milwaukee and Chicago. I got the job writing advertising copy, mostly. Then, at a radio station, little opportunities turn up. I did a children's program, a little of this, and a little of that, but mostly what came out of that was my lifetime life with what became my husband. The commander became my husband.

DAVID: Did he own the station, or manage it?

SANDRA:	No, no, no. He was Program Director. Then, he went to an advertising agency and got me a job there at the advertising agency. This was before we were married. We were just co-workers at the radio station. He apparently thought . . . .
DAVID:	Apparently, he thought you had talent.
SANDRA:	Yeah, I think he thought so.
DAVID:	In those days, we had something called "network radio," which doesn't seem to exist today, and many of these stations around the country fed in what they got from Chicago or New York or the west coast. Was there much original broadcasting done in your region?
SANDRA:	Much local?
DAVID:	Yeah.
SANDRA:	It was all local. We had a few—what did we used to call them?
DAVID:	Sustainers?
SANDRA:	Yeah, remotes.
DAVID:	From the historical point of view, I'm wondering whether or not the station that you worked at was affiliated with one of the networks.
SANDRA:	WISN?
DAVID:	Was that at NBC, CBS, or Mutual?
SANDRA:	It's silly, but I can't remember that. It was Hearst, I know that. I remember that very vividly.

DAVID: You sound like it was influenced by the Hearst philosophy.

SANDRA: (Laughs) Influence is one word. Control is another. I think that's the one that fits.

DAVID: The stories about that gentleman were probably very accurate.

SANDRA: I'm afraid so. Look, Mr. Siegel, you are asking me to talk about myself, and I don't like to do that (laughs). I want to know where and how you came about these things, how we can get control of some of them again—get copies. I need them very badly for some gaps in the *Lone Journey.*

DAVID: I'd be more than happy to share anything I have with you, or with Gretta.

SANDRA: If you would just tell me about it. Do you have any number of *Lone Journeys*?

DAVID: No, I think I only have—I sent her two and think I may have two more.

SANDRA: They're actually discs?

DAVID: Well, they're tapes. I put them on cassette tapes for her. She said she was coming out to see you, so she should be bringing those with her.

SANDRA: Well, she doesn't live too far away. Los Gatos is not more than an hour's flight.

DAVID: Right. She's a wonderful person, by the way. I've only spoken with her twice, but she certainly seems very enthusiastic about learning more about you and your career in radio. Basically you can call me somewhat of either an archivist, or a historian. There are a lot of books that have been written about radio from different perspectives—Lone Ranger, Jack Benny—biographies have been done, etc. There are some general books. Some people have written books about the soaps. What I have tried to do as mostly a fan—a collector—I attend a convention that takes place on the east coast every year. Some of the performers like Jackson Beck, who are still around, show up. It takes place in October, and if you were of a mind to, I'm sure that they'd love to have you as a guest, talking about your career as a radio person.

SANDRA: I'm a shy violet.

DAVID: Well, one of the nice things about these programs is that so many of the folks who have been away from radio for many years meet people that they have known years ago. I was telling this to Gretta. I don't know if you know the name Stella Reynolds? She's no longer with us. She was married to Arnold Moss. I understand she wrote radio broadcasts.

SANDRA: Arnold Moss. He was a star on one of our shows.

DAVID: Arnold Moss used to attend these meetings. He's no longer with us, but he did attend the meetings. They reenact some of the scripts from the old radio programs.

SANDRA: Well, this is one thing that's interesting to me: that you have the actual tapes, because when people try to do the programs over again . . . . There was a fan in Montana, quite a wonderful woman actually, who heard about my brother's work. She asked for permission to use some scripts, and they were done by a little local play group. They were very good, but when I heard their interpretation, it was *so* far off from the original concepts, that it was kind of sad. But that doesn't mean that one couldn't redo shows. As a matter of fact, that brings me back to *Harvest* again, because that was why I wanted, if possible, to find not so much the broadcast *Harvest*—I think we have a copy of that here, and there's one in Montana—but I would like to get the original script, and that's very difficult to do. Have you ever encountered . . . .

DAVID: No. As a matter of fact, it's not even a program that I'm familiar with. I've heard of *The Affairs of Anthony.*

SANDRA: This was a television show.

DAVID: Oh, no, no. I'm not into TV at all.

SANDRA: Yeah, because we wrote television shows, too.

DAVID: Did you know the advertisers sometimes would keep those things?

SANDRA: Oh, I suppose that might be possible.

DAVID: Sometimes, these things come up because they were in the files of agencies, for example, *Fibber McGee and Molly.* All of their programs were held or kept by the Johnson Wax Company.

SANDRA: That was clever of them.

DAVID: That's one of the reasons that you can still listen to *Fibber McGee and Molly* today, because Johnson Wax kept the tapes.

SANDRA: Oh, I see.

DAVID: *Cavalcade of America* is available because the DuPont Company kept the programs. Some of the sponsors were very, very respectful of the work that was done, and other sponsors treated it like it's here today gone tomorrow. There was no thought of the historical value.

SANDRA: *The Omnibus*, I don't remember their sponsors.

DAVID: Aluminum, I think. Wasn't that the British person, Alistair Cook?

SANDRA: Oh, yes, yes. It could have been Aluminum. You know, they should have been preserved because those were wonderful shows. Now, you mentioned that someone somewhere said that I got angry. I don't think I permit myself to be angry. There are bigger things to be angry about. I was *unhappy* because I was not *trying* to write a soap opera. I was trying the reverse. I was trying to write something that would be legitimate, that I wouldn't have to blush about. When we met Mr. Ramsey from Proctor & Gamble, he was the first person to believe that that kind of writing would do well on commercial television. His faith was certainly justified, because *Against the Storm* had a very fast success. So much so that John, my husband and the producer of the show, was besieged by other advertising agencies. They wanted him to come up with some more dramatic programs.

DAVID: Right.

SANDRA: You can't go out and buy dramatic programs like that, but you have to have somebody who *wants* to write that kind of show. You can't write according to somebody's orders. Again, I don't like to think that I was arrogant enough to be angry, but I was unhappy.

DAVID: (Laughs) Well, as I said, it was a quote from one of the reference books on radio. I can read it to you exactly as it appears here. Let's see if I can find it. *Against the Storm* was so high brow, that to call it a soap opera made its creator-writer see red. Sandra Michael had long believed that daytime radio needed an antidote for the mindless formulas of *Our Gal Sunday* and *Stella Dallas*. Michael disdained the cliffhanger, that well-worn device that made listeners wonder, "Will John's wife finally meet John's other wife?"

SANDRA: (Laughs).

DAVID: And it goes on. I don't know where the gentleman who wrote that got it, but he got it somewhere.

SANDRA: Now, he uses the word disdained, which I think is unbecoming.

DAVID: Don't be so modest.

SANDRA: Well, I don't know about that. I'm just kind of a realist, but for him to say that I saw red, that would have been extremely dangerous at that time. In fact, I had to try to call myself not red. I didn't honor them by telling them I was not red, I just didn't pay any attention to them. It was a bad time. I don't know if you know anything about that.

DAVID: I know a little bit about the Red Channels, was it?

SANDRA: It was a terrible time.

DAVID: Elia Kazan and Company.

SANDRA: Oh, gosh.

DAVID:	We won't get into that. I'm not sure that has anything to do with radio.
SANDRA:	That's too bad. He shouldn't have done that.
DAVID:	Let me try to keep track of where we are going. You were in the Midwest and you ended up in New York writing a major daytime drama. How did that happen?
SANDRA:	Well, because of Mr. Ramsey. Mr. Ramsey bought *Against the Storm*. I must say they put me through a little training problem first before they decided to buy my show. They asked if I would do a month of the show by Mrs. Elaine Carrington. Wait a minute—have I got that straight?
DAVID:	Yes. There was Elaine Carrington, Irna Phillips . . . .
SANDRA:	Not that one. No, no, no. I'm so sorry. No, this was a genuine writer, and she had a daytime show, which was intelligent at the very least. It was something you could listen to and you could sort of believe the people. She was going on vacation, and would I do her program for a month? I said I would if I could do it in my own way, take her characters, and put them in another setting. I set them in Texas for some strange reason. My big brother, Gunner, went with me down to Texas to look at the scenery, to see what it was like, and get a feel of the country. After that, they gave me a chance to do *Against the Storm*. I wrote the first episode on the day that war was declared.
DAVID:	1941. December 7.
SANDRA:	No, 1939.

DAVID: That was in Europe. That's September 1939.
            Neville Chamberlain came back—peace in our
            times.

SANDRA: That's the one. The war was a part of the program
            from then on. We followed the events. It reflected
            the actions of the day. It was a normal thing to do,
            because it was set in a university town.

DAVID: Were you getting much reaction from the listeners
            to the program?

SANDRA: Oh gosh, yes. We got to know a lot of interesting,
            nice people that way. I mean, on paper, and some
            of them actually in person.

DAVID: Do you have any memory of what programs you
            ran against? In other words, whatever time of
            day you were on, clearly the other network was
            carrying a different program.

SANDRA: All of the other things you were talking about:
            *Elaine Carrington, When a Girl Marries, Ma
            Perkins, Stella Dallas*, the whole range. We used to
            have a good term. We used to call cheap novels
            "pulps."

DAVID: Pulps, yes, because of the paper they were made
            with.

SANDRA: To me, most of the radio stuff, with notable
            exceptions was pulp. We had wonderful people
            like the comedy series.

DAVID: *Vic and Sade*. Paul Rhymer. Did you know Paul
            Rhymer?

SANDRA: Yes. I had the pleasure of meeting him once.

DAVID: Very talented. I don't know what kind of personality he had. It's interesting there are two books in print that contain the scripts for the "halfway up the next block." Two hardcover books. I don't know how well they did, but they collected some of those scripts, because they stand alone, those scripts.

SANDRA: They were absolutely wonderful. They tried television, but for some reason or another, it didn't quite work. I don't know why. I think that *Vic and Sade* is an American classic all by itself in that genre. If anybody ever captured the funny side of small town life . . . .

DAVID: I think there's only one person still alive who had anything to do with that program, a gentleman named Billy Idelson. He used to play the young Rush.

SANDRA: He was the son (laughs). Yeah, what funny names his father called him besides his own name. He always had funny nicknames for him. I loved that show. We all did. It was great.

DAVID: There were redeeming qualities to radio, weren't there?

SANDRA: Yes, indeed there were, thank goodness.

DAVID: So again, I'm trying to tell a story here. You were in the Midwest. You've come up with the idea for *Against the Storm*. You've interested Mr. Ramsey. You're then writing a series of substitute scripts for another writer who's on vacation.

SANDRA: That was before I met Mr. Ramsey.

DAVID: Then, you end up in New York, or in Connecticut working in New York.

SANDRA: We lived in New York for a few months on Fifth Avenue. I remember that was nice. Our little dog didn't like being walked in Washington Square with all the noise after the peace and quiet of Connecticut.

DAVID: Greenwich Village, Washington Square, New York University. I knew it well.

SANDRA: Eighth Street with the wonderful rye bread and corn beef sandwiches. I remember them. It was a great time.

DAVID: Okay, now was *Against the Storm* the first long series of radio programs that you were involved in?

SANDRA: Yeah.

DAVID: Because I see some of these others I don't know: *Open Door, Party Line*, and *The Affairs of Anthony.*

SANDRA: Well, *Party Line* was one that I wrote while I was in Milwaukee at the advertising agency. It wasn't local. It was picked up by many stations. That was a very successful program. It was kind of a funny small town milieu.

DAVID: I remember in those days if you picked up the phone and someone else was on it, you couldn't use it. You'd be listening to other people's conversations.

SANDRA: That wasn't how we worked it, but that was true. There is a little operator who gets to know everybody in town and everybody knows everybody else's business, but not necessarily over the telephone. It didn't have much to do with the phone itself, actually.

DAVID: Do you have any copies of that program in your collection?

SANDRA: No, I don't think so.

DAVID: That's one that I don't think is well-known at all.

SANDRA: No. It was well-known at the time, goodness knows. I remember we gave out a little pamphlet of recipes that two of the lady characters got as an offer and we got five million responses.

DAVID: Wow. That's quite a listenership.

SANDRA: My mother was an absolutely marvelous artist in many ways, and one of her artistic achievements was the best food in the world. I had to ask her would she please give me some recipes. She did, and we gave a kind of Midwestern touch to the names, not to the recipes. Well, look, this is running up an enormous telephone bill, and you are an indefatigable and inescapable interviewer. I told you a heck of a lot more than I really have ever told anybody.

DAVID: You haven't told me half of what I want to know about.

SANDRA: Well, I'll have to send you my own resume when I write it.

DAVID: I was going to ask you how in the world you work with collaborators on those programs? Did you come up with a theme and they just filled it out, or are they doing the actual writing?

SANDRA: No, no, no. We wrote our own shows. If there
            would be a scene I would especially like my brother
            to write or my sister—it was my own show for a
            long, long time—when Proctor & Gamble wanted
            another program, I thought well, this would be a
            great one for my brother who knows an awful lot
            about the West, and whom I also told you was a
            far greater writer than I could ever hope to be.

DAVID: I know your brother wrote most of it, but your
            name is still associated with it.

SANDRA: With *Lone Journey?* Yeah, of course, because, again,
            that's the way stuff works. They had one show that
            was a surprise to everybody, so they wanted another
            one. I can't write the kind of thing I would like to
            write if I had two shows going at the same time. I
            asked them if it would be okay if my brother wrote
            it, and they said yes, it was. He did, and it worked
            out fine. On *Against the Storm*, when I felt that I
            really needed fresh help for something, my brother
            and my sister were there to give it. We thought
            so much alike that sometimes we'd almost use the
            same symbol for something, which was rather
            curious.

DAVID: How far in advance are the scripts written before
            the actual broadcast date?

SANDRA: That scares me, because I was always just up to the
            deadline. They should be ahead, certainly, two
            weeks, a week and a half.

DAVID: Were you actually present at any of the programs—
            the broadcasts?

SANDRA: Yes. If there was something critical about a casting,
            I always wanted to hear it.

DAVID: Did you select the cast in any case, or did you play a role in the selection of casts?

SANDRA: Yes, both. Sometimes, after all, I lived out in Greenwich in the country, and sometimes if there was a new character they would make some tests. And again, John, my husband, knew so well what was wanted that he could choose at least as well as I could.

DAVID: I'm just looking at the cast for *Against the Storm*. Roger DeKoven?

SANDRA: He was Professor Allen.

DAVID: Katherine Anderson.

SANDRA: Don't remember her.

DAVID: Gertrude Warner.

SANDRA: Oh, yes. I remember her very well.

DAVID: Claudia Morgan.

SANDRA: Claudia Morgan, yeah.

DAVID: Wasn't she Frank Morgan's niece?

SANDRA: Yes, quite a girl.

DAVID: Joan Tompkins.

SANDRA: Oh, yeah, Joan Tompkins. As a matter of fact, she lives not terribly, terribly far from here. I would like to see her, but there hasn't been much chance. She has written to me, and we were especially in communication when Anne Seymour died. We both loved Anne Seymour, a great actress and friend.

DAVID: Arnold Moss, Alexander Scourby.

SANDRA: Yep. Oh, he was good, very good.

DAVID: So, you had quite a very, very distinguished cast on that program.

SANDRA: They were awfully good.

DAVID: Without getting too nosy, how expensive was it to put on a fifteen-minute drama each day? Is that the producer's problem?

SANDRA: Yes, it was the producer's problem. I wish I remembered, but I think the figures would sound pretty silly today. They weren't much.

DAVID: You had a script writer, engineers, actors, and director.

SANDRA: There was a tremendous amount of stuff connected with—I don't know. It was just three years ago, two days ago that my husband died. If he were here, he would know everything. He had a *fantastic* memory, and he was always interested in what was going on. The last few years of his life, he had a lively interest in what was going on, in television, particularly. But he would remember *all* the radio stuff, too. The price—I can't even remember how we were paid, but I do know this—we owned the show. If we got an advance, then we'd pass 10 percent on to the actors, because we thought that was only fair. But aside from that . . . .

DAVID: So, as the owners of the program, you actually were able to select the cast.

SANDRA: Yeah.

DAVID: Was it the sponsor that paid you, or the network that paid you?

SANDRA: The network.

DAVID: So, the sponsor paid the network and the network paid the owners of the program.

SANDRA: Right.

DAVID: That's interesting.

SANDRA: That was the way it went.

DAVID: What are the factors that end up in the show going off the air? In some cases is it the listenership, the sponsor, the producers themselves who decide they've had enough?

SANDRA: It was something known as Nielson Ratings, and they were phony. They're not phony in that they gave you false reports directly, but they—do you know how they made those ratings? By calling people.

DAVID: Then, was Hooper and Nielson . . . .

SANDRA: They were both bad. In the city of Chicago, for example, where you had at the time how many millions of people—two million—whatever it was at the time. They would check on the telephone to see what people were listening to, and out of all the calls they made—and there weren't very many. Actually, they might have completed twelve calls. Someplace I have, perhaps my brother has a whole record. We investigated to see how they came up with the figures that they came up with. It was appalling, because the number of calls they made would be indications of nothing except specifically the calls that they made. It had no reference at all to the larger population. It didn't matter who answered the phone, whether it was a child, or an invalid, or somebody past compos mentis.

DAVID: I just wondered whether or not they would decide based on the fact that sales of the product were going up or were improving.

SANDRA: Well, that was the silly part of it. They *never ever* correlated those facts.

DAVID: Because if they're selling soap, or—Phillip Morris was one of your sponsors.

SANDRA: (Laughs) Yes, I'm sorry to say. I actually am sorry to say.

DAVID: They're trying to make up for it now with some other type of advertising showing what good folks they are.

SANDRA: I know, I know. It doesn't salve my conscious any, but there it is.

DAVID: How do you feel that those programs would fare if they were broadcast or televised today? Would they hold up do you think?

SANDRA: I think *Storm* would, yeah. And I think *The Lone Journey* would, because they are concerned more with people and people's minds and hearts. But you said something that reminded me of something. Robert Montgomery's son, Skip Montgomery, who lives in Florida and is an attorney, I think, has wanted *very* much to get me interested in old Montgomery shows. I don't want to be involved in something that I don't know very much about. It seemed to me such a tenuous thing. I don't see how they could do anything with the Montgomery shows. Perhaps they could, and perhaps, they will, but . . . .

DAVID: Do they want to redo them or reissue them?

SANDRA: Yes, not redo them, but they want to reissue them, but that would mean of course getting them transcribed into another medium.

DAVID: He had a television program. Are you talking about a radio program that Robert Montgomery did?

SANDRA: Television. *Robert Montgomery Presents.*

DAVID: Why would they transcribe it? That was an anthology, I think.

SANDRA: I guess you could call it that. My husband produced that for seven years. One new complete hour dramatic show every . . . .

DAVID: Wasn't that done live?

SANDRA: It was done live, yeah.

DAVID: Not on tape. Did they have kinescopes of the shows?

SANDRA: Yes, I think they did. Yes, they did. Of course they did. It was done live, yes. I remember on one broadcast my husband was in the studio, and they were supposed to use some recorded music in the background, and they didn't have the particular one they needed. It was a dance record. He ran out on Seventh Avenue, looking for that record. It was around 7:30 or 8:00 at night when most stores were closed and he just managed to hit the store that had that particular record . . . .

DAVID: Tower Records.

SANDRA: . . . and he raced back and they got it on the machine just in time. That's how live that was.

DAVID: That's interesting because again, one of the subjects that is always raised when panelists who were involved in radio meet and speak at the conventions, are people dropping their scripts at the last-minute, or playing practical jokes on other performers. One person tells a story of Orson Wells coming into a broadcast, and just before the beginning of the show, he drops his script. Everybody rushes to help him pick it up, and he just pulls the real script out of his pocket (laughter). So, do you have any stories to tell that might amuse people who are interested in radio history?

SANDRA: Do I? No, I don't think so.

DAVID: People mispronouncing a word on the radio? I don't want to get sexy, but something that someone has said that has the wrong meaning?

SANDRA: No, it was just silly. One actor, a wonderful actor—I can't think of his name—had quite a career in movies as a comedian. Not exactly a comedian, a comic actor. He was awfully good at comedy.

DAVID: He started in radio?

SANDRA: Yeah, he was on our show. He played the part of a young professor at this university on *Against the Storm*. One day, in speaking to somebody in the script, he uses a couple of French words, and the actor took it upon himself to say to the other character, "That's French, you know."

DAVID: (Laughs).

SANDRA: Well, this was so crazy and so wrong that one of the listeners that we had begun corresponding with sent me a letter saying the only thing I would criticize is that Professor Wintergreen shouldn't have said, "That's French, you know." I couldn't tell her . . . .

DAVID: I didn't write that! That was an ad-lib.

SANDRA: That kind of thing makes you a little nervous at the time.

DAVID: No ad-libbing on my show!

SANDRA: (Laughs). Well, look Mr. Siegel, it was really kind and sweet of you to call. I hope I've given you something you've wanted here, but I know I haven't told it completely correctly the way it should be told."

DAVID: I've had the pleasure of having conversations like this in the past with people like—I'm trying to think of some of the folks who have been kind enough to speak with me—one who lived right here before he passed away—and that was the actor who was on *The Fred Allen Show*, "Titus Moody"—Parker Fennelly. Parker lived in Peekskill, New York when I first moved to this region. I had been upstate and always collected radio programs. Somebody told me that Parker Fennelly lived nearby, and I called his house and spoke to his wife, and told her I was a radio fan, and would it be possible for me to come over and speak with him. I brought my tape recorder, and for ninety minutes, I have Parker Fennelly talking about his career on radio. Not just with Fred Allen, but he also had a very distinguished stage career. There have been a few other people who have been involved with radio, who have been kind enough to share their thoughts and memories with me.

SANDRA: Of course they would be *glad* to have a call from you. It's very, well, I don't know what word I want . . . .

DAVID: I don't want to tire you out, and I don't want to get you angry. The last thing I want to do is that.

SANDRA: You know about my viscous temper? (Laughs).

DAVID: Yes, I've been told you're a terrible person. Please don't hit me. I'm hoping that when Gretta comes up or down to see you, I'm not sure which direction.

SANDRA: Rancho Santa Fe is south.

DAVID: If you have a collection of scripts, if you have tapes, by the way, if you do have transcriptions, you can't play those on a regular turntable. You need a very large table to play those.

SANDRA: We had one.

DAVID: I have one.

SANDRA: You do?

DAVID: So, if you ever want to get those transferred so you can put those on tapes, you can tell Gretta. Usually those are metal. I hope they're not glass. If they're metal, they will travel well, and I would be more than happy to make copies of those transcriptions for you.

SANDRA: That's wonderful, that's great to know. Well, I repeat that I'm grateful to you for your call, and I wish I were more articulate, not so garrulous.

DAVID: Well, it's the garrulous part that I like, because I assume who you really are—the real Sandra Michael—not someone who's pretending to be Sandra Michael. You have been extremely kind. If you let me, I'd be happy to talk to you for another two hours. But I won't impose on you, because I get the sense that you want to say goodbye.

SANDRA: No, no, no, no, no. Except for your telephone bill.

DAVID: Don't worry about my telephone bill. I keep telling everybody I married my wife because she's wealthy.

SANDRA: Oh, that's nice.

DAVID: It's not true, but you have to say something.

SANDRA: (Laughs). Apropos of that, may I ask where you live?

DAVID: Yes. I live in Westchester County in a place called Yorktown Heights, New York.

SANDRA: How close is that to Greenwich?

DAVID: Probably about a thirty-minute drive.

SANDRA: Oh, really? That long, huh?

DAVID: I think so. My wife is much better on geography than I am.

SANDRA: My sister and brother-in-law live in Greenwich on the Sound.

DAVID: Oh, let me ask this: were they involved with radio? Your sister was. Didn't she write with you?

SANDRA: Yes.

DAVID: I wonder whether or not I could contact her sometime?

SANDRA: She got married and had three children, which was the end of her writing career. It's a crime because she's a great writer.

DAVID: I see. Well, I certainly don't want to impose on her, but if you thought that she'd like to be interviewed or spoken to . . . .

SANDRA: I'll ask her. She's not quite as tough and sturdy as I am. She's rather frail right now.

DAVID: If she were interested, I could bring some of those tapes over to her place and she could listen to them.

SANDRA: I'll tell her, Mr. Siegel. Thank you very much, and in the meantime, I have a pen here, which is odd, because you never have one when you need it. Could I have your name and address?

DAVID: Of course, of course. (Gives information). I've sent Gretta some print material and also two copies of *Against the Storm* and two copies of *Lone Journey.*

SANDRA: Really? Wonderful.

DAVID: So, please remind her to bring them with her when she comes to visit with you.

SANDRA: I'll do that.

DAVID: I'm hoping, from the point of view of history, that any materials that you might have—advertising materials, photos of the cast, anything at all—if you have duplicates of any of those materials that you could share with Gretta or me, I would love to have them.

SANDRA: As I say, I will keep that in mind. I will remember. This is very, very nice of you. I hope you and Mrs. Siegel have a happy Valentine's.

DAVID: Well, that's very kind of you. I hope you have a sweet Valentine's. If you like, I'll send you a chocolate valentine.

SANDRA: (Laughs) That's nice.

DAVID: You're a sweetheart. I don't need your address because I don't want to bother you. I have your phone number. I won't call you again unless you want me to.

SANDRA: Yes, I'd like to talk again sometime.

DAVID: This has been a wonderful opportunity for me and I really, really appreciate it. You're a very kind person.

SANDRA: No, no, no I'm not. Next time, the telephone call will be on me, okay? (Laughs).

DAVID: No, no, no. Look, when you have a hobby, you will do anything to enhance your hobby.

SANDRA: Yeah, I know. I'm a rose nut and a cat nut. I *love* cats.

DAVID: I love what I call the Golden Age of radio.

SANDRA: Oh (laughs).

DAVID: Believe me, it is a pleasure to make this call. It's not a problem in terms of the—AT&T gives me 7¢ a minute, so I'm not worried. I won't go broke on this phone call, I assure you.

SANDRA: Out here, they advertise 5¢ a minute, so 7¢ sounds awfully big. Okay, Mr. Siegel. Thank you so much.

DAVID: Thank you.

SANDRA: Bye-bye.

DAVID: Bye-bye.

Chapter 14
PEGGY MOYLAN
(1932-)

INTERVIEW: NOVEMBER 3, 2001

Speaking with Peggy Moylan was a real step back to my earlier childhood and memories of listening to a program called *The Horn and Hardart Children's Hour.* If you were not raised on the east coast, you may not be familiar with this show. The sponsor owned a chain of restaurants, the likes of which most readers will find difficult to imagine: Mr. Horn and Mr. Hardart conceived of a restaurant in which the food was placed behind glass doors in sealed cubby holes. Next to each cubby hole was a sign indicating the price of the item and a slot in which nickels could be inserted. Only when the patron inserted the required number of nickels, would the glass door open, enabling to patron to remove the food.

The Horn and Hardart program featured talented children, including singers, comedians, instrumentalists, and yes, even dancers. Among the most popular guests were two little girls, Peggy Joan and her sister, Marianne. Over time, the sisters' sweet voices attracted enough listener attention to earn them their own radio program sponsored by Thrivo dog food. In addition to having their own radio program, the pre-teen sisters were also featured guests on the Fred Allen program and managed to star in two or three episodes of *Treasury Star Parade.* Peggy and I got along very nicely on the phone when it was discovered that we were both born the same year. I hope you'll enjoy the following interview as much as I did conducting it.

DAVID: Today is Saturday, November 3, 2001, and it is my great pleasure to be speaking with Peggy Moylan, one of the two very famous Moylan Sisters, who entertained children and their parents during the late 1930s and early 1940s. Peggy Joan, may I ask you when you and your sister, Marianne, first began to sing together?

PEGGY: Oh dear, I was about three and a half. I was born in 1932, so that would be what?

DAVID: Well, I was born in 1932, and I'm 69 years old now.

PEGGY: So am I. When's your birthday?

DAVID: August.

PEGGY: Mine's January.

DAVID: Okay.

PEGGY: So, we began when I was about three.

DAVID: And your sister is two years older than you?

PEGGY: Yes.

DAVID: What got you started, just listening to the radio?

PEGGY: Yes. My aunt called *The Horn & Hardart Children's Hour* because my sister used to sing a lot when he was little and we used to sing. Excuse me, I'm getting a cold.

DAVID: You sound just fine, by the way.

PEGGY: No, I'm getting a terrible cold. We used to sing when we'd hear the songs on the radio.

DAVID: So, you listened to *The Horn & Hardart Children's Hour*?

PEGGY: No, no, no. It was any other program.

DAVID: Any program.

PEGGY: Any music program. So, to make a long story short, my aunt wrote to *The Horn & Hardart Children's Hour* and said she had a niece who could sing. They said to come in, and we went in. My sister got up to sing, and she says, "Oh, my sister can sing, too." And she grabs me and out I went, and I didn't even know I was going to do it.

David: (Laughs).

Peggy: So, that was the beginning. We went to *The Horn & Hardart Children's Hour* every Sunday until we got our own program, which was I think in 1940 or 1939. And as I remember, we were in New York on December 7, 1941, when Pearl Harbor—and they took us off the air that day, so I guess that's about all I can tell you about that.

David: Did you live on Long Island at the time?

Peggy: Yes. I was born and raised in Sag Harbor.

David: How did you get into the city each week?

Peggy: Drove.

David: You and your parents?

Peggy: No, my aunt used to drive my mother, my sister, and I in. My father used to stay home most of the time. He'd come in once in a while, but he stayed home.

David: Did that program have rehearsals, or were they just on without rehearsals on Sundays?

Peggy: You'd go in and sing your song once, and that was it, and then you'd go on.

David: So, it was one preview and then you'd go on live, and that was on Sunday, as well?

Peggy: Yes. There were an awful lot of kids on that.

DAVID: Did you get to know any of them?

PEGGY: No. I shouldn't say no. One, Olivio Santoro. He was . . . .

DAVID: The Boy Yodeler.

PEGGY: Yes.

DAVID: He was on *The Horn & Hardart Hour* also?

PEGGY: Yes he was. He was very, very nice. I don't know whatever happened to him.

DAVID: I see. Was it Bobby Hookey and some of the others you never got to meet or talk to?

PEGGY: No. We didn't get friendly with them. We did our thing, and then left and came home because it was a long drive.

DAVID: Was it always singing, or did you have any dialog?

PEGGY: No. It was mostly always singing on *The Horn & Hardart Children's Hour.*

DAVID: And how did you decide which song you were going to do on a week to week basis?

PEGGY: My father would pick them out. He had a lot of sheet music and songs that he thought we could do well. He'd teach us 'cause he was a pianist.

DAVID: Oh, he was?

PEGGY: And a violinist. He played the violin beautifully.

DAVID: Well, and music ran in your family?

PEGGY: Oh yeah, it runs in my family. My three sons are all very musically inclined.

DAVID: Do you remember Ed Herlihy at all? Was he the person who was the emcee during the whole time that you and your sister were on?

PEGGY: Yes he was. I remember him.

DAVID: Any special memories of Ed Herlihy in terms of personality or how he participated?

PEGGY: Is he still alive, do you think?

DAVID: I think he passed away about a year or two ago.

PEGGY: Then, I can say this. (Laughs). I thought he was very loud. I don't know, not my type of person.

DAVID: Loud? Boisterous, you mean?

PEGGY: Yes, very loud and boisterous. Somebody I wouldn't want to become friendly with.

DAVID: (Laughs) How did he interact with the children, or did he interact with the children?

PEGGY: Not much. He just introduced everybody and that was about it. Everybody just did their own thing, and then left.

DAVID: Now, was that a program that paid the children, or did . . . .

PEGGY: No, no, no. That was nothing. No pay.

DAVID: You just did it for the fun of it?

PEGGY: Uh-huh.

DAVID: They didn't even give you a pie?

PEGGY: Not even a pie.

DAVID: You didn't get anything from Horn & Hardart on Christmas?

PEGGY: We used to go eat at Horn & Hardart.

DAVID: But you had to pay for it.

PEGGY: Absolutely. Put the nickel in the slot.

DAVID: Oh, my gosh, that was an inexpensive show for them to sponsor. And you were there for so many years. Now, while you were on *The Horn & Hardart Show*, did you guest on any of the other programs?

PEGGY: Not until we got our own show. Then, we went and did Fred Allen a lot.

DAVID: There was another children's program on about the same time as *Horn & Hardart* was on—*Coast to Coast on a Bus*. Are you familiar with that one?

PEGGY: No, I never listened to it.

DAVID: Never heard it. I see.

PEGGY: I might have heard of it, but I didn't listen to it.

DAVID: Did you and your sister perform outside of radio? You know, in theaters at all, while you were on *Horn & Hardart*?

PEGGY: Not in the city. We would do things at home, you know, like benefits and stuff like that.

DAVID: But still not for salary, not for pay?

PEGGY: No, no. We didn't get paid until we got our own show.

DAVID: That's almost abusive.

PEGGY: Really.

DAVID: And you got your own show with the dog food company?

PEGGY: That's right, Thrivo.

DAVID: How did that develop?

PEGGY: You have to remember, I was very young, and I don't remember. My mother was on the phone with somebody. I don't even remember his name, and he said—oh, I know—his name was Sammy Weisbord, and he was with the William Morris . . . .

DAVID: An agency?

PEGGY: Yes. He wanted to be our agent. He had heard us on *Horn & Hardart*, and we did go to meet him. I remember that in the city, and he became our agent, and then he got us the Thrivo show and shows on the other one, the one we were just talking about.

DAVID: Oh, Fred Allen.

PEGGY: Yes, Fred Allen. Very nice.

DAVID: So he got you some money for a change?

PEGGY: Yes. Mr. Weisbord. He became the head of the
            agency, by the way.

DAVID: Well, obviously, he knew talent when he saw it.

PEGGY: He started out as a clerk, working just running
            errands and everything. He worked himself up. A
            very nice man.

DAVID: I've heard a few of the Thrivo shows, and they
            describe your singing, you, and your sister, in a
            very, very unique way. Could you kind of help us
            to understand why the two of you sang in a way
            that would be different than any other two
            children might be singing together?

PEGGY: I think they're talking about three-part harmony.

DAVID: I'm not sure that I understand that.

PEGGY: All right, we'd start a song, and my sister would
            sing the lead and I'd sing the alto, and then we'd
            switch, and I'd sing the lead and she'd sing the
            soprano. So it would go, back and forth.

DAVID: I see.

PEGGY: Kind of hard to explain.

DAVID: But that was unique in terms of the sound, and it
            sounded very, very lovely.

PEGGY: Yes. It's called three-part harmony.

DAVID: I see, and do you recall the number of years that
            you were on for Thrivo?

PEGGY: Well, we were on until when the war came. Everything, you know, changed.

DAVID: Right.

PEGGY: I think we were on another year after that, and then they stopped because the tin cans, you know.

DAVID: Oh yes, rationing.

PEGGY: Right. All the rationing, and they stopped the show because of the war.

DAVID: Right. Now, while you were on for Thrivo, is that when you began to make records, or did that happen later?

PEGGY: We made records then, yes.

DAVID: And mostly for Decca?

PEGGY: Decca, right.

DAVID: Do you know how many records you've made altogether, the two of you?

PEGGY: I have no idea.

DAVID: But you do recall making records and the sheet music that had your pictures on them?

PEGGY: Yes.

DAVID: Any other kind of advertising that popularized you around the country?

PEGGY: Not that I can remember.

DAVID: Did you get a lot of fan mail?

PEGGY: Ah, so much fan mail you wouldn't believe it—
                from all over the world.

DAVID: How did you handle the fan mail?

PEGGY: My mother did the best she could, and my
                aunts. My mother had three sisters, and they
                helped and they answered most of it, an awful lot
                from servicemen.

DAVID: Servicemen? Did they know how old you were?

PEGGY: Oh, yes.

DAVID: And they responded?

PEGGY: Yes.

DAVID: Thomas DeLong, whom you may have met, wrote
                a book about music in that period, and he must
                have spoken to you because he commented on the
                fact that in 1941 and thereafter, you and your sister
                were corresponding with many, many servicemen.

PEGGY: Yes, that's true.

DAVID: Then you made some movies.

PEGGY: They were shorts. They called them shorts. You
                know, they'd come on before the feature film. I
                think they were made mostly in Philadelphia.

DAVID: How did you get involved in that?

PEGGY: That was Sammy Weisbord.

DAVID: Your agent again. And somewhere it said that you were called "The Angels of the Airwaves."

PEGGY: Yes, I don't know who gave us that name. One of the announcers, I think, came up with it.

DAVID: When you started working for Thrivo, did you then begin to do some public appearances?

PEGGY: Not really, no. My mother didn't want us to do too much. She wanted to keep us as normal as possible.

DAVID: You were going to school at this time?

PEGGY: Yes.

DAVID: Any interference between school work and radio work, or singing?

PEGGY: When we got into—I can't remember what grade it was, but it was getting to be too much, so my mother had us tutored by one of the nuns. We went to a Catholic school.

DAVID: Well that was a good upbringing.

PEGGY: Oh yeah. I graduated from Catholic school. She taught us in the afternoon, so we only had to go in the afternoon for a while until we got to high school, and then we went to regular Catholic high school.

DAVID: Did the children in your community know that you and your sister were performing on the radio each week?

PEGGY: Oh, yeah.

DAVID: Did they treat you any differently, do you think?

PEGGY: No, no. Not in our little town. We had a great little town.

DAVID: You weren't special celebrities?

PEGGY: No, no, no. There were only 4,000 people in the town. Everybody knew everybody else.

DAVID: Yeah, but everybody else wasn't on the radio.

PEGGY: It wasn't any different for them than it was for us.

DAVID: Do you recall any of the lyrics to the old Thrivo theme song?

PEGGY: (Sings) "I feed my doggie Thrivo. He's very much alive-o. Full of pep and vim. If you want a peppy pup, you better hurry up. Give Thrivo to him."

DAVID: That's beautiful. Each year in October, there's a radio convention that we hold at the Holiday Inn, which is a hotel right outside of the airport in Newark. They have guests who performed live on radio, mostly in the 1930s, 1940s, some in the 1950s. Of course, after the 1950s, radio stopped being what we remember it as. But if you're able to attend next year, even if only on Saturday, and you can bring anyone that you'd like along with you as a guest, I have a feeling that you would thrill an awful lot of people.

PEGGY: Okay, that's very nice. I'll keep that in mind.

DAVID: I'll leave the scheduling of that up to you, just in case I'm not able to make it. You said you were on

Fred Allen's program a few times. Do you remember Fred at all?

PEGGY: Yes, he was very nice.

DAVID: Any particular memories of those shows in terms of his personality?

PEGGY: Yes, he was a very normal person. He didn't own anything. He didn't own a car. He didn't own a house. He rented an apartment in New York City. He told my mother, he said, "I don't believe in owning anything. I rent my apartment." And he rented a house out in Montauk during the summer, but he was very nice. I liked him very much.

DAVID: He must have liked you and your sisters, or he wouldn't have had you back several times.

PEGGY: Oh, yeah, we got along great with him.

DAVID: Now, on those shows, I'm sure you had some dialog. It wasn't only singing.

PEGGY: With him, we did.

DAVID: Did you have to come in early for rehearsal, or how did that work out?

PEGGY: I can't remember. I think we came maybe an hour before. We only had to do our song once and that was it. We knew what we were doing.

DAVID: Did you meet any of the other cast members and have any acquaintance with any of the others who were on the program?

PEGGY: We just met his wife, Portland.

DAVID: Portland Hoffa.

PEGGY: Yes.

DAVID: What kind of lady was Portland?

PEGGY: She wasn't as friendly as he was, but she was nice. Do you remember the stage actress, Shirley Booth?

DAVID: Oh, yes, she had been married at one time to Ed Gardner.

PEGGY: Yes. She was on one time when we were on Fred Allen. She was very nice.

DAVID: I'm trying to think. She played the maid . . . .

PEGGY: *Come Back Little Sheba*, on Broadway, I think.

DAVID: She played it in the film also, I think, with Burt Lancaster.

PEGGY: That's right.

DAVID: And didn't she also play a famous maid?

PEGGY: I don't know.

DAVID: She had a series. I'm trying to think . . . .

PEGGY: Oh, yes. I can't remember.

DAVID: *Hazel. Hazel.*

PEGGY: Very nice.

DAVID: A wonderful woman. Anyone else you might remember from radio?

PEGGY: Well, do you want me to tell you the people I met?

DAVID: Share it, share it.

PEGGY: Okay, we met Tyrone Power . . . .

DAVID: Wow.

PEGGY: . . . and he was horrible.

DAVID: Really?

PEGGY: Oh! He was rude, very badly mannered. We were having dinner in a restaurant somewhere in New York with our agent. He said, "Oh, there's Tyrone Power at the bar. You wanna go over and meet him?" I didn't care, because I didn't think much of him to begin with. He wasn't one of my favorites. But my mother and my sister said "yes." We went over and he didn't even stand up. He just sat at the barstool. He said a few words. I said to my mother, "I'm going back to the table." Waste my time, you know? He was really very rude. Then, we met Lana Turner, who was the most delightful, lovely, beautiful person I think I ever met in my life. She was grand. We met her at the Sherry Netherland Hotel. Our agent arranged it, and she was just lovely.

DAVID: You were two teenagers at the time?

PEGGY: Yes, I was twelve. I remember that. I was twelve years old.

DAVID: Your sister was fifteen?

PEGGY: No, she was two years older. She was fourteen.

DAVID: Fourteen.

PEGGY: I'll remember her until the day that I die. She was such a lovely, lovely person. Let's see, we met Joe DiMaggio and his son. He was very nice. And we met Gary Cooper, and I can't remember who else. I'm going to lose my voice.

DAVID: That's the beauty of being on tape. You don't have to keep repeating it. We have it now on the record.

PEGGY: Right, but I can't remember anybody else.

DAVID: Did you work with Alec Templeton at one time, the blind pianist?

PEGGY: Yes. Oh, no, no, no. We might have one time, I think. Yes, I think we did, now that you mention it.

DAVID: On his radio program.

PEGGY: I think so. I really don't remember much about that.

DAVID: And what about Ilka Chase? Does that name ring a bell?

PEGGY: No, it doesn't.

DAVID: Again, Tom DeLong had mentioned those two as people who, in addition to Fred Allen, you might have performed with.

PEGGY: I don't remember her.

DAVID: Were you a guest on any other programs?

PEGGY: We just did those shorts, and then we did the *Treasury Star Parade* during the war.

DAVID: Now how did that work out? Wasn't that a bond program?

PEGGY: Yes, for the war effort.

DAVID: Those were fifteen-minute shows, and you and your sister sang. Was that also the same agent that got you on that one?

PEGGY: Yes, he did everything. He became the head of the agency in California.

DAVID: Well, as I said before, he had good taste in selecting you and your sister.

PEGGY: Yes. Not only that, he was a very, very nice man, very smart.

DAVID: At what point did you and your sister decide—or was it your mom who decided enough was enough, and you were not going to be performing anymore?

PEGGY: When we got into high school.

DAVID: And was it because of the school?

PEGGY: Yes, it was just too much.

DAVID: So you were not tempted by show business?

PEGGY: Oh, no, not at all. I wasn't. I'd had enough of it. I'd been doing it for so many years.

DAVID: And you never missed it, never wanted to go back?

PEGGY: Never.

DAVID: Sister also?

PEGGY:	Same thing. We had plenty of it.
DAVID:	That's interesting.
PEGGY:	Well, we were so young when we started.
DAVID:	You think of people like Deanna Durbin and Bobby Breen, who continued.
PEGGY:	No, we didn't have any interest in it. My sister became a lab technician in high school.
DAVID:	I tell you, I'm absolutely thrilled to have been able to speak with you today.
PEGGY:	Well, thank you for calling.
DAVID:	It's been my pleasure. I'm not sure if we can make it next week, but my wife and I have been thinking about it. It's a long trip out there.
PEGGY:	Yes, it is. We're way out on the end of the island.
DAVID:	I want to thank you so very much for being kind in allowing me to tape this interview.
PEGGY:	It was nice of you to call.
DAVID:	You're a very sweet woman.
PEGGY:	Thanks a lot.
DAVID:	I look forward to meeting you next year.
PEGGY:	Thank you very much. Bye-bye.
DAVID:	Bye-bye.

PART II
A RESOURCE GUIDE TO RADIO'S ORAL HISTORY

CHAPTER 1

This is the first ever compilation of oral history interviews devoted exclusively to the Golden Age of radio. Much of the information comes from the collection of the author, David S. Siegel, who has been collecting audio and print material relating to the Golden Age for forty-five years.

The list includes the wide range of personalities who made radio happen, from the writers, producers, and directors to the performers, technical people, and the individuals responsible for the business side of radio. Some of the personalities made themselves available for multiple interviews, but others were available for only one.

The interviews were conducted by different people, in different venues, and over a period of years. Some, like those of John Dunning and Chuck Schaden, were broadcast as part of radio programs that also rebroadcast old-time radio programs. Many of the SPERDVAC interviews were taped as part of presentations at the group's monthly meetings. Still others, such as the Friends of Old-Time Radio interviews, were recorded as panel discussions, and some were conducted via the telephone.

Of the thirteen sources of oral history interviews included in this compilation, all but three list interviews conducted by a specific person or organization. The three exceptions are sources that include a combination of original interviews as well as copies of interviews done by others: the Library of American Broadcasting and the private collections of Barbara Watkins and Bobb Lynes.

The interviews survive in a variety of formats, including reel-to-reel tape, cassettes, CDs, videos, DVDs, in some cases, print transcripts. Access to the interviews is equally diverse, which is why the author has included, where appropriate, contact information for the source of the interview.

I recognize that the list is by no means complete. That said, what I have attempted to do is identify sources of significant collections of interviews that are, for the most part, accessible to the public. For practical reasons, I have omitted interviews conducted by individuals who have not made the existence of their efforts known to collectors or researchers. Leads to these and other potential sources of interviews are, however, identified below.

In the course of my research, I have also learned that, for a variety of reasons, some lists of interviews were not available, at least not at the present time. For example, the list of interviews done by the Pacific Pioneer Broadcasters is not accessible due to environmental issues. Another well-known interviewer is in the process of deciding if, how and when, he will make copies of all his interviews available to the public. And a third interviewer, for reasons that he did not share with the author, declined to provide a list of his oral history interviews.

Long-time collectors will no doubt recognize some of the sources on this list and indeed may already have copies of some of the interviews. I suspect, however, that other sources are likely to be less well-known and will be of interest. For new fans, as well as the new generation of radio scholars, I hope that the list will enrich your appreciation and knowledge of radio's Golden Age.

How This List is Organized

Names

The list is arranged alphabetically by last name. In a few instances where the personality might have been known by more than one name, a cross reference is provided.

Anyone researching the Golden Age of radio knows that it is not uncommon to find a name spelled more than one way and that verifying the "correct" spelling is not always possible. The "spelling problem" was compounded since the 1,000 names in this compilation came from multiple sources. While I have tried to verify as many spellings as possible, I humbly acknowledge my limitations in not being familiar enough with every name to be able to associate a particular spelling with a reference to a particular person.

Also, in some cases where two sources listed the same first and second name, but only one listed a middle initial, it was not always possible to determine with any degree of certainty if the two names identify the same person.

Category Codes

To the right of most names, readers will find a category code that is designed to help identify personalities associated with specific aspects of the Golden Age, e.g., actor, writer, music, business, etc. The codes are meant as a general guide only, since some personalities could easily be placed in more than one category. In a few instances, more than one category code is shown. Some of the category codes are based on information provided by the source; others were added by the authors based on either their own familiarity with the name or by matching the name to listings in John Dunning's *On the Air: The Encyclopedia of Old-Time Radio*. When the author is not able to assign a category code with any degree of certainty, the column is left blank.

a = actor
an = announcer
b = business
bd = broadcaster (includes sportscasters, farm broadcasters, general interest programs, etc.)
d = director
f = family (family members of personalities)
m = music (includes singers, band leaders, disc jockeys)
n = news
p = producer
w = writer

Source Codes

Each of the sources has been assigned a number 1 through 13, as identified below. Since many of the personalities gave more than one interview, the reader will find a series of sources code numbers to the right of the category code. In some instances, a source may have multiple interviews with the same personality. This occurs mostly with the John Dunning and SPERDVAC interviews.

What follows is a brief description of the source of the interviews included in this book, as well as contact information on how to obtain copies of the interviews. The sources are listed without regard to the time frame in which the interviews took place or the number of interviews available from the source.

1. ARCHIVE OF AMERICAN TELEVISION

Although the oral history video interviews conducted by the Archive of American Television, part of the Academy of Television Arts and Sciences, focus on television, some of the interviews are of personalities who got their early start in the entertainment business in radio. A complete list of those interviewed, and the ability to view the interviews online, is available at http://emmytvlegends interviews.blogspot.com. Additional information is available at Archive of American Television, 5220 Lankershim Blvd, N. Hollywood, CA 91601, 818-509-2262.

2. BARBARA WATKINS

A private collector and long-time member of SPERDVAC (see below), many of Barbara "Sunday" Watkins's oral history interviews were conducted as part of the radio program she co-hosted, *Don't Touch That Dial.* Additional interviews in her collection were conducted by other broadcasters and interviewers. As of June 2009, the collection is not available to the public, but Ms. Watkins can be contacted by e-mail at kinseyfan@hotmail.com.

3. BOBB LYNES

Also a private collector and long-time member of SPERDVAC, many of the interviews in Bobb Lynes's collection were first aired on *Don't Touch That Dial,* the program he co-hosted with fellow collector Barbara Watkins. Additional interviews originated on *The Old-Time Radio Show,* another radio program he hosted with Ms. Watkins, or are from other miscellaneous sources. As of June 2009, the collection is not available to the public, but Mr. Lynes can be contacted by e-mail at iairotr@hotmail.com.

4. CHUCK SCHADEN

Over the thirty-nine years from 1970 through June 2009 that he hosted the radio program, *Those Were the Days*, Chuck Schaden interviewed countless numbers of radio personalities. Forty-six of the interviews are available in Mr. Schaden's book, *Speaking of Radio: Chuck Schaden's Conversations with the Stars of the Golden Age of Radio*, (Nostalgia Digest Press, 2003, and available at www.nostalgiadigest.com). Additional interviews known to be in private collections are also shown in the listing. An interview with Mr. Schaden is included in the list below. As of June 2009, Mr. Schaden had not yet decided on the future disposition of his remaining interviews.

5. FRANK BRESEE

A radio personality in his own right, Frank Bresee was also the host of his own program, *The Golden Days of Radio*, for more than fifty years. During that time, he had the opportunity to interview countless legendary figures from radio's past. Some interviews are also available from private collectors. An interview with Bresee is included in the list below. Mr. Bresee can be contacted at 8282 Hollywood Boulevard, Hollywood, CA 90069, (323) 650-7984. In June 2009, Mr. Bresee made known his intention to transfer his interview tapes to the American Radio Archives located at the Thousand Oaks Public Library in Thousand Oaks, CA.

6. FRIENDS OF OLD TIME RADIO (FOTR)

Under the leadership and guidance of Jay Hickerson, Friends of Old Time Radio has been hosting annual conventions since 1970. Most of the conventions have included one-on-one panels with radio personalities or group panels devoted to a specific program. Most of the sessions have been recorded, initially on audiotape and in later years on video. Only those interviews recorded since 2002 are included in the list. For information about these and earlier interviews, contact Fred Berney at Satellite Media Production, P.O. Box 638, Walkersville, MD 21793, (301) 845-2737, www.satellite mediaproduction.com.

7. THE GOLDEN AGE OF RADIO

The Golden Age of Radio was a joint project of WTIC (Hartford, CT) announcer Dick Bertel and a dedicated radio fan, Ed Corcoran. Beginning in April 1970, and continuing over the next seven years, the team conducted eighty-nine broadcasts featuring interviews with radio actors, writers, producers, engineers, and musicians from radio's early days. The interviews are all available today on the Internet at www.goldenage-wtic.org/log.html.

8. JOHN DUNNING

The name John Dunning is synonymous with radio history since both his books, *Tune in Yesterday* and *On the Air: The Encyclopedia of Old-Time Radio*, have become the Bibles for radio researchers. The owner of a used bookstore who also loved radio, Mr. Dunning was one of the first pioneers of radio history to conduct interviews of radio personalities for his radio program, Old-Time Radio Show. Copies of the Dunning interviews are available to members of the Radio Historical Association of Colorado (see below), can also be found at the Library of American Broadcasting (see below), and in many private collections.

9. LIBRARY OF AMERICAN BROADCASTING (LAB)

One of the major repositories of audio and print material pertaining to the Golden Age of radio, the LAB has an extensive collection of oral history interviews, only a portion of which are shown below. The collection is particularly strong in capturing the often overlooked business side of radio history. For more information, including a complete list of the available interviews, contact Michael Henry, Library of American Broadcasting, University of Maryland, 3210 Hornbake Library, College Park, MD 20742, (301) 314-0397, www.lib.umd.edu/LAB.

10. RADIO PIONEERS PROJECT, COLUMBIA UNIVERSITY

The Radio Pioneers Project is part of the Columbia University Oral History Collection consisting of over 8,000 taped interviews of people from the 20th century who have contributed significantly to society or who were close affiliates of world leaders. The radio collection includes engineers, station and network executives, writers, directors, government officials, and performers. More information about the collection is available by contacting the Oral History Research Office, Butler Library, 535 West 114th Street, New York, NY 10027, (212) 854-7083, http://www.columbia.edu/cu/lweb/indiv/oral.

11. RICHARD LAMPARSKI

Known as the "crown prince" of nostalgia, Richard Lamparski, began broadcasting his *Whatever Became Of?* series on two community radio stations, KPFA in Berkeley, California and WBAI in New York City. Mr. Lamparski delighted movie, stage and radio fans by locating folks who had been out of the public eye for many years but who, in earlier years, had been extremely well known and famous. Sadly, there is little evidence that either station retained copies of the interviews although Lamparski did publish the highlights of these interviews in his series of *Whatever Became Of?* books. Some of the original interviews have survived, however, through the efforts of a few private collectors.

12. THE SOCIETY TO PRESERVE AND ENCOURAGE RADIO DRAMA, VARIETY, AND COMEDY (SPERDVAC)

Organized in 1974, SPERDVAC has been and continues to be one of the leading sources of radio oral history interviews. Located on the west coast, the organization has had unprecedented access to countless radio personalities, some of whom appeared as featured guests at the group's regular monthly meetings and annual conventions. A full listing of the interviews, including the date the interview took place, is available on the group's web site, www.sperdvac.org, or by contacting the organization at PO Box 669, Manhattan Beach, CA 90266-0669, (877) 251-5771. Copies of the interviews are available on reel-to-reel, cassette, VHS, or DVD to members only. Membership is available at a modest cost.

13. WALDEN HUGHES

A collector who hosts a program about old-time radio on satellite radio's Yesterday USA Radio Network, Walden Hughes has conducted countless interviews at radio conventions and also via telephone. He can be reached via email at waldenhughes@yesterdayusa.com.

ADDITIONAL SOURCES

JOHN AND LARRY GASSMAN

For many years, John and Larry Gassman conducted oral history interviews as part of the radio program they co-hosted, *Same Time Same Station*. While the brothers are no longer active in the radio hobby, readers wanting to get in touch with them are advised to try the following e-mail addresses: johngassman@roadrunner.com or lgsinger@sbcglobal.net.

PACIFIC PIONEER BROADACASTERS (PPB)

Founded by individuals who actually participated in radio's Golden Age, PPB is said, by those in the know, to have one of the richest collections of oral history interviews. Alas, as of June 2009, the collection, along with a list of the interview tapes, is inaccessible because it is stored in the basement of a building with PCB contamination. Once the environmental problem is resolved, the collection will be transferred to the American Radio Archives located at the Thousand Oaks Public library in Thousand Oaks, CA.

RADIO HISTORICAL ASSOCIATION OF COLORADO (RHAC)

An organization of area collectors, RHAC is one of two sources for a complete set of the John Dunning interviews. A catalog of the holdings can be downloaded from the web site, www.rhac.org. While the Dunning tapes are available only to members, membership is available at a modest cost. Additional information about the organization is available at PO Box 1908, Englewood, CO 80150.

OTHER REGIONAL OLD-TIME RADIO CLUBS AND ORGANIZATIONS

The authors are aware of the following three groups that have held annual conventions or monthly meetings that featured interviews of radio personalities.

- Golden Radio Buffs (GRB). Although this group based in Baltimore, Maryland may no longer be active, copies of many of the interviews done at its meetings are in the hands of private collectors.

- Cincinnati Old-Time Radio and Nostalgia Convention. Contact Bob Burchett, 10280 Gunpowder Road, Florence, KY 41042, haradio@msn.com.

- Radio Enthusiasts of the Puget Sound (REPS), www.repson line.org.

MAX SCHMID

The host of *The Golden Age of Radio* program broadcast on WBAI (NYC), Max Schmid has, over the years, conducted numerous interviews of radio personalities. Mr. Schmid can be contacted at www.oldtimeradio.com.

DAVID GOLDIN

The host of the popular web site, www.radiogoldindex.com, David Goldin's private old-time radio collection also includes several interviews of radio personalities.

Chapter 2
LIST OF ORAL HISTORIES

CATEGORY CODE:

a = actor
an = announcer
b = business
bd = broadcaster
d = director
f = family
m = music
n = news
p = producer
t = technician
w = writer

SOURCE CODE:

1 = AAT
2 = Watkins
3 = Lynes
4 = Schaden
5 = Bresee
6 = FOTR
7 = GAR
8 = Dunning
9 = LAB
10 = RPP
11 = Lamparski
12 = SPERDVAC
13 = Hughes

Ace, Goodman	w, a	7, 11	Alexander, Joan	a		11
Ackerman, Harry	d	12	Alexander, John	b		9
Adams, Uncle Bill	an	11	Alexanderson, Werner			10
Adams, Douglas	w	2	Alland, William	w		12
Adams, Mason	a	2, 7, 11	Allen, Barbara Jo	a		11
			Allen, Ed			10
Adler, Larry	m	2, 11	Allen, Mel	bd		7
Adrian, Iris	a	12	Allen, Steve	a		8, 9
Agronsky, Martin	n	9	Allman, Elvia	a		8, 9, 12
Albert, Eddie	a	1				

Beck, Jackson	a	7, 12
Bee, Molly	m	6, 12
Bell, Mary		12
Belviso, Thomas H.	m	9
Benedict, Chuck		12
Bennis, Charles L.	t	9
Benny, Jack	a	4, 5, 7
Benny, Joan	f	12, 13
Benson, Court	a	9
Benson, Sam		
Bergen, Edgar	a	3, 4, 5, 7, 9
Bergman, Ted (see Reed, Alan)		
Berle, Milton	a	1
Berliner, Oliver		12
Berwin, Bernice	a	8, 9, 12
Bilby, Kenneth W.	b	9
Billsbury, Rye	an	12
Binyon, Conrad	a	12
Bishop, Jack	w	7
Blair, Don	n	9
Blanc, Mel	a	5, 7, 8, 12
Bliss, Edward, Jr.	w	9
Bliss, Lucille		12
Blue, Ben	a	
Boardman, True	w	9, 11
Boles, Jim	a	4, 9
Bontsema, Peter H.	bd	9
Borroff, Edwin Raymond	b	9
Bosler, Gustave A.		10
Boswell, Connee	m	11

Boswell, Vet	m	11
Boulton, Milo	bd	11
Bower, Roger	bd	7, 9
Boyd, Rita Ascott	a	4
Bradbury, Ray	w	3, 5, 8, 9
Bradley, Curley	a	3, 8, 9
Bradley, Dr. Preston	bd	9
Bradley, Will	m	11
Bragdon, Everett L.	w	10
Bratone, June Hiett		13
Brecher, Irving	w	12
Breen, Bobby	m	11
Breitenbach, Harry P.		10
Bresee, Frank	bd	8, 9, 12
Brickhouse, Jack	bd	4
Bride, Esther Lee	bd	9
Brito, Phil	m	11
Britton, Barbara	a	7
Brock, Para Lee	bd	9
Broderick, Gertrude	bd	9
Brown Les Jr.		13
Brown, Carleton	m	9
Brown, Himan	p, d	2, 7, 9
Brown, Jack		2, 12
Brown, Lucky		12
Brown, Vanessa	a	11
Brown, Walter		12
Brown, Walter R.	t	9
Brown, William Wilbur		10
Browne, Olivia	bd	9
Bruce, Bob		2, 12
Bryson, Ace		12

Hoover, Herbert		
Clark	b	10
Hope, Bob	a	5
Horlilck, Harry	m	9, 11
Horseford, Dennis		8, 9
Hosley, Pat	a	6
Houseman, John	w, d	8, 9
Howard, Moe		11
Howe, James L.	b	9
Howe, Quincy	n	9, 11
Hul, Albert Wallace		10
Hull, Henry	a	7
Hunt, Marsha	a	12
Hunt, Mary	b	9
Hunter, W. Lee	t	9
Hyman, Elaine	a	6
Idelson, Billy	a	3, 5, 8, 9, 11, 12
Ives, Burl	m	2
Jaeger, Ed		12
James, E.P.H.		10
James, Harry	m	5
Jameson, House	a	11
Janis, Eddie	a	10
Janiss, Vivi	a	12
Janney, Leon	a	7
Jeffreys, Anne	a	13
Jeffries, Herb		13
Jenson, Bob		12
Jerome, Jerry	m	9
Jessel, George	a	5
Jewell, James	a	9
Johnson, Bill	f	9
Johnson, Edwin C.	b	9
Johnson, Len	b	9
Johnson, Raymond		

Edward	a	7, 8, 9
Johnson, Russell		13
Johnstone, Jack	a	3, 8, 9, 12
Jonas, Kirby		13
Jones, Dick	a	12
Jordan, Jim	a	3, 4, 5, 7, 8, 9, 11, 12
Jordan, Will	a	7
Josephsberg, Milt	w	3
Josephson, Larry	p, d	9, 13
Jostyn, Jay	a	4, 5, 9
Joy, Dick	a	8
Judson. Judson		10
Julian, Joseph	a	7
Julliard, A.		12
Juster, Evie	a	7
Kadderly, Wallace	bd	9
Kaland, William J.		10
Kallen, Kitty	m	13
Kaltenborn,, H.V.	n	10
Kane, Byron	a	3
Kanter, Hal	w	1, 9, 11
Kaplan, Dr. Morris	b	9
Kaplan, Marvin	a	12
Karloff, Boris	a	5
Karloff, Sara	f	13
Kasey, Mike J,		12
Kasner, Hank		12
Katz, Bernard	m	12
Keach, Stacy, Sr.	a	12
Kearney, Donald	bd	9

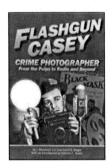

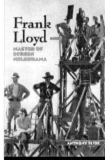

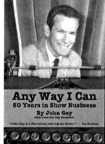

Breinigsville, PA USA
01 June 2010
238980BV00002B/5/P